A 2003 HOMETOWN COLLECTION

America's Best Recipes

Oxmoor
House®

©2003 by Oxmoor House, Inc.
Book Division of Southern Progress Corporation
P.O. Box 2463, Birmingham, Alabama 35201

ISBN: 0-8487-2731-2
ISSN: 0898-9982

Printed in the United States of America
First Printing 2003

Editor-in-Chief: Nancy Fitzpatrick Wyatt
Executive Editor: Susan Carlisle Payne
Art Director: Cynthia R. Cooper
Copy Chief: Allison Long Lowery

America's Best Recipes: A 2003 Hometown Collection

Editors: Allison Long Lowery, Leah Marlett, Kelly Hooper Troiano
Copy Editor: Donna Baldone
Editorial Assistants: Megan Graves, Diane Rose
Designer: Kelly Davis
Director, Test Kitchens: Elizabeth Tyler Luckett
Assistant Director, Test Kitchens: Julie Christopher
Recipe Editor: Gayle Hays Sadler
Test Kitchens Staff: Kristi Carter, Nicole L. Faber, Kathleen Royal Phillips,
   Jan A. Smith, Elise Weis, Kelley Self Wilton
Senior Photographer: Jim Bathie
Photographer: Brit Huckabay
Senior Photo Stylist: Kay E. Clarke
Photo Stylist: Ashley Wyatt
Director, Production and Distribution: Phillip Lee
Books Production Manager: Larry Hunter
Production Assistant: Faye Porter Bonner
Publishing Systems Administrator: Rick Tucker

CONTRIBUTORS
Indexer: Mary Ann Laurens
Test Kitchens Interns: Mary Beth Brookby, Traci Higgins
Project Consultant: Jean Wickstrom Liles
Editorial Intern: Terri Laschober

To order additional copies, call 1-800-765-6400.

For more books to enrich your life, visit oxmoorhouse.com

Cover: Tomato, Cheese, and Herb Tart *(page 160)*

Contents

Introduction

Discover the best that America has to offer in this newest collection of *America's Best Recipes–A 2003 Hometown Collection.* Inside you'll find local culinary treasures and favorite family recipes from fund-raising community cookbooks across our nation. Don't be surprised if you uncover a recipe reminiscent of your childhood. Share it with your family and continue the tradition. And try one of the many new recipes that you'll find inside this edition of *America's Best Recipes.* Our recipes appeal to cooks of every skill level who enjoy the adventure of making creative recipes from around our diverse country. Throughout these pages, you'll find:

- A party primer giving you a versatile collection of recipes, tips, and ideas to simplify entertaining. From appetizers to desserts, you'll find the perfect recipes you'll need to awe your guests. Also in this chapter, you'll find ideas on themes, guidelines to determining the right amount of food and beverages you'll need, no-fuss tips for easy entertaining plus a handy countdown do-list of tasks to check off before your event.
- Speedy solutions when time is of the essence. Our Quick & Easy chapter gives you a variety of recipes that can be cooked and prepared in 45 minutes or less—using only a handful of ingredients.
- Recipes for every taste and occasion throughout these 17 delicious food chapters. From Cajun Meat Loaf to Beef Tenderloin Stuffed with Goat Cheese, you'll delight in the enticing range of traditional to contemporary dishes.

We're excited to provide these hometown recipes to you as well as introduce you to some of the many charitable organizations across America that make this book possible. If a cookbook featured in this edition interests you and you'd like to buy a copy, you'll find the address beginning on page 320. With your purchase of these books, you're not only receiving outstanding recipes, you're lending a helping hand to these charitable organizations across our country. In turn, the communities of the sponsoring charitable organizations benefit from the proceeds of the sale of these cookbooks. What a great way to show your generosity and give back to America.

The Editors

Party Pleasers

Tulip Cups with Lemon Curd Filling, page 39

Party Pleasers

Whether you're hosting a lavish party or taking a dish to a potluck, this chapter offers spectacular recipes to "make" or to "take." From appetizers to dessert, from elegant to just plain fun, you'll find a versatile collection of recipes, tips, and ideas to simplify party planning.

Golden Rule of Hospitality

Attend your own party; be sure you have a good time, too. Entertaining is not about impressing your guests. It's about being yourself and making guests feel welcome and comfortable.

Decisions, Decisions

Begin your party planning by making the following important decisions:

- Budget—conservative or splashy
- Time of day—morning, midday, or evening
- Setting—indoors, outdoors, or offsite
- Style—formal or informal, intimate or large, seated or buffet
- Guest list—children, adults, or multigenerational
- Menu—catered, homemade, or a combination of the two
- Invitations—oral or written
- Entertainment—game playing, spectator (watching sports or a movie), conversation, background music, or entertainers (birthday clowns, magicians, etc.)
- Decorations—Plan decorations and flowers around your menu and party theme. See our theme ideas on the opposite page.

Planning Checklist

Here's a handy countdown to-do list.

1 to 2 months ahead—Plan menu; send invitations (if large event); do major housecleaning

3 weeks—Rent or borrow extra chairs and special equipment; make shopping list

2 weeks ahead—Send invitations (if small informal party); shop for staples; clean out refrigerator and freezer; cook food ahead, and freeze

1 week ahead—Clean house; confirm RSVP numbers; buy beverages; iron napkins; polish silver

1 or 2 days ahead—Shop for perishables; do light housecleaning

1 day ahead—Prepare some perishables; arrange fresh flowers; set table; select serving dishes and utensils; chill beverages

Party Themes

Birthdays and anniversaries are natural times to celebrate. For even more fun, consider a theme party. Here are some ideas:

Time of day	sunrise, breakfast, brunch, lunch, afternoon tea, sunset, sleepover
Ethnic	Italian pasta, Japanese sushi, Mexican fiesta, Texas barbecue, Indian buffet
Holiday	Christmas to Thanksgiving and all in between—highlighting special foods like spectacular lamb roast, wild game, fish fry, dessert party, wine and cheese party, cookie swap, or pizza
Dress up	hat party; attire from a decade, century, or other period of time
Work/Play	painting, leaf-raking, landscaping, cooking (making homemade pasta, enchiladas, etc.)
Outdoor	beach party, picnic, barbecue, tailgate, clambake
Milestone	graduation, bar/bas mitzvah, first job, new job, first house, retirement, garden harvest
Sports	skating, swimming, baseball, Super Bowl, skiing
Media	re-creating food scenes from movies or books
Family favorites	potluck featuring a collection of your family's favorite recipes, from Uncle Louie's famous chili to Grandma's best cookies
Fun 'n' Games	role-playing games, board or video games, cook-off competition, sports play-offs, girls-night-out

Frazzle Fighters

- Use convenience foods—everything doesn't have to be from scratch
- Buy a bakery cake, and decorate it with fresh flowers
- Delegate cleaning, cooking, and decorating
- Resist last-minute panic—guests won't know you didn't make extra dip
- Station snacks in several rooms to encourage mingling
- For large parties, consider hiring someone to clear and wash dishes
- If serving alcohol, hire a bartender—it's easier on the budget if you have multiple hosts for the party

How Much Serves How Many?

You want to have enough to serve your guests adequately, but without tons of left-overs. Use the following guidelines to determine your food and beverage needs. When in doubt, err on the side of generosity.

Appetizers	4 to 6 pieces per guest before dinner
Beer	1 keg per 30 to 40 guests
Beverages (alcoholic)	17 drinks per 750 ml bottle of liquor (Figure 1 to 2 drinks per guest per hour.)
Bread/Rolls	Rolls—2 per guest
Cakes (sheet)	¼ sheet (8"x12") = 24 (2"x2") servings ½ sheet (12"x16") = 48 (2"x2") servings Full sheet (16"x24") = 96 (2"x2") servings
Cakes (round)	8-inch round double-layer cake = 8 servings 9-inch round triple-layer cake = 10 to 12 servings
Cheeses	2 ounces per guest
Chips	2 ounces per guest
Dip	3 to 4 tablespoons per guest
Ice (crushed)	¾ to 1 pound per guest
Ice cream	½ gallon = 16 (½-cup) servings 1 gallon = 32 (½-cup) servings
Luncheon meats	3 to 4 ounces per guest
Meats	½ to 1 pound per guest (bone-in cooked) ¼ to ½ pound per guest (boneless cooked)
Mixers	1 (10-ounce) bottle per guest
Napkins	2 or 3 per guest
Punch (nonalcoholic)	1 gallon per 20 to 24 guests
Salads	Green—4 ounces per guest Chicken, Tuna, or Potato—½ cup per guest
Vegetables/Sides	⅔ cup per guest
Wine/Champagne	Wine—1 (750 ml) bottle per 4 (6-ounce) servings Champagne—1 case per 50 guests

Party Poopers: too many things that need to be baked in the oven at once; any menu that takes you away from your guests for more than 15 minutes at a time; waiting until the last minute to clean the house; forgetting to prepare food or order equipment ahead; inviting more people than your house can accommodate

Stuffed Mushrooms

These Greek-inspired stuffed mushrooms contain a creamy feta filling and are topped with Parmesan cheese.

30 large fresh mushrooms
2 tablespoons butter or margarine, divided
2 tablespoons olive oil, divided
2 tablespoons finely chopped green onions
2 tablespoons dry white wine
½ teaspoon pepper
¼ teaspoon salt
1 cup crumbled feta cheese
1 tablespoon chopped fresh dill
2 tablespoons heavy whipping cream
¼ cup grated Parmesan cheese

Rinse mushrooms; pat dry. Remove and discard stems. Melt 1 tablespoon butter in a large skillet; add 1 tablespoon olive oil. Sauté half of mushrooms over medium heat 5 minutes. Place mushrooms on an ungreased 15- x 10-inch jellyroll pan, stem side up. Repeat procedure with remaining mushrooms, butter, and oil, reserving drippings in skillet; set pan aside.

Sauté green onions in drippings over medium heat 1 minute. Add wine, pepper, and salt; cook, uncovered, 30 seconds or until liquid evaporates. Remove from heat, and stir in feta cheese, dill, and whipping cream. Stuff mushroom caps with cheese mixture; sprinkle with Parmesan cheese, and bake at 350° for 10 minutes. Yield: 30 appetizers.   Maria Garifalakis

Flavor It Greek! A Celebration of Food, Faith and Family
Philoptochos Society of Holy Trinity Greek Orthodox Church
Portland, Oregon

Cheese Soufflé Sandwiches

These bite-size sandwiches take time to assemble, but their buttery goodness is well worth the effort. Chill the bread the night before you make these to make assembly easier. After assembling, you can freeze the unbaked sandwiches up to a month and bake them as you need them. And you don't need to thaw them before baking!

2　cups butter or margarine, softened

4　(5-ounce) jars sharp process cheese spread, softened

1　teaspoon onion powder

1　teaspoon Beau Monde seasoning

1½　teaspoons minced fresh dill

1½　teaspoons Worcestershire sauce

1　teaspoon hot sauce

3　(16-ounce) loaves sandwich bread, chilled (we tested with Pepperidge Farm)

Beat butter and cheese at medium speed with an electric mixer until light and fluffy. Add onion powder and next 4 ingredients.

Work with one loaf of bread at a time, leaving remainder chilled. Stack 3 slices of bread; using an electric knife or bread knife, remove crust from bread stack; reserve crust for other uses. Spread cheese mixture between 3 bread slices, restacking slices. Cut stack into 4 squares, and spread cheese mixture on top, bottom, and sides of each square. Place stacks on ungreased baking sheets. Repeat procedure with remaining bread and cheese mixture, loaf by loaf. (Sandwiches may be frozen in an airtight container up to 1 month at this stage. No need to thaw before baking.)

Bake at 325° for 15 to 18 minutes or until edges are golden. Yield: 6 dozen.

Note: Chill bread before spreading with cheese mixture to prevent bread slices from crumbling.

From Black Tie to Blackeyed Peas: Savannah's Savory Secrets
St. Joseph's Foundation of Savannah, Inc.
Savannah, Georgia

Carolina Caviar

This isn't a real caviar but rather black-eyed pea salsa that makes enough for a crowd. It marinates in Italian dressing, so serve the spicy blend with a slotted spoon.

2 (15.8-ounce) cans black-eyed peas, rinsed and drained
1 (16-ounce) bottle Italian dressing
1 (10-ounce) can white shoepeg corn, drained
1 large firm tomato, chopped
1 green bell pepper, chopped
1 small onion, chopped
1 cup chopped fresh parsley
4 green onions, chopped
1 tablespoon chopped fresh cilantro
2 garlic cloves, minced
Tortilla chips

Stir together all ingredients except chips in a large bowl. Cover and chill 8 to 24 hours. Spoon mixture into a serving bowl, using a slotted spoon. Serve with tortilla chips. Yield: 8 cups.

Carolina Thyme
The Junior League of Durham and Orange Counties, Inc.
Durham, North Carolina

Eggplant Cookies with Goat Cheese and Tomato Basil Sauce

Two slices of eggplant hold a goat cheese filling to make "cookies" that are then placed in a homemade tomato sauce for an elegant seated appetizer. The recipe calls for Oriental eggplant, which is narrow and straight and ranges in color from solid to striated shades of purple. Look for it in the produce section of most supermarkets.

2 teaspoons olive oil
1 large garlic clove, minced
1 small shallot, minced
1 tablespoon golden tequila or dry red wine
1½ tablespoons dry red wine
2 large tomatoes, peeled, seeded, and chopped
⅛ teaspoon salt
⅛ teaspoon freshly ground pepper
2 tablespoons julienne-sliced fresh basil

2 Oriental eggplants, peeled and cut into 12 (½-inch) slices each
½ cup all-purpose flour
1 large egg, lightly beaten
1 cup soft breadcrumbs (homemade)
6 tablespoons olive oil, divided
1 (4-ounce) log goat cheese, cut into 12 rounds

Heat 2 teaspoons olive oil in a medium saucepan over medium heat. Add garlic and shallot, and cook 1 minute or just until tender. Add tequila and wine; cook 1 minute or until liquid is absorbed. Stir in tomato, salt, and pepper; cook 5 minutes or until slightly thickened. Stir in basil; remove from heat. Cover and keep warm.

Dredge eggplant in flour; dip in egg. Dredge in breadcrumbs.

Heat 2 tablespoons oil in a large skillet over medium-high heat; add one-third of eggplant; cook 3 to 4 minutes on each side or until golden brown. Drain on paper towels. Repeat procedure twice with remaining oil and eggplant slices.

Place 1 slice of goat cheese between 2 eggplant slices; repeat with remaining eggplant and cheese. Spread tomato sauce evenly over individual serving plates, and top with eggplant "cookies." Serve warm. Yield: 6 servings.

Secret Ingredients
The Junior League of Alexandria, Louisiana

Pear, Brie, Brown Sugar, and Pecan Pizza

No one will be able to resist a slice of this gooey pizza that's both sweet and savory with each bite.

8 ounces Brie	1 (16-ounce) Italian bread
2 tablespoons butter or	shell (we tested with Boboli)
margarine	2 teaspoons olive oil
2 pears, peeled, cored, and	½ cup chopped pecans
thinly sliced (we tested with	3 to 4 tablespoons light brown
Bartlett)	sugar
½ teaspoon ground	
cinnamon	

Remove and discard rind from cheese. Cut cheese into cubes; set aside.

Melt butter in a large skillet over medium heat. Add pear, and sauté 3 minutes or until tender; sprinkle with cinnamon.

Place bread shell on a large pizza pan or baking sheet. Brush shell with olive oil, and top with cheese cubes. Spread cooked pear mixture over cheese; sprinkle with pecans and brown sugar. Bake at 500° for 5 minutes. Slice pizza into wedges, and serve immediately. Yield: 8 servings.

Sharla Sanderson

Look Who Came to Dinner
The Junior Auxiliary of Amory, Mississippi

Layered Pesto Terrine

Got extra basil? Make a batch of pesto. This appetizer is a great way to showcase homemade pesto.

1 (8-ounce) package cream cheese, softened
1 (4-ounce) package goat cheese, softened
1 cup loosely packed fresh basil
1 cup loosely packed fresh spinach
1½ teaspoons minced garlic
¼ cup extra-virgin olive oil
1 cup freshly grated Parmesan cheese

¼ teaspoon freshly ground pepper
⅓ cup dried tomatoes in oil, drained and chopped
¼ cup chopped walnuts
Olive oil (optional)
Chopped dried tomatoes (optional)
Chopped fresh basil (optional)

Beat cream cheese and goat cheese at medium speed with an electric mixer until smooth; set aside.

Pulse 1 cup basil, spinach, and garlic in a food processor until minced, stopping to scrape down sides. With processor running, gradually pour ¼ cup olive oil through food chute. Process until well blended. Add Parmesan cheese and pepper; process just until blended.

Line a 3-cup bowl with a 14-inch piece of heavy-duty plastic wrap, smoothing any wrinkles. Place one-third of cream cheese mixture in an even layer in prepared bowl; top with half of pesto mixture. Sprinkle with half each of tomatoes and walnuts. Repeat layers, using remaining cheese mixture, pesto mixture, tomatoes, and walnuts, ending with cheese mixture. Fold plastic wrap over top, and pack down lightly. Chill at least 8 hours.

About 30 minutes before serving, unfold plastic wrap, and invert mold onto a serving platter. Carefully peel away plastic wrap. Drizzle with oil, and sprinkle with dried tomatoes and basil, if desired. Yield: 12 appetizer servings.

Carolina Thyme
The Junior League of Durham and Orange Counties, Inc.
Durham, North Carolina

Cocktail Meatballs

These scrumptious meatballs, covered with sauerkraut, cranberry sauce, and chili sauce are delicious served alone or on sandwich rolls with melted Swiss. They're superquick to make and will be the first to go at any party.

2 pounds lean ground beef
1 cup fine, dry breadcrumbs (store-bought)
1 (1.4-ounce) envelope dry onion soup mix
3 large eggs
1 (16-ounce) can sauerkraut, drained

1 (16-ounce) can whole-berry cranberry sauce
1 (12-ounce) bottle chili sauce
½ cup water
1 cup firmly packed light brown sugar

Combine ground beef, breadcrumbs, onion soup mix, and eggs in a large bowl, and stir until blended. Shape into 1-inch meatballs. Place meatballs in a greased 13- x 9-inch baking dish.

Stir together sauerkraut and remaining 4 ingredients. Spoon over meatballs.

Bake, uncovered, at 450° for 25 minutes. Yield: 3 dozen.

Tucson Treasures: Recipes & Reflections
Tucson Medical Center Auxiliary
Tucson, Arizona

Chinese Spareribs

These spareribs are the ultimate finger food for true party-goers.
They're infused with a gingery garlic sauce and bathed in a glaze.

1 (10-ounce) jar plum jelly
⅓ cup dark corn syrup
⅓ cup soy sauce
2 green onions, sliced

2 garlic cloves, minced
2 teaspoons ground ginger
2 pounds pork back ribs

Combine first 6 ingredients in a medium saucepan; cook over medium heat 5 minutes or until jelly melts. Remove from heat, reserving ½ cup sauce for basting. Set aside.

Cut ribs into serving-size portions. Place ribs and sauce in a large heavy-duty zip-top plastic bag; seal. Chill at least 8 hours, turning bag occasionally.

Remove ribs from marinade, discarding marinade. Place ribs in a single layer on a rack in a large shallow aluminum foil-lined pan.

Bake at 350° for 1 hour, brushing often with reserved sauce. Yield: 6 to 8 servings.   Veronica Marsh

Lake Waccamaw United Methodist Church Cookbook
Lake Waccamaw United Methodist Church
Lake Waccamaw, North Carolina

Skewered Chicken Teriyaki

Try a variety of Oriental dipping sauces with these for fun!

½ cup lite soy sauce
½ cup dry white wine
5 garlic cloves, minced
1 teaspoon grated fresh ginger
3 tablespoons light brown
    sugar

2 tablespoons olive oil
2 pounds skinned and boned
    chicken breast halves, cubed
¼ cup sesame seeds, toasted

Stir together first 6 ingredients in a bowl; reserve ½ cup marinade.

Place chicken in a heavy-duty zip-top plastic bag; pour remaining marinade over chicken. Seal bag securely, and marinate in refrigerator 8 hours.

Soak 16 (6-inch) wooden skewers in water at least 30 minutes.

Drain chicken; discard marinade. Thread chicken onto skewers. Place skewers on a lightly greased rack in a broiler pan.

Broil 3 inches from heat 3 minutes on each side, brushing often with reserved marinade. Sprinkle with sesame seeds, and transfer to serving plate. Yield: 16 appetizers. Hisako Nakano

Flavors of the Tenderloin
Sidewalk Clean-Up, Recycling & Urban Beautification (SCRUB)
San Francisco, California

Mahogany Chicken Wings

These beautifully glazed chicken wings look as good as they taste. Make sure you serve them with lots of napkins!

1½ cups soy sauce
¾ cup dry sherry
¾ cup cider vinegar
1 cup hoisin sauce
¾ cup plum sauce
½ cup honey

12 green onions, minced (about 2 cups)
6 large garlic cloves, minced
32 chicken wings (6 to 7 pounds)

Combine first 8 ingredients in a large saucepan. Bring to a boil; reduce heat, and simmer, uncovered, 5 minutes. Cool sauce; cover and chill ½ cup sauce.

Cut off and discard wing tip; cut wings in half at joint.

Place chicken in a large plastic container. Pour remaining sauce over chicken; cover and marinate in refrigerator at least 8 hours.

Remove chicken from marinade, discarding marinade. Place chicken into 2 lightly greased roasting pans. Bake chicken at 375° for 1 hour or until done, basting with reserved ½ cup sauce marinade every 20 minutes. (Discard any remaining marinade.) Yield: 16 appetizer servings. Jackie Metzger and Livia Weinstein

Note: For easy cleanup, line roasting pans with aluminum foil.

Look What's Cooking . . .
Temple Sinai Sisterhood
Cranston, Rhode Island

Oriental Chicken Won Tons

Won ton wrappers are sold in the refrigerated produce section of most supermarkets. Use your favorite Asian dipping sauce to serve alongside these bite-sized treats. Cut leftover won ton wrappers into thin strips and add to broth-based soups in place of noodles.

8 ounces ground chicken or turkey	1 tablespoon dry sherry
½ cup shredded carrot (about 1 small carrot)	2 teaspoons cornstarch
½ cup finely chopped celery (about 1 rib)	½ (16-ounce) package won ton wrappers
1 tablespoon soy sauce	2 tablespoons butter or margarine, melted
2 teaspoons grated fresh ginger	Sweet-and-sour sauce (optional)

Cook ground chicken in a large nonstick skillet coated with cooking spray over medium heat, stirring until it crumbles and is no longer pink; drain. Add carrot, celery, soy sauce, and ginger. Combine sherry and cornstarch, stirring well; add to meat mixture. Cook, stirring constantly, 2 minutes or until thoroughly heated.

Lightly brush edges of won ton wrappers with water. Spoon about 1 teaspoon of filling in center of each won ton wrapper. Bring 2 opposite points of wrapper over filling; bring remaining 2 points to center, pressing together firmly. Place on lightly greased baking sheets.

Bake at 375° for 12 minutes or until golden. Brush with melted butter. Serve warm with sweet-and-sour sauce, if desired. Yield: 32 won tons.

Peg Gordon

Gifts from Our Heart
Mercy Special Learning Center
Allentown, Pennsylvania

Turkey and Chutney Rolls

If you could put the taste of Thanksgiving in a sandwich, this would be it, and nothing could be easier than using prepackaged rolls that you slice, fill, and then bake in the pan they came in.

1 (8-ounce) package cream cheese, softened
2 tablespoons mayonnaise
2 tablespoons sour cream
2 tablespoons chutney
1 tablespoon Dijon mustard
½ teaspoon curry powder
½ teaspoon ground red pepper

3 tablespoons minced onion
1 cup whole-berry cranberry sauce
4 (7½-ounce) packages party rolls in aluminum trays
1 pound smoked turkey, thinly sliced

Beat first 7 ingredients at medium speed with an electric mixer until blended. Stir together onion and cranberry sauce.

Remove rolls from aluminum tray. Slice rolls in half horizontally, using a serrated knife; do not separate rolls. Spread a thin layer of cream cheese mixture over top and bottom halves of each package of rolls.

Layer one-fourth of the turkey slices over bottom half of each package of rolls. Spread a thin layer of cranberry mixture over turkey. Cover with top halves of rolls. Cut rolls into individual sandwiches, and return rolls to aluminum trays.

Cover and bake at 350° for 25 minutes or until warm. (Bake, uncovered, during last 10 minutes, if desired, for crispier rolls.) Yield: 80 appetizers.

Note: These sandwiches freeze well.

Tapestry: A Weaving of Food, Culture and Tradition
The Junior Welfare League of Rock Hill, South Carolina

Junior League Punch

Jell-O, lemonade, and pineapple juice bring a splash of color and fruity flavor to this all-purpose punch that can be made ahead and frozen. You determine the final flavor and color of the punch by the flavor of gelatin you choose.

2 cups boiling water
2 (3-ounce) packages any flavor gelatin
1 (12-ounce) can frozen lemonade concentrate, undiluted

1 cup sugar
1 (46-ounce) can unsweetened pineapple juice
4 quarts water
1 tablespoon almond extract
2 (1-liter) bottles ginger ale

Combine boiling water and gelatin, stirring about 2 minutes or until gelatin dissolves. Stir in lemonade concentrate and sugar.

Add pineapple juice, water, and almond extract. Pour evenly into 2 large containers; cover and freeze at least 8 hours. Remove punch from freezer 4 hours before serving. Stir 1 bottle ginger ale into each container just before serving. Yield: 2 gallons.

Ropin' the Flavors of Texas
The Junior League of Victoria, Texas

White Sangría

Sangría is usually made with red wine, but this white wine version is a refreshing change. To keep the sangría cold when serving, freeze a cluster of grapes to put in it as a garnish, along with the orange, lime, and lemon slices. The frozen grapes will keep the sangría cold without diluting it.

1 (750-milliliter) bottle dry white wine
1 lemon, thinly sliced
1 orange, thinly sliced
1 lime, thinly sliced
½ cup orange juice

¼ cup orange liqueur (optional)
2 cups lemon-lime soft drink (we tested with Sprite)
1 cup crushed ice

Combine first 6 ingredients in a large container. Cover and chill thoroughly. Add soft drink and ice just before serving; stir gently. Yield: 6 cups.   Lourdes C. Gaztambides

De Nuestra Mesa: Our Food, Wine, and Tradition
New Hope Charities, Inc.
West Palm Beach, Florida

Thunder Valley Frozen Margaritas

This classic slushy concoction is guaranteed to liven up any party or celebration, and quench everyone's thirst. Plan ahead because the mixture needs to freeze at least 24 hours, then stir it and let stand until it reaches the desired slushy consistency. Thaw it all at once for a large party or stir it and spoon out portions for a glass or two at a time.

6 cups white tequila
16 cups water
2 cups Triple Sec
4 (12-ounce) cans frozen
   limeade concentrate, thawed
   and undiluted

2 (10-ounce) cans frozen
   margarita mix, thawed
Lime juice
Coarse salt

Combine tequila, water, Triple Sec, limeade, and margarita mix in a very large plastic container. Cover and freeze at least 24 hours or until frozen to a slushy consistency. Moisten rims of margarita glasses with lime juice, and dip into coarse salt. Pour margarita mixture into glasses. Yield: 2 gallons.

Start Your Ovens: Cooking the Way It Ought'a Be
The Junior League of Bristol, TN/VA
Bristol, Virginia

December Cider

If you're feeling jolly during the holidays, add extra rum to this fruity cider. Keep the cider warm in a slow cooker and let guests serve themselves.

1 (12-ounce) can frozen apple juice concentrate, undiluted
1 (11.5-ounce) can frozen cranberry-apple juice concentrate, undiluted
9 cups water
1 (6-ounce) can frozen lemonade concentrate, undiluted

5 (3-inch) cinnamon sticks
1 teaspoon ground nutmeg
7 whole cloves
⅓ cup rum or cinnamon schnapps

Combine first 3 ingredients in a Dutch oven. Stir in lemonade concentrate, cinnamon sticks, nutmeg, and cloves; bring to a boil. Cover, reduce heat, and simmer 15 minutes. Remove and discard cloves and cinnamon sticks before serving. Stir in rum or schnapps. Serve warm. Yield: 12 cups. Lindsay Lockett

Southern Elegance: A Second Course
The Junior League of Gaston County
Gastonia, North Carolina

After-Dinner Coffees

After a dinner party, treat your guests to an international coffee tasting. Place the ingredients on a tray, display recipes on cards, and let your guests prepare their own flavored coffee!

Café Brûlot

1 cup hot, strong brewed coffee
3 tablespoons warmed brandy or cognac

Sugar to taste
3 strips orange rind
Garnish: cinnamon stick

Combine first 4 ingredients in a large cup or mug; stir until sugar dissolves. Garnish, if desired. Yield: about 1¼ cups.

Irish Coffee

1 cup hot, strong brewed
  coffee
1½ teaspoons light brown
  sugar

¼ cup Irish whiskey
Whipped cream

Combine first 3 ingredients in a large cup or mug; stir until sugar dissolves. Dollop with whipped cream. Yield: 1¼ cups.

Hungarian Coffee

1 cup hot, strong brewed
  coffee
2 tablespoons brandy or
  cognac

1 tablespoon grated German
  chocolate
Whipped cream
Garnish: cinnamon stick

Combine first 3 ingredients in a large cup or mug; stir until chocolate melts. Dollop with whipped cream, and garnish, if desired. Yield: 1¼ cups.

Mexican Coffee

1 cup hot, strong brewed
  coffee
3 tablespoons coffee liqueur
1 tablespoon grated semisweet
  chocolate

Whipped cream
Garnish: cinnamon stick

Combine first 3 ingredients in a large cup or mug; stir until chocolate melts. Dollop with whipped cream, and garnish, if desired. Yield: about 1¼ cups.

Settings on the Dock of the Bay
ASSISTANCE LEAGUE® of the Bay Area
Houston, Texas

Quick Onion Buns

These rolls are delicious by themselves, but add a slice of roast beef and a dollop of horseradish, and you've got something special.

2 (¼-ounce) envelopes active
   dry yeast
½ cup warm water (100° to 110°)
1 teaspoon sugar
1 cup warm milk (100° to 110°)
½ cup butter or margarine,
   melted

3 large eggs
½ cup sugar
1 teaspoon salt
5½ cups all-purpose flour
1 (1.4-ounce) envelope dry
   onion soup mix
¼ cup butter or margarine

Combine yeast, warm water, and 1 teaspoon sugar in a 1-cup glass measuring cup; let stand 5 minutes. Combine milk and ½ cup butter in a small bowl; stir well.

Combine yeast mixture, milk mixture, eggs, ½ cup sugar, salt, and 2 cups flour in a large mixing bowl; beat at medium speed with an electric mixer until well blended. Gradually stir in enough of remaining flour and onion soup mix to make a soft dough. Place in a well-greased bowl, turning to grease top. Cover and let rise in a warm place (85°), free from drafts, 1 hour or until doubled in bulk.

Punch dough down; turn out onto a heavily floured surface. Roll dough to ¾-inch thickness. Cut dough with a 2-inch round cutter. Place rolls on greased baking sheets. Cover and let rise in a warm place, free from drafts, 30 minutes or until doubled in bulk.

Bake at 350° for 14 minutes or until buns are lightly browned. Rub ¼ cup butter across tops of buns while still hot. Serve warm. Yield: 41 buns.

Pamela Virostko

Divine Offerings: Recipes and Hints for the Kitchen
St. Charles Presbyterian Women
St. Charles, Missouri

Sausage and Biscuit Bites

These little bites taste like Mom's homemade sausage gravy, but in the form of a biscuit. The yeast is in the biscuits for flavor only; no rising time is needed.

1 pound ground pork sausage
1 (¼-ounce) envelope active
   dry yeast
¼ cup warm water (100° to 110°)
2⅔ cups all-purpose flour
2 tablespoons sugar

1 teaspoon baking powder
½ teaspoon baking soda
¾ teaspoon salt
½ cup shortening
¼ cup buttermilk

Cook sausage in a large skillet, stirring until it crumbles and is no longer pink. Drain; set aside.

Combine yeast and warm water in a 1-cup glass measuring cup; let stand 5 minutes. Combine flour and next 4 ingredients in a large bowl; cut in shortening with a pastry blender until mixture is crumbly. Add yeast mixture and buttermilk; stir just until dry ingredients are moistened. Knead in sausage. Turn dough out onto a lightly floured surface, and knead 6 to 8 times.

Roll dough to ½-inch thickness; cut with a 1¾-inch round biscuit cutter. Place on ungreased baking sheets. Bake at 425° for 10 minutes or until golden brown. Yield: 4 dozen.   Jean Starkey

Down Home Dining in Mississippi
Mississippi Homemaker Volunteers, Inc.
Water Valley, Mississippi

Cranberry Pistachio Biscotti

Don't be deterred by the crumbly dough; the biscotti will hold its shape once baked.

1 (6-ounce) package dried
  cranberries (about 1⅓ cups)
1 cup hot water
2½ cups unbleached
  all-purpose flour
1 cup sugar
½ teaspoon baking soda
½ teaspoon baking powder
½ teaspoon salt
3 large eggs, lightly beaten
1 teaspoon vanilla extract
1 cup pistachios, coarsely
  chopped
1 large egg, lightly beaten
1 teaspoon water

Combine cranberries and hot water in a small bowl; let stand 5 minutes. Drain well, and pat dry with paper towels.

Stir together flour and next 4 ingredients in a large bowl. Combine 3 eggs and vanilla; stir until blended. Add egg mixture to flour mixture; beat at medium speed with an electric mixer until well blended (mixture will be crumbly). Stir in cranberries and pistachios.

Knead mixture 6 to 8 times on a lightly floured surface. Divide mixture in half, and shape each portion into a 13- x 2-inch log. Place logs 3 inches apart on a lightly greased baking sheet (logs will spread).

Combine 1 egg and 1 teaspoon water. Brush each log with egg mixture. Bake at 325° for 30 minutes. Remove from oven, and cool in pan on a wire rack 10 minutes. Cut each log diagonally into ¾-inch slices with a serrated knife, using a gentle sawing motion. Place biscotti, cut side down, on ungreased baking sheets. Bake at 325° for 12 minutes; turn and bake 12 more minutes. Cool on wire racks. Yield: 3 dozen.

The Bounty of Chester County: Heritage Edition
Chester County Agricultural Development Council
West Chester, Pennsylvania

Shrimp Supreme

2 pounds unpeeled, large fresh shrimp

¾ cup butter or margarine, divided

1 small bunch green onions, finely chopped (about ¾ cup)

½ cup finely chopped parsley

3 tablespoons all-purpose flour

2 cups half-and-half

3 tablespoons dry sherry

⅛ teaspoon Worcestershire sauce

1 (4.5-ounce) jar sliced mushrooms, drained

¼ teaspoon salt

⅛ teaspoon ground red pepper

⅛ teaspoon black pepper

Peel shrimp, and devein, if desired.

Melt ¼ cup butter in a medium skillet over medium-high heat; add shrimp, and sauté 5 minutes or until shrimp turn pink; drain and set aside.

Melt remaining ½ cup butter in a large skillet over medium-high heat. Add green onions and parsley; sauté 2 minutes or until tender. Add flour, stirring well. Gradually add half-and-half, and cook over medium-high heat, stirring constantly, until thickened. Stir in sherry and remaining 5 ingredients; add shrimp to skillet. Cook until thoroughly heated. Serve over rice or pasta. Yield: 4 to 6 servings.

Crawfish Supreme

Substitute 1 pound frozen, peeled, and cooked crawfish for shrimp. Omit sautéing in ¼ cup butter. Add to sauce, and cook until thoroughly heated. Yield: 4 to 6 servings.

Secret Ingredients
The Junior League of Alexandria, Louisiana

Cold Poached Salmon with Lemon Dill Sauce

Salmon offers great make-ahead potential for a party. You can poach and chill this salmon and make its sauce a day ahead. Serve it either as a luncheon or dinner entrée or as an elegant seated appetizer.

2 quarts water	2 teaspoons salt
1 onion, sliced	2 bay leaves
¼ cup fresh lemon juice	6 (1-inch-thick) salmon steaks
10 black peppercorns	Lemon Dill Sauce

Combine first 6 ingredients in a fish poacher or a large skillet; bring to a boil. Cover, reduce heat, and simmer 30 minutes. Add salmon; simmer 8 to 10 minutes or until fish flakes with a fork. Transfer steaks to a platter. Cover and chill 8 to 10 hours. Serve with Lemon Dill Sauce. Yield: 6 servings.

Lemon Dill Sauce

1 cup mayonnaise	2 teaspoons dried dillweed
¼ cup buttermilk	2 teaspoons fresh lemon juice
1 tablespoon minced fresh parsley	1 garlic clove, crushed

Combine all ingredients in a small bowl. Cover and chill at least 1 hour. Yield: 1¼ cups.

Start Your Ovens: Cooking the Way It Ought'a Be
The Junior League of Bristol, TN/VA
Bristol, Virginia

Company's Best Chicken

Convenient packaged long-grain and wild rice shines through in this chicken dish that gets dolled up with a buttery mushroom cream sauce.

2 (6-ounce) packages long-grain and wild rice mix (we tested with Uncle Ben's)
12 (4-ounce) skinned and boned chicken breast halves
½ teaspoon salt
½ teaspoon pepper
½ cup butter or margarine, melted
1 (8-ounce) package sliced fresh mushrooms
1 tablespoon grated onion
2 cups whipping cream
¼ cup dry sherry

Prepare rice according to package directions. Spread rice in a greased 13- x 9-inch baking dish.

Sprinkle chicken with salt and pepper. Cook 6 chicken breast halves in ¼ cup butter in a large skillet over medium-high heat 5 minutes on each side or until done. Remove chicken from skillet, and arrange over rice; discard browned butter. Wipe skillet with a paper towel. Repeat procedure with remaining chicken breast halves and butter. Arrange chicken over rice. (Do not wipe skillet with a paper towel.)

Add mushrooms and onion to pan drippings; sauté 2 minutes. Stir in whipping cream and sherry. Bring to a simmer; simmer 10 minutes. Pour over chicken and rice.

Bake, uncovered, at 350° for 25 minutes or until thoroughly heated. Yield: 12 servings.

From Black Tie to Blackeyed Peas: Savannah's Savory Secrets
St. Joseph's Foundation of Savannah, Inc.
Savannah, Georgia

Grilled Chicken with Mango Salsa

How to choose a ripe, juicy mango? Pick one that yields to slight pressure and has a reddish-orange blush. Mangoes are available year-round, but are at their peak May through September. This recipe can easily be cut in half.

¾ cup olive oil
½ cup white wine vinegar
3 tablespoons grated fresh ginger
3 tablespoons Dijon mustard
1 tablespoon ground coriander

1 tablespoon ground cumin
¼ teaspoon freshly ground pepper
24 skinned and boned chicken breast halves
Mango Salsa
Garnish: fresh cilantro sprigs

Combine first 7 ingredients in a small bowl, stirring well; set aside. Place chicken in a large shallow dish. Reserve ¼ cup marinade, and pour remaining marinade over chicken, turning to coat. Cover and marinate in refrigerator at least 8 hours.

Remove chicken from marinade, discarding marinade. Grill chicken, without grill lid, over medium-high heat (350° to 400°) 6 to 8 minutes on each side or until done, basting often with reserved ¼ cup marinade. Serve with Mango Salsa. Garnish, if desired. Yield: 24 servings.

Mango Salsa

6 cups chopped peeled mango (about 6 mangoes)
1 cup finely chopped purple onion
½ cup chopped fresh cilantro
6 tablespoons fresh lime juice

4 jalapeño peppers, seeded and minced
2 large garlic cloves, minced
½ teaspoon dried crushed red pepper
1 teaspoon salt

Combine all ingredients in a large bowl; stir well. Cover and chill. Yield: 8 cups.

Austin Entertains
The Junior League of Austin, Texas

Sautéed Chicken in Lemon Cream Sauce

Tender chicken breasts bathed in a lemon cream sauce make a company-worthy main dish when served with buttered pasta and sautéed asparagus.

6 skinned and boned chicken breast halves	2 tablespoons fresh lemon juice
¼ teaspoon salt	¾ cup whipping cream
¼ teaspoon freshly ground pepper	½ cup low-sodium chicken broth
¼ cup butter or margarine, divided	½ cup freshly grated Parmesan cheese, divided
2 tablespoons dry vermouth or fresh lemon juice	¼ cup chopped fresh parsley
2 teaspoons grated lemon rind	Garnish: lemon wedges

Place chicken between 2 sheets of heavy-duty plastic wrap; flatten to ¼-inch thickness, using a meat mallet or rolling pin. Sprinkle chicken evenly with salt and pepper.

Melt 2 tablespoons butter in a large skillet over medium-high heat; add half of chicken, and cook 4 to 5 minutes on each side or until done. Set aside. Repeat procedure with remaining butter and chicken. Transfer chicken to a platter, and keep warm.

Wipe butter from skillet with a paper towel. Add vermouth, lemon rind, and juice; bring to a boil, and cook 1 minute, stirring to loosen particles from bottom of skillet.

Add cream, broth, and any liquid from cooked chicken to skillet; boil 8 minutes or until slightly thickened. Stir in ¼ cup Parmesan cheese; cook 30 seconds.

Pour sauce over chicken, and sprinkle with remaining ¼ cup cheese and parsley. Garnish, if desired. Yield: 6 servings.

Creating a Stir
The Lexington Medical Society Auxiliary
Lexington, Kentucky

Pork Roast with Apples and Bourbon

Bourbon combines with the natural sweetness of apples to add even more flavor to the roasted pork. Use the extra sauce atop noodles or mashed potatoes as a side dish.

1 (3½-pound) boneless pork loin roast
2 tablespoons vegetable oil
⅔ cup Dijon mustard
⅓ cup firmly packed light brown sugar
2 cups beef broth
½ cup bourbon

¼ teaspoon salt
½ teaspoon dried thyme
¼ teaspoon dried sage
3 apples, peeled and sliced (we tested with Braeburn)
½ cup half-and-half
1 tablespoon cornstarch

Cook pork in hot oil in a large skillet over medium-high heat until browned on all sides.

Place roast in a large roasting pan, reserving drippings in skillet. Spread mustard evenly over roast, and sprinkle with brown sugar; set aside.

Add beef broth and next 4 ingredients to skillet. Bring to a boil; reduce heat, and simmer, uncovered, 20 minutes. Add broth mixture to roasting pan; cover and bake at 375° for 20 minutes. Add apple slices; cover and bake 1 hour or until a meat thermometer inserted in center of roast registers 160°. Remove roast from pan, reserving apples and drippings in pan; cover roast with aluminum foil, and let stand 10 minutes before slicing.

Bring apples and pan juices to a boil in roasting pan over medium-high heat on cooktop. Combine half-and-half and cornstarch, stirring with a wire whisk until smooth. Stir cornstarch mixture into apple mixture; cook, stirring constantly, until thickened and bubbly. Serve sauce with pork. Yield: 8 to 10 servings.

Note: Omit half-and-half and cornstarch if you prefer a thinner sauce.

A Thyme to Remember
Dallas County Medical Society Alliance
Dallas, Texas

Veal Verrette

Tender veal topped with mushrooms, artichokes, and pearl onions makes a showstopping entrée. Pair it with a mixed greens salad, pasta tossed with olive oil, crusty bread, and your favorite wine for a sensational meal.

20 (4-ounce) veal cutlets
2 cups all-purpose flour
2 cups fine, dry breadcrumbs (store-bought)
1 teaspoon salt
1 teaspoon black pepper
2 tablespoons olive oil
5 tablespoons butter or margarine
1 (8-ounce) package sliced mushrooms

2 cups chopped artichoke hearts
1 cup pearl onions, peeled
¼ cup dry sherry
¼ teaspoon salt
¼ teaspoon garlic powder
¼ teaspoon black pepper
⅛ teaspoon ground white pepper
⅛ teaspoon ground red pepper

Place veal between 2 sheets of plastic wrap, and flatten to ¼-inch thickness, using a meat mallet or rolling pin.

Combine flour and next 3 ingredients in a shallow dish. Dredge veal in flour mixture; set aside.

Heat 1½ teaspoons olive oil in a large skillet over medium-high heat; add one-fourth of veal, and cook 1 to 2 minutes on each side or until lightly browned. Remove veal to a warm platter; cover and keep warm. Repeat procedure with remaining oil and veal.

Melt butter in skillet over medium-high heat. Add mushrooms, artichokes, and pearl onions; sauté 8 to 10 minutes or until tender. Add sherry and remaining 5 ingredients; cook 2 to 3 minutes or until thoroughly heated. Top veal with mushroom mixture. Serve immediately. Yield: 10 servings.

Jesse Verrette

Settings on the Dock of the Bay
ASSISTANCE LEAGUE® of the Bay Area
Houston, Texas

Bourbon Baked Ham

Basting this ham with bourbon as it bakes creates an awfully tasty ham. Be sure to flame the bourbon to burn off the alcohol and prevent possible oven flare-ups.

1 cup bourbon
1 cup firmly packed light
   brown sugar
1 (12- to 13-pound) smoked,
   fully cooked ham half

¾ cup water
⅓ cup Dijon mustard
1½ teaspoons pepper

Place bourbon in a small long-handled saucepan; heat just until warm (do not boil). Remove from heat. Ignite with a long match. Let flames die down.

Combine bourbon and brown sugar in a saucepan, stirring well. Bring to a boil, and cook 1 minute.

Remove and discard skin from ham. Score fat on ham in a diamond design. Place ham, fat side up, in a shallow roasting pan. Insert a meat thermometer, making sure it does not touch bone or fat. Pour water into pan. Bake, uncovered, at 350° for 1 hour, basting often with bourbon mixture.

Combine mustard and pepper; coat exposed portion of ham with mustard mixture. Cover and bake 2 hours or until thermometer registers 140°, basting often with bourbon mixture in pan. Transfer ham to a serving platter; let stand 10 minutes before slicing. Yield: 18 to 20 servings.

Mary Elliott

Cooking with Friends
Brunswick Community Hospital
Supply, North Carolina

Jamaican Beef Brisket

Serve this saucy, melt-in-your-mouth brisket alone or shredded on party rolls.

1 (6-pound) beef brisket
2 tablespoons vegetable oil
3 onions, sliced
3 garlic cloves, crushed
1 cup ketchup
1 cup water

¾ cup firmly packed light
    brown sugar
½ cup red wine vinegar
2 to 3 tablespoons
    pickapepper sauce

Trim excess fat from brisket. Heat oil in a Dutch oven over medium-high heat until hot. Add beef; brown on all sides. Remove beef from pan. Add onion and garlic; sauté 5 minutes or until onion is tender. Return beef to pan.

Combine ketchup and remaining 4 ingredients in a small bowl; stir well. Pour ketchup mixture over beef.

Cover and bake at 350° for 4 hours or until beef is very tender. Remove beef from pan, reserving pan juices. Let beef stand 10 minutes before serving. Slice beef diagonally across the grain, and serve with pan juices. Yield: 12 to 15 servings.   Susan Hughes

Breakfast in Cairo, Dinner in Rome
International School of Minnesota Foundation
Eden Prairie, Minnesota

Spectacular Beef Tenderloin with Port Sauce and Puff Pastry Garnish

This succulent tenderloin with its rosemary-infused sauce and buttery pastry caught our attention. It makes a great first impression and a lasting one, too!

½ (17.3-ounce) package frozen puff pastry sheets, thawed
1 (3- to 4-pound) beef tenderloin, trimmed
2 cups beef broth
¾ cup tawny port
3 tablespoons minced shallots (about 2)
½ teaspoon dried rosemary
1 bay leaf
3 tablespoons butter or margarine, melted
3 tablespoons all-purpose flour
Garnish: fresh rosemary sprigs

Cut puff pastry into leaf shapes, using small cookie cutters or a knife. Carefully transfer to baking sheets. Bake at 400° for 10 minutes or until pastry is puffed and golden. Gently remove pastry from baking sheets with spatulas, and cool on wire racks; set aside.

Place tenderloin on a rack in a shallow roasting pan. Bake at 400° for 45 to 55 minutes or until a meat thermometer inserted into thickest portion registers 145° (medium rare) or 160° (medium). Let stand 10 minutes before slicing.

Combine broth and next 4 ingredients in a large saucepan; place over medium-high heat. Bring to a boil; boil until mixture is reduced to 1½ cups. Reduce heat, and simmer 20 minutes. Combine butter and flour, stirring until smooth. Slowly whisk into broth mixture. Cook, stirring constantly, 5 minutes or until thickened. Discard bay leaf. Serve sliced tenderloin with sauce and puff pastry leaves. Garnish, if desired. Yield: 10 servings.

Creating a Stir
The Lexington Medical Society Auxiliary
Lexington, Kentucky

Tulip Cups with Lemon Curd Filling

Dress up these dainty bite-sized cups filled with lemon curd with a dollop of whipped cream and a berry for pizzazz.

½ (16-ounce) package frozen phyllo pastry, thawed (20 sheets)
½ cup butter or margarine, melted
½ cup butter or margarine
1 tablespoon grated lemon rind
⅓ cup fresh lemon juice
¼ teaspoon salt
1½ cups sugar
3 egg yolks
3 large eggs

Working with 1 phyllo sheet at a time, place phyllo sheet on a large work surface (keep remaining phyllo covered with a slightly damp towel). Brush each phyllo sheet with melted butter. Layer 3 more phyllo sheets on top, brushing each sheet with butter. Repeat procedure 4 more times, making 4 more stacks of 4 buttered sheets. Cut each stack into 3-inch squares, using kitchen shears.

Press squares of layered phyllo into lightly greased miniature (1¾-inch) muffin pans, pressing gently in center to form pastry shells. Bake at 350° for 12 to 14 minutes or until golden brown. Gently remove from pan, and cool on wire racks. (Phyllo cups may be made up to 2 days in advance and stored in an airtight container.)

Place ½ cup butter and next 4 ingredients in top of a double boiler. Cook over simmering water, stirring constantly, until butter melts. Combine egg yolks and eggs. Gradually stir about one-fourth of hot mixture into eggs; add to remaining hot mixture, stirring constantly. Cook over simmering water, stirring constantly, until mixture thickens and coats a spoon (about 10 minutes). Remove from heat; cool.

Fill cups with lemon curd up to 4 hours before serving. Chill until ready to serve. Yield: 40 pastries.

A Taste Tour
Gingko Twig of Muhlenberg Hospital, Plainfield, New Jersey
Westfield, New Jersey

Black and White Torta

Silky, creamy, and sinful with every bite, this double chocolate torta is a dream come true for chocolate lovers.

2 cups graham cracker crumbs	Dark Chocolate Filling
½ cup cocoa	White Chocolate Filling
1 cup sugar	Garnish: dark and white
½ cup unsalted butter, melted	chocolate shavings or curls

Combine first 4 ingredients. Press into bottom and 1 inch up sides of a 10-inch springform pan. Bake at 350° for 5 minutes on center rack of oven. Cool on a wire rack.

Prepare Dark Chocolate Filling, and pour into prepared pan; cover and chill 30 minutes. Prepare White Chocolate Filling, and spread over chilled dark chocolate layer. Cover and chill at least 8 hours.

Run a knife around sides of pan to loosen torta. Place on a serving plate, and remove sides of pan. Garnish, if desired. Yield: 12 to 16 servings.

Dark Chocolate Filling

16 (1-ounce) bittersweet chocolate baking squares, coarsely chopped (we tested with Baker's)	1½ cups heavy whipping cream

Place chocolate and cream in top of a double boiler. Place over warm but not simmering water, and cook, stirring occasionally, until chocolate melts. Yield: 2¾ cups.

White Chocolate Filling

4 (4-ounce) packages white chocolate baking bars, coarsely chopped (we tested with Ghirardelli)	2 teaspoons unflavored gelatin
	2 tablespoons cold water
3 cups heavy whipping cream, divided	1½ teaspoons vanilla extract

Combine chocolate and 1 cup cream in top of a double boiler. Place over warm but not simmering water, and cook, stirring occasionally, until chocolate melts. Cool 5 minutes; set aside.

Sprinkle gelatin over cold water in a saucepan; let stand 1 minute. Cook over low heat, stirring until gelatin dissolves; cool 5 minutes.

Beat remaining 2 cups whipping cream and vanilla at medium speed with an electric mixer. Gradually add cooled chocolate mixture and dissolved gelatin. Increase to medium speed, and beat until mixture begins to thicken and soft peaks form. Yield: 6 cups.

Savor the Moment
The Junior League of Boca Raton, Florida

Fresh Strawberry Cream Torte

A unique walnut crust topped with a fluffy cream cheese filling and adorned with mouthwatering strawberries is the essence of summer.

½ cup pecans or walnuts
1½ cups all-purpose flour
2 tablespoons sugar
¾ cup butter or margarine, cut into pieces
1 (8-ounce) package cream cheese, softened

½ cup sugar
1½ cups whipping cream
4 cups fresh strawberries, halved

Pulse nuts in a food processor until finely ground. Add flour and 2 tablespoons sugar. With processor running, add butter in pieces through food chute. Process just until dough starts to leave sides of bowl.

Press dough on bottom and 1 inch up sides of a 10-inch tart pan with a removable bottom. (Dough will be crumbly.) Bake at 325° for 40 minutes. Cool completely in pan on a wire rack.

Beat cream cheese and ½ cup sugar at high speed with an electric mixer until fluffy. Gradually add whipping cream in a thin stream. (Mixture thins if added too fast.) Spread cream cheese mixture over cooled crust. Arrange strawberries on top. Remove sides of tart pan before serving. Yield: 10 servings.

Molto Bene
Salvatore Mancini Lodge #2440
North Providence, Rhode Island

Cranberry Baked Alaska

2 (3-ounce) packages
  ladyfingers
2 quarts vanilla ice cream,
  slightly softened
1 (16-ounce) can whole-berry
  cranberry sauce, chilled

6 tablespoons brandy
3 egg whites
¾ cup sugar
⅛ teaspoon salt
⅛ teaspoon cream of tartar
Brandy Sauce

Line bottom of a 9-inch springform pan with ladyfingers. Place ladyfingers upright around outer edge of pan, arranging ladyfingers on bottom so sides fit together. Place ice cream in a large bowl. Add cranberry sauce and brandy; swirl into ice cream. Spoon ice cream mixture into prepared pan. Cover with plastic wrap, and freeze at least 8 hours.

Combine egg whites, sugar, salt, and cream of tartar in top of a double boiler. Place over simmering water. Cook, stirring constantly with a wire whisk, 5 minutes or until temperature registers 160° on an instant-read thermometer. Remove from heat. Beat at high speed with an electric hand mixer 5 minutes or until soft peaks form. Remove dessert from freezer; remove plastic wrap. Quickly spread meringue over entire surface, making sure edges are sealed. Return, uncovered, to freezer.

Just before serving, bake at 475° for 5 minutes or until meringue peaks are lightly browned. Remove sides of pan; transfer dessert to a cake plate. Slice; serve immediately with warm Brandy Sauce. Yield: 12 servings.

Brandy Sauce

¼ cup brandy
2 teaspoons cornstarch

1 (16-ounce) can whole-berry
  cranberry sauce

Place brandy in a long-handled saucepan; heat until warm (do not boil). Remove from heat. Ignite with a long match; let flames die down.

Combine cornstarch and cranberry sauce, stirring until blended. Stir into brandy. Cook over medium heat, stirring constantly, until thickened. Yield: 1½ cups.

Yuletide on Hilton Head: A Heritage of Island Flavors
United Way of Beaufort County
Hilton Head Island, South Carolina

Quick & Easy Recipes

Candy Bar Pizza, page 63

Chicken and Cheese Crostini

Enjoy these delectable bites of chicken and cheese hot from the oven as is or dolloped with a little guacamole.

1 **French baguette, cut into about 48 (¼-inch-thick) slices**
2 **cups (8 ounces) shredded mozzarella cheese**

2 **cups chopped cooked chicken**
½ **cup chunky salsa**
¼ **teaspoon garlic powder**

Arrange baguette slices on aluminum foil-lined baking sheets. Bake at 400° for 5 minutes or until golden.

Combine cheese and remaining 3 ingredients in a large bowl; spread about 1 tablespoon cheese mixture on each slice. Bake 4 more minutes or until cheese melts. Serve immediately. Yield: about 4 dozen.

Forget Me Not: Recipes and Stories to Remember
Hospice and Palliative Care of Greensboro, North Carolina

Onion and Cheese Spread

Just three ingredients make up this cheesy spread that's great as a topper for Melba toast or flavored bagel chips.

4 **cups (16 ounces) shredded Swiss cheese**

1 **cup mayonnaise**
1 **large onion, diced**

Stir together cheese and mayonnaise in a microwave-safe bowl. Microwave at HIGH 2½ minutes or until cheese melts. Stir in onion. Spoon cheese mixture into a greased 1-quart baking dish. Bake at 350° for 30 to 35 minutes or until lightly browned. Serve cheese spread with bagel chips or assorted crackers. Yield: 3 cups.

Faithfully Charleston
St. Michael's Episcopal Church
Charleston, South Carolina

Hot Ryes

A favorite finger food for parties, these party ryes are easy to prepare ahead. Simply make the topping up to a day ahead, and refrigerate it. Top bread slices with the spread just before baking.

4 bacon slices, cooked and crumbled
1 cup (4 ounces) shredded Swiss cheese
1 (4½-ounce) can chopped ripe olives
¼ cup mayonnaise
3 green onions, chopped
1 teaspoon Worcestershire sauce
½ teaspoon salt
Cocktail rye bread

Combine first 7 ingredients in a small bowl. Spread 1½ teaspoons cheese mixture onto each bread slice. Arrange slices on an ungreased baking sheet. Bake at 375° for 10 minutes or until lightly browned. Serve warm. Yield: about 3 dozen.

A Taste Tour
Gingko Twig of Muhlenberg Hospital, Plainfield, New Jersey
Westfield, New Jersey

Grab 'n' Go Gorp

Go ahead and dig into this merry mix of dried berries, chocolate, and nuts! It's high in fiber, vitamins, and protein, and is perfect for an after-school snack.

2 cups crispy wheat cereal squares
2 cups mixed nuts
1 cup dried cherries
1 cup dried cranberries
1 cup dried blueberries
1 cup semisweet chocolate morsels

Combine all ingredients; store in an airtight container. Yield: 8 cups.

Vintage Virginia: A History of Good Taste
The Virginia Dietetic Association
Centreville, Virginia

Crunch Sticks

1 (12-ounce) can buttermilk
  biscuits
3 tablespoons milk
1½ cups crisp rice cereal,
  coarsely crushed

2 tablespoons caraway seeds
2 tablespoons celery seeds
2 tablespoons dillseeds
1 teaspoon salt

Cut each biscuit in half. Roll each half into a pencil-thin stick. Brush with milk. Combine cereal and seasonings in a shallow pan. Roll sticks in cereal mixture. Place 2 inches apart on lightly greased baking sheets. Bake at 450° for 8 to 10 minutes or until lightly browned. Yield: 20 breadsticks.   Corey Fuselier

Sharing Our Best
Bull Run Parent Teacher Club
Sandy, Oregon

Frothy Orange Soda

This refreshing soda will remind you of that popular Dreamsicle ice cream bar. It's guaranteed to quench your thirst on hot summer days.

1 cup orange juice
1 cup vanilla ice cream

1 cup lemon-lime soft drink

Process orange juice and ice cream in a blender 1 minute or until smooth. Add lemon-lime soft drink; stir well. Pour into glasses; serve immediately. Yield: 3 cups.   Sylvia Autrey

Cooking with the Original Search Engine
Fort Worth Public Library All Staff Association
Fort Worth, Texas

Strawberry-Melon Soup

1 ripe cantaloupe, cubed
   (about 6¼ cups)
1 pint fresh strawberries
4 cups orange juice, divided
3 tablespoons fresh lemon
   juice

1 tablespoon strawberry
   liqueur (optional)
¼ teaspoon ground ginger
Garnishes: sour cream or
   lemon yogurt, fresh mint
   sprigs

Process half of cantaloupe, half of strawberries, and ½ cup orange juice in a food processor or blender until smooth. Pour into a 2½ quart pitcher; set aside. Process remaining cantaloupe, strawberries, and ½ cup orange juice; add to pitcher.

Add remaining 3 cups orange juice, lemon juice, liqueur, if desired, and ginger to pitcher, stirring well. Cover and chill until ready to serve. Garnish, if desired. Yield: 10 cups.

Lighthouse Secrets: A Collection of Recipes from the Nation's Oldest City
The Junior Service League of St. Augustine, Florida

Greek Bread

A hefty slice of this gooey bread that's loaded with olives, onions, and garlic would be a perfect accompaniment with a dinner salad or soup.

1½ cups (6 ounces) shredded
   mozzarella cheese
¼ cup butter or margarine,
   softened
2 tablespoons mayonnaise

6 green onions, chopped
1 (2¼-ounce) can sliced ripe
   olives, drained
¼ teaspoon garlic salt
1 (1-pound) loaf Italian bread

Stir together first 6 ingredients until well blended. Cut bread in half lengthwise. Spread butter mixture over each cut side of bread.

Wrap bread in aluminum foil, and bake at 350° for 20 minutes. Open foil, and bake bread 10 more minutes or until lightly browned. Yield: 6 servings.
                                Kimm Looney

Cookin' with Pride
4th Infantry Division
Ft. Hood, Texas

Baked Fish Fillets in Lime Juice and Sour Cream

Grated lime rind adds pretty flecks of color and hints at the flavor of these fish fillets drenched with a lime juice-spiked sour cream sauce. Be sure to grate the lime before juicing it.

6 (1-inch-thick) halibut or other whitefish fillets (about 2 pounds)
¾ teaspoon salt
½ teaspoon pepper
3 tablespoons fresh lime juice
1 (8-ounce) container sour cream
1 tablespoon chopped fresh parsley
1 teaspoon grated lime rind

Place fish fillets in a greased 13- x 9-inch baking dish; sprinkle with salt and pepper.

Combine lime juice, sour cream, and parsley, stirring well; pour over fish. Sprinkle with lime rind.

Bake at 400° for 20 minutes or until fish flakes with a fork. Yield: 6 servings.

Flavors of the Gardens
Callaway Gardens
Pine Mountain, Georgia

Golden Catfish Fillets

A crisp, crunchy coating of cornmeal accented with garlic powder plus ground red pepper and black pepper adds zip to this easy catfish dish.

1 cup cornmeal
1 teaspoon salt
¼ teaspoon garlic powder
¼ teaspoon ground red pepper
⅛ teaspoon black pepper
1 egg white
1 cup milk
6 (6-ounce) catfish fillets (½ inch thick)
Vegetable oil
Garnish: lemon wedges

Combine first 5 ingredients in a shallow dish; stir well. Set aside.

Whisk together egg white and milk in a shallow dish. Dip fillets in egg mixture; dredge in cornmeal mixture.

Pour oil to a depth of ¼ inch into a large heavy skillet. Fry fillets in hot oil over medium-high heat 4 minutes on each side or until golden. Garnish, if desired. Yield: 6 servings.   Joyce Ogle

Lake Waccamaw United Methodist Church Cookbook
Lake Waccamaw United Methodist Church
Lake Waccamaw, North Carolina

Feta Chicken with Fresh Oregano

An unusual marinade of plain yogurt laced with garlic and oregano flavors and tenderizes this Greek-inspired entrée. Feta cheese sprinkled on top carries out the Mediterranean theme.

1 (8-ounce) container plain
  yogurt
2 large garlic cloves, minced
1 tablespoon chopped fresh
  oregano or 1 teaspoon dried
  oregano

½ teaspoon freshly ground
  pepper
4 skinned and boned chicken
  breast halves
¾ cup crumbled feta cheese

Combine first 4 ingredients in a large bowl. Add chicken; turn to coat. Cover and marinate in refrigerator 30 minutes, turning after 15 minutes.

Preheat broiler.

Remove chicken from marinade, reserving marinade. Place chicken on a lightly greased rack in a broiler pan; brush with remaining marinade. Broil 5½ inches from heat 8 to 10 minutes. Turn chicken; sprinkle evenly with feta cheese. Broil 4 to 5 more minutes or until chicken is done and golden. Serve immediately. Yield: 4 servings.

California Fresh Harvest: A Seasonal Journey through Northern California
The Junior League of Oakland-East Bay
Lafayette, California

Summer Lime Chicken

Generous amounts of fresh lime juice, cilantro, and garlic create a marinade that only needs to mingle with the chicken for an hour to infuse it with flavor.

⅓ cup olive oil
¼ cup fresh lime juice
3 garlic cloves
3 tablespoons minced fresh
  cilantro

½ teaspoon salt
½ teaspoon pepper
4 skinned and boned chicken
  breast halves

Combine first 6 ingredients in a small bowl; stir with a whisk. Reserve 2 tablespoons marinade for basting.

Place chicken in a large heavy-duty zip-top plastic bag. Pour remaining marinade over chicken, and seal. Marinate in refrigerator 1 hour, turning occasionally.

Remove chicken from marinade; discard marinade. Grill, covered with grill lid, over medium-high heat (350° to 400°) about 20 minutes or until done, turning once and basting occasionally with reserved marinade. Yield: 4 servings.

It's About Time: Recipes, Reflections, Realities
National Association Teachers of Family and Consumer Sciences
Bowling Green, Kentucky

Bill Bolcom's Pork Scaloppine with Green Peppercorns

A scant but tangy green peppercorn sauce flavors these pork medaillons nicely. Pounding the pork loin tenderizes the meat and allows it to cook faster. Look for pickled green peppercorns on the condiment aisle of your supermarket.

1 pound pork tenderloin or
   boneless pork loin
¼ teaspoon salt
¼ teaspoon freshly ground
   black pepper
2 tablespoons olive oil,
   divided

2 tablespoons butter or
   margarine, divided
1 garlic clove, crushed
2 tablespoons pickled green
   peppercorns, drained
1 teaspoon fresh lemon juice

Cut pork crosswise into 8 slices. Place pork between 2 sheets of heavy-duty plastic wrap, and flatten to ¼-inch thickness, using a meat mallet or rolling pin. Sprinkle pork evenly with salt and pepper.

Heat 1 tablespoon olive oil and 1 tablespoon butter in a large non-stick skillet over medium-high heat until hot. Add garlic and half of pork; cook 2 minutes on each side. Transfer pork to a platter, and keep warm. Repeat process with remaining oil, butter, and pork; remove to platter.

Discard garlic clove. Add peppercorns and lemon juice to skillet; cook 30 seconds. Pour sauce over pork. Serve immediately. Yield: 4 servings.

Bravo! Recipes, Legends & Lore
University Musical Society
Ann Arbor, Michigan

Lamb Chops Stilton

No one would ever guess that this 3-ingredient dish is such a snap to prepare because it tastes like something from a five-star restaurant! We were so impressed with its look and flavor that we awarded it our highest rating.

8 (1-inch-thick) lamb loin chops
8 teaspoons Dijon mustard, divided

6 ounces Stilton cheese, crumbled

Place lamb chops on a lightly greased rack in a broiler pan. Brush top of each chop with ½ teaspoon mustard.

Broil chops 5 minutes. Turn chops; brush each with ½ teaspoon mustard. Broil 5 more minutes.

Sprinkle chops evenly with crumbled cheese, and broil 1 minute or until cheese melts. Serve immediately. Yield: 4 servings.

Settings on the Dock of the Bay
ASSISTANCE LEAGUE® of the Bay Area
Houston, Texas

Ravioli with Roasted Red Pepper Cream

If you're looking for a simple, yet rich-tasting, dish that tastes like it took hours, this 15-minute miracle fits the bill. A salad and bread-sticks are all you need to complete the meal.

1 (24-ounce) package frozen cheese ravioli
2½ quarts boiling water
1 (7-ounce) jar roasted sweet red peppers, drained, seeded, and cut into strips

½ cup dry white wine
1 cup whipping cream
¾ cup freshly grated Parmesan cheese

Cook ravioli in boiling water 5 minutes or until tender. Drain; set aside, and keep warm.

Meanwhile, combine peppers and wine in a saucepan. Bring to a boil; reduce heat, and simmer, uncovered, 5 minutes or until reduced to 2 tablespoons. Stir in whipping cream. Bring to a boil; reduce heat, and simmer, uncovered, 3 to 5 minutes or until slightly thickened, stirring often. Add Parmesan cheese; cook, stirring constantly, until cheese melts.

Divide ravioli among 4 individual serving bowls. Spoon sauce over pasta. Serve immediately. Yield: 4 servings.

Cooks of the Green Door
The League of Catholic Women
Minneapolis, Minnesota

Rotini with Artichokes and Sun-Dried Tomatoes

Instead of using Italian dressing, prepare a homemade one with equal parts balsamic vinegar and olive oil for the salad, and top it with 8 ounces of crumbled herb-flavored feta cheese.

1 (16-ounce) package rotini pasta
2 (6-ounce) jars marinated artichoke hearts, drained and quartered
¾ to 1 cup Italian dressing
1 (6-ounce) can pitted black olives, drained and quartered

1 (7-ounce) jar marinated dried tomatoes in oil, drained and chopped
10 fresh basil leaves, thinly shredded
1 large red bell pepper, diced
½ teaspoon salt

Cook pasta according to package directions. Drain pasta, rinse, and place in a large bowl.

Combine artichoke hearts, ¾ cup dressing, and remaining 5 ingredients. Toss with pasta, adding additional dressing, if desired. Yield: 8 servings.

The Kosher Palette
Joseph Kushner Hebrew Academy
Livingston, New Jersey

Easy Skillet Eggplant Lasagna

Serve this superquick Italian favorite alone or on an Italian roll for sandwiches.

1 cup Italian-seasoned
  breadcrumbs
1 (1-pound) eggplant, cut into
  ¼-inch slices
2 large eggs, beaten

¼ cup vegetable oil, divided
1 (26-ounce) jar marinara
  sauce
1 cup (4 ounces) shredded
  mozzarella cheese

Place breadcrumbs in a shallow dish. Dip eggplant slices in egg; dredge in breadcrumbs, shaking off excess.

Pour 2 tablespoons oil into a large skillet; place over medium heat until hot. Fry half of eggplant slices in hot oil until golden on each side. Remove from skillet; keep warm. Add remaining oil to skillet; fry remaining eggplant slices until golden on each side. Return reserved eggplant slices to skillet.

Pour marinara sauce over eggplant. Bring to a boil; cover, reduce heat, and simmer 5 minutes or until eggplant is tender. Sprinkle with cheese; cover and simmer 1 to 2 minutes or until cheese melts. Yield: 4 servings.   Effie Karambelas

Flavor It Greek! A Celebration of Food, Faith and Family
Philoptochos Society of Holy Trinity Greek Orthodox Church
Portland, Oregon

Greens and Berries Salad

4 cups loosely packed torn
   salad greens
¼ cup red wine vinaigrette
2 tablespoons honey
¼ cup thinly sliced purple
   onion

2 cups fresh strawberries,
   quartered
½ cup chopped walnuts,
   toasted

Place salad greens in a large bowl.

Combine vinaigrette, honey, and onion in a small microwave-safe bowl. Microwave, covered, at HIGH 2 minutes or until onion is tender, stirring once. Drizzle hot dressing over greens; toss to coat. Add strawberries and walnuts, tossing gently. Serve immediately. Yield: 4 servings.   Elizabeth Tiffany

Breakfast in Cairo, Dinner in Rome
International School of Minnesota Foundation
Eden Prairie, Minnesota

Sugared Asparagus

When buying asparagus, choose firm, bright green stalks with tight tips.

2 pounds fresh asparagus
3 tablespoons butter or
   margarine

2 tablespoons light brown
   sugar
½ cup chicken broth

Snap off tough ends of asparagus; cut asparagus into 2-inch pieces.

Melt butter and brown sugar in a skillet over medium-high heat, stirring until sugar dissolves. Add asparagus, and sauté in butter mixture 2 minutes. Stir in chicken broth; bring to a boil. Cover, reduce heat, and simmer 8 minutes or until asparagus is crisp-tender. Remove asparagus to a serving dish; keep warm.

Cook sauce, uncovered, until reduced by half. Pour over asparagus, and serve immediately. Yield: 4 to 6 servings.   Paula Underwood

Bread from the Brook
The Church at Brook Hills
Birmingham, Alabama

Broiled Tomatoes

A slathering of cheese topping richly crowns ripe-from-the-garden tomatoes that are a must for this dish.

½ cup mayonnaise
½ cup shredded Gruyère
    cheese or grated Parmesan
    cheese
½ cup minced shallots

2 tablespoons minced fresh
    parsley
2 large ripe tomatoes, cut into
    ½-inch slices

Combine first 4 ingredients in a small bowl. Gently spread mixture over tomato slices. Place tomato slices on a lightly greased rack in a broiler pan. Broil 5½ inches from heat 2 to 3 minutes or until cheese melts. Serve immediately. Yield: 4 to 5 servings.   Diann Howell

Sharing Our Best
Hackensack American Legion Auxiliary Unit 202
Hackensack, Minnesota

Parmesan Corn on the Cob

Parmesan cheese and Italian seasoning brushed on farm-fresh corn on the cob snap your taste buds to attention!

4 ears fresh corn
¼ cup water
¼ cup butter or margarine,
    melted

¼ cup grated Parmesan cheese
½ teaspoon dried Italian
    seasoning
½ teaspoon salt

Remove and discard husks and silks from corn; place corn in a microwave-safe dish. Add water; cover and microwave at HIGH 10 to 12 minutes or until tender. Drain.

Combine butter, Parmesan cheese, and Italian seasoning in a small bowl. Brush butter mixture over corn; sprinkle corn evenly with salt. Yield: 4 servings.   Ruth Hart

Future Generations
Robertson County Family and Community Education Clubs
Springfield, Tennessee

Curried Sweet Potatoes

Curry powder, a spice mix from India, ranges in flavor from mild to hot. It adds a bold accent to a variety of dishes, even sweet potatoes.

3 **pounds sweet potatoes, peeled**
1 **cup firmly packed light brown sugar**

2 **teaspoons curry powder**
½ **cup butter or margarine, melted**

Cut potatoes into ½-inch-thick slices.

Arrange potato slices in a single layer in a lightly greased 15- x 10-inch jellyroll pan. Combine sugar and curry powder; sprinkle over potato. Drizzle with melted butter.

Bake, uncovered, at 350° for 50 minutes or until potato is tender. Yield: 8 servings.

To Your Health: Recipes for Healthy Living from Lahey Clinic
Lahey Clinic
Burlington, Massachusetts

Roasted New Potatoes

Dress up any plate with a helping of these golden potatoes infused with the flavors of paprika and rosemary.

1 **large garlic clove, minced**
1 **teaspoon salt**
¼ **teaspoon paprika**
¼ **teaspoon dried rosemary, crushed**

⅛ **teaspoon pepper**
1½ **tablespoons olive oil**
1½ **pounds small red potatoes, cut in half**

Combine first 6 ingredients in a large bowl. Add potato; toss well. Spoon potato mixture onto a lightly greased 15- x 10-inch jellyroll pan. Bake at 450° for 30 minutes or until tender and brown, stirring after 20 minutes. Yield: 4 to 6 servings.   Tonya Baldwin

McInnis Bobcat Favorites
McInnis Elementary PTA
DeLeon Springs, Florida

Peach Trifle

Several convenience products make this trifle a snap to prepare, but insist on fresh peaches if they're in season.

1 (9-inch) round angel food cake
⅓ cup orange juice
2 cups milk
1 (3.4-ounce) package vanilla instant pudding mix
1 (12-ounce) container frozen whipped topping, thawed
6 fresh ripe peaches, peeled and coarsely chopped

Cut cake horizontally into 3 layers. Brush orange juice over cake layers. Cut into 1-inch cubes. Combine milk and pudding mix in a medium bowl. Beat 30 seconds with a wire whisk. Let stand 2 minutes or until thickened. Fold in 2 cups whipped topping.

Layer half each of cake cubes, peaches, and pudding mixture in a 3-quart trifle dish or glass bowl. Repeat layers. Top with remaining whipped topping. Cover and chill 1 hour. Yield: 8 to 10 servings.

At Your Service: Southern Recipes, Places and Traditions
The Junior League of Gwinnett and North Fulton Counties
Duluth, Georgia

Chocolate Peanut Clusters

1 cup butterscotch morsels
1 cup semisweet chocolate
  morsels

2 tablespoons creamy peanut
  butter
2 cups salted Spanish peanuts

Place first 3 ingredients in a heavy saucepan. Cook over low heat, stirring constantly, until smooth. Remove from heat; stir in peanuts.

Drop by rounded teaspoonfuls onto a baking sheet lined with wax paper. Chill 10 minutes before serving. Store in refrigerator. Yield: 2½ dozen.

Everything But the Entrée
The Junior League of Parkersburg, West Virginia

Drop Brownies

Chocolate morsels, butter, flour, and sweetened condensed milk are all you need to prepare these drop-dead delicious, chewy fudge brownielike cookies.

2 cups semisweet chocolate
  morsels
1 (14-ounce) can sweetened
  condensed milk

½ cup butter or margarine
1 cup all-purpose flour

Combine first 3 ingredients in a medium saucepan; cook over low heat, stirring constantly, until melted. Stir in flour.

Drop dough by rounded teaspoonfuls onto ungreased baking sheets. Bake at 350° for 7 minutes. (Cookies will be soft; do not over-bake.) Cool on baking sheets 2 minutes; remove to wire racks to cool completely. Yield: about 4 dozen.   Diane Paul

Moon River Collection
The Landings Landlovers
Savannah, Georgia

Almond Spice Bars

This cakelike bar cookie recipe starts with a convenient cake mix and ends with an easy two-ingredient orange glaze. Substitute carrot cake mix if spice isn't available.

1 (18.25-ounce) package spice
   cake mix
2 tablespoons sugar
2 large eggs
½ cup butter or margarine,
   melted

1¼ cups water
½ cup chopped slivered
   almonds, toasted
Orange Glaze

Combine first 5 ingredients in a large mixing bowl. Beat at medium speed with an electric mixer until blended. Stir in almonds. Pour into a greased 15- x 10-inch jellyroll pan. Bake at 375° for 20 to 25 minutes or until a wooden pick inserted in center comes out clean. Cool slightly. Drizzle with Orange Glaze. Cool. Cut into bars. Yield: 2½ dozen.

Orange Glaze

1½ cups sifted powdered
   sugar

3 tablespoons orange juice

Combine sugar and orange juice, stirring until mixture is smooth. Yield: ½ cup.

Specialties of the Haus
TCM International, Inc.
Indianapolis, Indiana

Apricot Squares

White chocolate morsels are a flavor surprise in these treats.

1 (18.25-ounce) package yellow
cake mix
½ cup butter or margarine,
melted
1 cup dried apricots, chopped

1 cup slivered almonds
1 cup flaked coconut
1 cup white chocolate morsels
1 (14-ounce) can sweetened
condensed milk

Combine cake mix and butter; press into a lightly greased 15- x 10-inch jellyroll pan. Top with apricots, almonds, coconut, and chocolate morsels; pour milk over cake. Bake at 350° for 25 minutes; cool and cut into squares. Yield: 32 squares.   Eleanor Bousquet

Recipes from the Heart of Maine
Friends of the Millinocket Memorial Library
Millinocket, Maine

Raspberry Bars

An oozing layer of jam forms a ribbon of flavor between a cakelike crust and an oat topping. Feel free to substitute your favorite preserves in place of raspberry.

1 (18.25-ounce) package yellow
cake mix
2½ cups uncooked quick-
cooking oats

¾ cup butter or margarine,
melted
1 (12-ounce) jar raspberry
preserves

Combine cake mix and oats. Stir in butter until mixture is crumbly. Press about 3 cups mixture evenly into a greased 13- x 9-inch pan. Spread preserves over crumb mixture. Sprinkle with remaining crumb mixture. Pat gently to level topping. Bake at 375° for 24 to 26 minutes or until lightly browned. Cool completely in pan on a wire rack. Cut into bars. Yield: 32 bars.   Paula Weil

The Western New York Federal Court Centennial Cookbook
U.S. District Court, Western District of New York
Buffalo, New York

Chocolate Fix

Since there's a caramel layer between these gooey brownies, they may not look done when removed from the oven. But we found that 20 minutes was the ideal cooking time because they set as they cool.

1 (18.25-ounce) package German chocolate cake mix (we tested with Duncan Hines)
¾ cup butter or margarine, melted
⅔ cup evaporated milk, divided
1 cup chopped pecans
1 cup (6 ounces) semisweet chocolate morsels
1 (14-ounce) package caramels, unwrapped (we tested with Kraft)

Combine cake mix, butter, ⅓ cup evaporated milk, and pecans in a large bowl; stir well. Press half of dough into a greased 13- x 9-inch pan.

Bake at 350° for 6 minutes. Sprinkle crust evenly with chocolate morsels.

Combine remaining ⅓ cup evaporated milk and caramels in a medium saucepan; place over low heat, and cook, stirring constantly, until smooth. Spread caramel mixture over chocolate morsels. Sprinkle remaining dough over caramel mixture. Bake 20 minutes. (Mixture will not be completely set.) Let stand 30 minutes. Chill 1 hour before serving. Yield: 2 dozen.   Trudy Sutherland

Bless This Food: A Collection of Prayers & Recipes
Steel Lake Presbyterian Church—Women's Ministries
Federal Way, Washington

Candy Bar Pizza

The ultimate treat for a children's party, this dessert pizza is studded with chopped candy bars and drizzled with caramel. It cuts easily into slices.

1 (18-ounce) tube refrigerated chocolate chip cookie dough
2 cups frozen whipped topping, thawed
2 (2.7-ounce) chocolate-coated caramel-peanut nougat bars, coarsely chopped (we tested with Snicker bars)
2 (1.4-ounce) chocolate-covered toffee candy bars, coarsely chopped (we tested with Skor bars)
2 (2.1-ounce) chocolate-covered crispy peanut-buttery candy bars, coarsely chopped (we tested with Butterfinger bars)
¼ cup caramel topping

Press cookie dough onto a greased 12-inch pizza pan. Bake at 375° for 15 to 18 minutes. Let cool completely.

Spread whipped topping evenly over cookie dough. Sprinkle chopped candies over whipped topping. Drizzle lightly with caramel topping. Refrigerate pizza until ready to serve. To serve, cut into slices. Yield: 10 to 12 servings.

Jan Went

Business is Cookin' with FBLA
Lakeview Future Business Leaders of America
Columbus, Nebraska

Tortoni Squares

Make this dessert up to a month ahead, freeze it, and relax! Dessert's done–what could be simpler?

⅓ cup chopped toasted
   almonds
3 tablespoons butter or
   margarine, melted
1⅓ cups finely crushed vanilla
   wafers

1 teaspoon almond extract
½ gallon vanilla ice cream,
   softened
1 (12-ounce) jar apricot
   preserves

Combine almonds, butter, vanilla wafer crumbs, and almond extract; press one-third of mixture into a buttered 9- x 5-inch loafpan.

Spread half of ice cream over crumb layer. Repeat layers once, and top with preserves. Press remaining crumb mixture on top. Cover and freeze 8 hours or up to 1 month. Let stand 10 minutes before serving. Yield: 9 servings.

Creating a Stir
The Lexington Medical Society Auxiliary
Lexington, Kentucky

Easy Orange Sherbet

1 (14-ounce) can sweetened
   condensed milk
1 (8-ounce) can crushed
   pineapple, undrained and
   chilled

1 (64-ounce) bottle orange
   soda, chilled

Combine all ingredients in freezer container of a 5-quart hand-turned or electric freezer, stirring well. Freeze according to manufacturer's instructions.

Pack freezer with additional ice and rock salt, and let stand for 1 hour before serving. Yield: 4 quarts.

Savoring the Seasons: Riverside
The Craven Regional Medical Center Foundation
New Bern, North Carolina

Appetizers & Beverages

Three-in-One Cheese Ball, page 74

Elegant Layered Torta

2 garlic cloves, cut in half
1 shallot, quartered
1 cup butter, cut into small
   pieces
12 ounces crumbled feta
   cheese
1 (8-ounce) package cream
   cheese, cut into pieces

½ cup dry vermouth or dry
   white wine
½ cup pine nuts, lightly
   toasted
1 cup dried tomatoes in oil,
   drained and minced
1 cup pesto

Lightly grease an 8- x 4-inch loafpan. Line pan with plastic wrap, allowing it to extend slightly over edges of pan. Set pan aside.

With food processor running, drop garlic and shallot through food chute. Process 3 or 4 seconds, stopping to scrape down sides. Process 3 or 4 more seconds or until minced. Add butter and next 3 ingredients; process until smooth, stopping to scrape down sides twice.

Layer half each of pine nuts, dried tomatoes, pesto, and cheese mixture in prepared pan, smoothing each layer to edges of pan. Repeat layers with remaining ingredients. Cover and chill at least 8 hours.

To serve, invert pan onto a serving platter; remove plastic wrap. Serve with crackers or baguette slices. Yield: 15 to 20 appetizer servings.

What Can I Bring?
The Junior League of Northern Virginia
McLean, Virginia

Figgy Bleu Torte

12 ounces dried figs
½ teaspoon sugar
2 (8-ounce) packages cream
   cheese, softened

4 ounces blue cheese,
   softened
Garnish: dried or fresh figs

Line a 6-inch springform pan or flat-bottomed bowl with plastic wrap, allowing it to extend slightly over edges of pan. Set aside.

Place figs in a medium saucepan, adding water to cover. Bring to a boil; reduce heat, and simmer, uncovered, 15 minutes or until figs are tender. Drain well. Place figs and sugar in a food processor, and process until smooth, stopping twice to scrape down sides. Set aside.

Process cream cheese and blue cheese in food processor until smooth. Layer half of cheese mixture in prepared pan. Top with fig mixture, ending with remaining cheese mixture. Fold plastic wrap over top, and cover with additional plastic wrap. Chill 8 hours. To serve, invert pan onto a serving platter; remove plastic wrap. Garnish, if desired. Serve with crackers or baguette slices. Yield: 12 to 15 appetizer servings.

America Celebrates Columbus
The Junior League of Columbus, Ohio

Pesto and Sun-Dried Tomato Cheesecake

A savory cheesecake makes a rich—and surprising—first course. And this appetizer serves a crowd, too.

3 slices sandwich bread, toasted
½ cup freshly grated Parmesan cheese
½ cup butter, melted
4 (8-ounce) packages cream cheese, softened
2 (8-ounce) jars pesto
¼ cup heavy whipping cream
4 large eggs
1 (7-ounce) jar dried tomatoes in oil, drained and chopped
Fresh basil sprigs (optional)

Place bread in a food processor; pulse 10 times or until coarsely crumbled. Measure 1 cup crumbs; discard remaining crumbs.

Combine breadcrumbs, Parmesan cheese, and butter in a medium bowl. Firmly press mixture into an ungreased 9-inch springform pan. Bake at 325° for 10 minutes or until lightly browned.

Beat cream cheese at medium speed with an electric mixer until creamy; gradually add pesto and cream, beating well. Add eggs, 1 at a time, beating after each addition. Pour batter into prepared pan.

Bake at 325° for 45 minutes (center will not be completely set). Turn oven off; leave cheesecake in oven 1 hour. Run a knife around edge of pan to release sides. Cool in pan on a wire rack 45 minutes. Cover and chill at least 8 hours. Remove sides of pan. Top cheesecake with dried tomatoes and, if desired, basil sprigs. Serve with assorted crackers or party bread. Yield: 20 to 24 appetizer servings.

Splendor in the Bluegrass
The Junior League of Louisville, Kentucky

Smoked Salmon Cheesecake

*If you love smoked salmon, add more to this cheesecake that can be
served as an appetizer or in wedges for a first course.*

6 tablespoons butter, melted
¼ cup freshly grated
   Parmesan cheese
1½ cups fine, dry breadcrumbs
   (store-bought), toasted
½ cup finely chopped onion
½ cup finely chopped green
   pepper
3 tablespoons butter, melted
3½ (8-ounce) packages cream
   cheese, softened

4 large eggs
⅓ cup heavy whipping cream
3 tablespoons freshly grated
   Parmesan cheese
½ cup (2 ounces) shredded
   Gruyère cheese
⅓ pound smoked salmon,
   diced
½ teaspoon salt
½ teaspoon pepper

Combine 6 tablespoons butter, ¼ cup Parmesan cheese, and bread-crumbs in a small bowl; press into bottom of an ungreased 9-inch springform pan. Bake at 300° for 6 minutes.

Sauté onion and green pepper in 3 tablespoons butter in a small skillet over medium-high heat until soft; set aside.

Combine cream cheese, eggs, and whipping cream; beat at medium speed with an electric mixer until smooth. Add 3 tablespoons Parmesan and Gruyère cheese, salmon, salt, and pepper. Beat at medium speed 5 minutes or until smooth. Fold in onion and green pepper. Pour into prepared pan. Place pan in a larger, shallow pan; add hot water to larger pan to a depth of 1-inch.

Bake at 300° for 1 hour and 40 minutes. Turn off oven, and let cheesecake stand 1 hour in oven. (Do not open oven door.) Remove from oven, and let cool in pan on a wire rack at least 2 hours. Serve at room temperature, or cover and chill up to 2 days.

Unmold and serve with assorted crackers or baguette slices. Yield: 16 to 20 appetizer servings.

Forget Me Not: Recipes and Stories to Remember
Hospice and Palliative Care of Greensboro
Greensboro, North Carolina

Tomato-Basil Squares

1 (10-ounce) can refrigerated
   pizza crust
2 cups (8 ounces) shredded
   mozzarella cheese, divided
4 plum tomatoes, thinly sliced

⅔ cup mayonnaise
¼ cup freshly grated
   Parmesan cheese
2 teaspoons dried basil
1 garlic clove, pressed

Unroll pizza crust, and press into a 15- x 10-inch jellyroll pan; sprinkle with 1 cup mozzarella cheese. Arrange tomato slices over cheese.

Combine remaining 1 cup mozzarella cheese, mayonnaise, and remaining 3 ingredients; stir well. Spread cheese mixture over tomato slices. Bake at 375° for 20 minutes. Cut into 16 rectangles. Yield: 8 appetizers.   Pam Boddicker

Christian Women's Fellowship
Oak Grove Christian Church
Shellsburg, Iowa

Garden Bruschetta

Use any leftover tomato mixture from this classic Italian appetizer to top pasta for a quick meal.

3 tomatoes, finely chopped
   (about 2 cups)
⅓ cup finely chopped fresh
   basil
1 tablespoon minced fresh
   garlic
2 teaspoons balsamic vinegar

¼ teaspoon salt
⅛ teaspoon freshly ground
   pepper
1 French baguette, sliced
   diagonally into 24 (½-inch-
   thick) slices
2 tablespoons olive oil

Stir together first 6 ingredients in a bowl. Cover and chill 1 hour.

Brush bread slices with oil; place on a baking sheet. Broil 5½ inches from heat 3 minutes or until lightly browned, turning once. Spoon tomato mixture on bread slices just before serving. Yield: 2 dozen.

The Bounty of Chester County: Heritage Edition
Chester County Agricultural Development Council
West Chester, Pennsylvania

Gruyère Onion Tarts

Slightly sweet caramelized onions and robust Gruyère make a delightful duo to fill flaky phyllo shells.

1½ tablespoons butter or margarine
2 cups thinly sliced onion
2 garlic cloves, chopped
¼ teaspoon salt
¼ teaspoon dried sage
¼ teaspoon dried thyme
¼ teaspoon pepper
⅛ teaspoon dried rosemary

¾ cup (3 ounces) shredded Gruyère cheese
¼ cup heavy whipping cream
24 frozen mini phyllo pastry shells, thawed
4 slices thick bacon, cooked and crumbled
Garnish: chopped parsley

Melt butter in a large skillet over medium heat. Add onion and next 6 ingredients. Cook, stirring often, 15 to 20 minutes or until lightly browned. Remove from heat; stir in cheese and whipping cream.

Place pastry shells on a baking sheet. Spoon onion mixture into shells. Sprinkle crumbled bacon on top. Bake at 350° for 9 to 11 minutes or until lightly browned. Garnish, if desired. Serve immediately. Yield: 2 dozen.

Key Ingredients
Le Bonheur Club, Inc.
Memphis, Tennessee

Chicken-Papaya Quesadillas

1 ripe papaya
1 tablespoon olive oil
2 skinned and boned chicken breast halves, cut into ½-inch strips
1 teaspoon paprika
⅛ teaspoon ground red pepper
1 (7-ounce) jar roasted red bell peppers, drained

¾ teaspoon chopped chipotle chile peppers in adobo sauce
4 (10-inch) flour tortillas
¼ cup pesto
2 cups (8 ounces) shredded Monterey Jack cheese
2 tablespoons butter or margarine

Peel papaya, and cut into thin slices; set aside.

Heat oil in a large skillet over medium-high heat until hot. Sprinkle chicken with paprika and red pepper. Sauté chicken in oil 6 minutes. Transfer chicken to a plate; cool completely. Shred chicken.

Process bell peppers and chipotle chiles in a food processor until smooth. Transfer mixture to a small serving bowl.

Place tortillas on a work surface. Spread 1 tablespoon pesto over half of each tortilla. Sprinkle chicken and arrange papaya evenly over pesto. Sprinkle ½ cup cheese over chicken and papaya on each tortilla. Fold tortillas in half.

Melt 1 tablespoon butter in a heavy skillet over medium-high heat. Add 2 quesadillas, and cook 2 minutes on each side or until golden brown. Repeat procedure with remaining 2 quesadillas and 1 tablespoon butter. Cut each quesadilla into 6 wedges. Arrange on a serving platter, and serve with bell pepper-chile sauce. Yield: 12 appetizer servings.   Nancy Nichols

Cookin' with Friends
National Presbyterian School Class of 2000
Washington, D.C.

Garden Greek Appetizer

1 (8-ounce) package ⅓-less-fat
   cream cheese, softened
1 (8-ounce) package feta
   cheese, crumbled
2 tablespoons plain yogurt
1 tablespoon chopped fresh
   mint leaves

1 garlic clove, minced
1 tomato, seeded and diced
1 small cucumber, diced
1 green onion, chopped

Combine first 5 ingredients in a medium bowl. Beat at medium speed with an electric mixer until well blended. Spread cheese mixture into a 9-inch pieplate. Cover and chill 2 hours. Top with tomato, cucumber, and onion just before serving. Serve with crackers or pita bread wedges. Yield: 10 to 12 appetizer servings.   Lois Ganter

On Course
Women Associates of the Buffalo Power Squadron
Lancaster, New York

Shrimp Toast Canapés

The French name for small pieces of bread topped with a savory topping is canapés. These are topped with a creamy shrimp and cheese mixture, and broiled until bubbly. Ask someone in the seafood market to steam the shrimp for you while you complete your shopping.

¾ **pound medium-size fresh shrimp, cooked, peeled, deveined, and chopped**
¾ **cup (3 ounces) shredded Cheddar cheese**
¾ **cup mayonnaise**
¼ **cup chopped onion**

1 **teaspoon Worcestershire sauce**
½ **teaspoon dry mustard**
¼ **teaspoon curry powder**
French baguette slices or cocktail rye bread

Combine first 7 ingredients in a medium bowl. Spread about 1½ tablespoons shrimp mixture on each bread slice. Place on ungreased baking sheets. Broil 5½ inches from heat for 7 minutes or until cheese is bubbly. Serve warm. Yield: 2 dozen.

Las Vegas: Glitter to Gourmet
The Junior League of Las Vegas, Nevada

Crab Havarti Pastries

1 **(15-ounce) package refrigerated piecrusts**
1 **large onion, chopped**
2 **garlic cloves, minced**
2 **tablespoons vegetable oil**
1 **tablespoon all-purpose flour**
⅓ **cup milk**

1 **cup (4 ounces) shredded Havarti cheese**
1 **(6-ounce) can crabmeat, drained, flaked, and cartilage removed**
¼ **cup chopped fresh parsley**
Milk

Let piecrusts stand at room temperature 10 minutes; unfold and roll each piecrust to press out fold lines. Place on a lightly greased baking sheet.

Sauté onion and garlic in hot oil over medium-high heat until tender; stir in flour and ⅓ cup milk. Cook 1 minute or until thickened and bubbly, stirring often. Add cheese; stir until melted. Remove from heat; stir in crabmeat and ¼ cup parsley.

Spoon half of crabmeat mixture onto half of each piecrust, leaving a ½-inch border around sides. Moisten edges with water; fold pastry, and seal with a fork. Prick tops with fork; brush with additional milk. Bake at 375° for 25 minutes or until golden brown. Cut each pastry into 8 wedges. Yield: 16 wedges.   Cindy Mitchell

Recipes from the Heart
Littleton Regional Hospital Helping Hands
Littleton, New Hampshire

Red Pepper Pastry Pockets

1 **tablespoon butter or margarine**	2 **tablespoons freshly grated Parmesan cheese**
2 **tablespoons finely chopped onion**	1 **teaspoon dried Italian seasoning**
1 **garlic clove, minced**	1 **(17¼-ounce) package frozen puff pastry, thawed**
1 **(7-ounce) jar roasted red bell peppers, drained**	3 **tablespoons milk**
½ **(8-ounce) package cream cheese, softened**	⅓ **cup freshly grated Parmesan cheese**

Melt butter in a medium skillet over medium-high heat. Add onion and garlic; cook 3 minutes, stirring often, or until onion is tender. Remove from heat. Stir in red peppers, cream cheese, 2 tablespoons Parmesan cheese, and Italian seasoning; set aside.

Unfold 1 pastry sheet on a lightly floured surface; roll into a 10-inch square. Cut sheet into 16 (2½-inch) squares. Spoon about 1 teaspoon cream cheese filling in center of each square. Fold opposite corners in half to form a triangle. Seal edges with a fork; cut slits in top of each pastry. Repeat procedure with remaining pastry sheet and cream cheese filling. Brush each pastry with milk, and sprinkle evenly with ⅓ cup Parmesan cheese. Arrange on an ungreased baking sheet.

Bake at 400° for 20 minutes or until golden. Cool on a wire rack 5 minutes. Serve warm. Yield: 32 appetizers.

Key Ingredients
Le Bonheur Club, Inc.
Memphis, Tennessee

Three-in-One Cheese Ball

What a bargain! From a basic cheese ball recipe, you can make 3 different balls by rolling one in cracked black pepper, one in chopped parsley, and the other in nuts. Variety is truly the spice of life!

1 (8-ounce) package cream
  cheese, softened
4 cups (16 ounces) shredded
  Cheddar cheese
2 tablespoons milk
2 tablespoons finely chopped
  onion
2 tablespoons Worcestershire
  sauce

2 teaspoons cracked black
  pepper or coarsely ground
  black pepper
½ cup crumbled blue cheese
2 tablespoons chopped fresh
  parsley
¼ teaspoon garlic powder
½ cup finely chopped pecans

Combine first 5 ingredients in a large mixing bowl; beat at medium speed with an electric mixer until creamy. Divide mixture evenly into thirds.

Shape 1 portion into a ball; roll in cracked black pepper.

Add blue cheese to second portion, mixing well. Shape into a ball; roll in chopped parsley.

Add garlic powder to remaining portion, mixing well. Shape into a ball; roll in chopped pecans. Cover and chill cheese balls 8 hours or until firm.

Remove from refrigerator 15 minutes before serving. Serve with crackers. Yield: 15 to 18 appetizer servings.   Irene Chelbana

Sharing Our Best
Hackensack American Legion Auxiliary Unit 202
Hackensack, Minnesota

Classic Hummus

2 (15.5-ounce) cans chickpeas
    (garbanzo beans), undrained
2 garlic cloves

2½ tablespoons tahini
¼ cup fresh lemon juice

Drain chickpeas, reserving ¼ cup liquid, and set aside.

Process garlic in a food processor until minced. Add chickpeas, reserved ¼ cup liquid, tahini, and lemon juice; process 3 minutes or until smooth, scraping down sides occasionally. Transfer to a serving bowl. Serve immediately, or cover and chill. Serve with pita chips or fresh vegetables. Yield: 1½ cups.

To Your Health: Recipes for Healthy Living from Lahey Clinic
Lahey Clinic
Burlington, Massachusetts

Skinny Guacamole

Skinny refers to the use of white beans instead of fat-laden avocados. When pureed, the beans help to thicken this otherwise traditional guacamole. The result is a flavorful dip ready to be scooped up by salty tortilla chips.

1 (15-ounce) can white
    cannellini beans, drained
2 large avocados, peeled and
    sliced
1 large garlic clove, minced
2 medium tomatoes, chopped

1 small onion, chopped
    (about 1½ cups)
¾ teaspoon salt
½ teaspoon pepper
½ teaspoon hot sauce
3 tablespoons lemon juice

Process beans in a food processor until smooth. Add avocado and garlic; pulse until blended. Combine tomato and remaining 5 ingredients in a large bowl; stir in avocado mixture. Cover and chill. Yield: 5 cups.   Frances Cunningham

Glen Haven Community Cookbook 1999
Glen Haven Area Volunteer Fire Department
Glen Haven, Colorado

Corn-Walnut Dip

This isn't your mother's dip. The corn and walnuts add depth and flavor to this creamy dip with a hint of heat from the chiles and ground red pepper.

2 (8-ounce) packages cream
   cheese, softened
¼ cup fresh lemon juice
1 tablespoon ground cumin
1 teaspoon salt
1 teaspoon ground red pepper
1 teaspoon black pepper

1 (8-ounce) can whole kernel
   corn, drained
1 cup chopped walnuts
1 (4.5-ounce) can chopped
   green chiles, undrained
3 green onions, chopped

Beat cream cheese at medium speed with an electric mixer until smooth; gradually add lemon juice, beating well. Add cumin and next 3 ingredients, beating well. Stir in corn and remaining ingredients. Cover and chill at least 1 hour. Serve with tortilla chips or large corn chips. Yield: 4⅓ cups.

The Guild Collection: Recipes from Art Lovers
The Guild, The Museum of Fine Arts, Houston, Texas

Pâté Chardonnay

A myriad of seasonings distinguishes this elegant appetizer that's best served cold.

½ cup butter or margarine
1 (8-ounce) package sliced
   fresh mushrooms
1 bunch green onions, thinly
   sliced
6 garlic cloves, minced
1 pound chicken livers

1½ teaspoons chopped fresh
   dill
1 teaspoon dry mustard
1 teaspoon salt
½ teaspoon dried rosemary
⅔ cup Chardonnay

Melt butter in a large skillet over low heat. Add mushrooms, green onions, and garlic; sauté 5 minutes. Remove vegetable mixture with a slotted spoon, and set aside.

Add chicken livers, and cook until done, turning occasionally. Stir in dill and next 3 ingredients. Add wine; cook, stirring often, until liquid is reduced by half. Remove mixture from skillet; place in food processor. Add vegetable mixture to processor. Process until smooth.

Line an 8½- x 4½-inch loafpan or shaped 4-cup mold with plastic wrap, allowing it to extend slightly over edges of pan. Spoon mixture into prepared loafpan. Cover and chill 8 hours. Invert pâté onto a serving platter; remove plastic wrap. Serve with baguette slices or crackers. Yield: 15 to 20 appetizer servings.　　　　　Lynn W. Weber

Menus & Memories
University of Oklahoma Women's Association
Norman, Oklahoma

Honey-Cardamom Crunch

Replace the traditional savory snack mix with this updated honey and cardamom mix. It's irresistible!

6　cups crisp rice cereal squares
2　cups tiny pretzel twists
1　cup whole natural almonds
1　cup sweetened flaked coconut
⅓　cup firmly packed light brown sugar

¼　cup butter or margarine
¼　cup honey
½　teaspoon ground cardamom
1　cup dried cranberries (we tested with Craisins)

Combine first 4 ingredients in a large roasting pan; stir well.

Combine brown sugar and next 3 ingredients in a saucepan. Place over medium heat, and cook until blended, stirring often. Drizzle brown sugar mixture over cereal mixture; toss to coat.

Bake at 300° for 40 minutes, stirring every 10 minutes. Stir in cranberries; spread mixture on a baking sheet. Cool completely. Store in an airtight container. Yield: 10 cups.　　　　　Hilda Olson

Cooking with the Original Search Engine
Fort Worth Public Library All Staff Association
Fort Worth, Texas

Iced Coffee

If you prefer a stronger coffee flavor, increase the amount of instant coffee to ¼ cup.

½ cup sugar
2 cups half-and-half
1 cup cold water
3 tablespoons instant coffee
  granules

¼ cup chocolate syrup
4 cups milk
1 teaspoon vanilla extract

Combine sugar and half-and-half in a large freezer-safe container. Combine water and coffee granules, stirring until granules dissolve; add to half-and-half mixture. Stir in syrup, milk, and vanilla. Freeze 4 hours or until slushy. Yield: 7 cups.   Elaine Frey

Cooking with Class
Forest Hills Elementary School PTO
Lake Oswego, Oregon

Mexican Fruit Punch

Pick papaya, pineapple, and juicy watermelon at the peak of their sweetness for a fruit explosion in this refreshing punch.

3 cups chopped papaya
3 cups chopped fresh
  pineapple
3 cups fresh orange juice

1 cup chopped watermelon
4 cups water
⅓ cup sugar
Garnish: pineapple chunks

Process first 4 ingredients in a blender until pureed. Pour puree into a pitcher. Stir in water and sugar. Serve over ice, and garnish, if desired. Yield: 10 cups.

Note: If desired, pour mixture through a wire-mesh strainer into a large bowl, discarding solids.

Tucson Treasures: Recipes & Reflections
Tucson Medical Center Auxiliary
Tucson, Arizona

Strawberry Lemonade

Nothing could be more refreshing on a lazy summer afternoon than sipping this strawberry-spiked lemonade with its addictive sweet and tart flavors.

2 cups sugar, divided
1 cup water
1½ cups strawberries, halved
2 cups fresh lemon juice
   (about 15 lemons)

6 cups sparkling water
Garnish: fresh mint leaves

Combine 1 cup sugar and 1 cup water in a small saucepan. Bring to a boil; reduce heat, and simmer, uncovered, 5 minutes or until sugar dissolves, stirring often. Cool.

Process strawberries, remaining 1 cup sugar, and sugar syrup in a blender or food processor until pureed. Pour mixture through a wire-mesh strainer into a large pitcher. Stir in lemon juice and sparkling water just before serving. Serve over ice. Garnish, if desired. Yield: 12 cups.

Lori Moses

On Course
Women Associates of the Buffalo Power Squadron
Lancaster, New York

Raspberry Sherbet Punch

If raspberry isn't your sherbet of choice, you could use any flavor in this versatile punch recipe that's always a party-pleaser.

2 (12-ounce) cans frozen pink
   lemonade concentrate,
   thawed and undiluted
½ gallon raspberry sherbet,
   softened

2 (2-liter) bottles ginger ale,
   chilled
Ice Ring

Combine lemonade concentrate and sherbet in a punch bowl; stir in ginger ale, breaking up sherbet. Unmold Ice Ring, and place in punch. Serve immediately. Yield: 18 cups.

Ice Ring

3½ cups water
1 (10-ounce) jar red
   maraschino cherries,
   drained

1 lemon, thinly sliced
1 lime, thinly sliced

Bring water to a boil; set aside to cool. Arrange cherries and lemon and lime slices in a 6-cup ring mold; add just enough cooled water to cover fruit mixture. Freeze until firm (about 4 hours). Fill ring with remaining cooled water; refreeze. Yield: 1 ice ring.

Everything But the Entrée
The Junior League of Parkersburg, West Virginia

Warm Golden Glow Punch

4 cups orange juice
3 cups apple cider
2 cups grapefruit juice
⅓ cup firmly packed light
  brown sugar

20 whole cloves
2 (3-inch) cinnamon sticks
¼ teaspoon ground allspice

Combine all ingredients in a large Dutch oven, and bring to a simmer; simmer 15 minutes, stirring occasionally. Serve warm. Yield: 9 cups.   Bessie Mae Louden

A Dab of This and a Dab of That
Bethlehem Baptist Church Senior Missionary
Ninety Six, South Carolina

Bloomer Droppers

The title says it all! Serve this fruity concoction with the funny title and enjoy your guests' reaction. Omit the liquor, and it's kid-friendly.

1 (6-ounce) can frozen
  lemonade concentrate,
  undiluted
2 fresh peaches, peeled and
  chopped

¾ cup vodka
½ (12-ounce) can lemon-lime
  soda
1 tablespoon powdered sugar
  Ice cubes

Place half each of first 5 ingredients in a blender; add enough ice to bring mixture to 3-cup level. Process until slushy. Pour mixture into a pitcher. Repeat procedure with remaining ingredients. Serve immediately. Yield: 5½ cups.

Splendor in the Bluegrass
The Junior League of Louisville, Kentucky

Glühwein (German Hot Spiced Wine)

If you want to keep warm on a wintry day, enjoy a mug of this traditional German favorite with pineapple, citrus juices, and, oh yes, plenty of red wine.

1 teaspoon whole cloves	1 orange, sliced
3 (3-inch) cinnamon sticks, broken	3½ cups pineapple juice
	1½ cups orange juice
1 teaspoon grated lemon rind	¾ cup sugar
1 lemon, sliced	5 cups dry red wine

Tie first 5 ingredients together in a cheesecloth bag. Combine spice bag, pineapple juice, orange juice, and sugar in a large saucepan or Dutch oven. Simmer mixture over medium heat 10 minutes, stirring occasionally.

Discard spice bag; add wine. Reduce heat to low, and cook just until thoroughly heated (do not simmer). Yield: 10 cups.

Sweet Pickin's
The Junior League of Fayetteville, North Carolina

Holiday Tea

12 whole cloves	½ cup red cinnamon candies
2 cups sugar	2 cups orange juice
8 cups cranberry juice	½ cup fresh lemon juice
8 cups water	

Tie cloves in a cheesecloth bag. Combine spice bag, sugar, and next 3 ingredients in a large saucepan or Dutch oven. Bring to a simmer over medium heat; cook, stirring occasionally, 10 minutes or until sugar and candies dissolve.

Discard spice bag; stir in orange juice and lemon juice. Serve warm or chilled. Yield: 20 cups.   Alice Hart

Our Daily Bread
First Presbyterian Church of Orlando—Weekday School
Orlando, Florida

Breads

Gingery Banana Waffles, page 84

Gingery Banana Waffles

These banana waffles bake up moist and tender as opposed to some waffles, which have crisp edges.

1½ cups all-purpose flour
2 teaspoons baking powder
¾ teaspoon salt
1 teaspoon ground cinnamon
¾ teaspoon ground ginger
⅓ cup firmly packed light
   brown sugar

2 large eggs
¾ cup milk
¼ cup molasses
1 ripe banana, mashed
¼ cup butter, melted
2 large bananas, sliced
Maple syrup

   Combine first 5 ingredients in a large bowl; set aside.

   Beat sugar and eggs at medium speed with an electric mixer until light and fluffy. Stir in milk, molasses, and mashed banana. Add egg mixture to flour mixture; stir just until dry ingredients are moistened. Stir in melted butter.

   Spread 1 cup batter onto a preheated, oiled 8-inch square waffle iron to edges. Bake until lightly browned. Repeat procedure with remaining batter. Cut each waffle into a 4-inch square. Serve with bananas and syrup. Yield: 12 (4-inch) waffles. Sue Mansfield

Plate & Palette: A Collection of Fine Art and Food
Beaufort County Arts Council
Washington, North Carolina

Autumn Apple Cakes

These tasty pancakes are cooked in a generous amount of oil, which makes them slightly crunchy on the outside, and moist and tender inside.

2 large eggs, beaten
1 cup milk
1 cup chunky applesauce
¾ cup firmly packed light
   brown sugar

2 cups biscuit mix
1 teaspoon ground cinnamon
4 to 5 tablespoons vegetable
   oil, divided

   Combine first 4 ingredients in a large bowl, stirring with a whisk until sugar dissolves. Combine biscuit mix and cinnamon; add to applesauce mixture. Stir with a wire whisk just until moistened.

Heat a 9-inch skillet or square griddle over medium-low heat until hot. Heat 1 tablespoon oil in skillet. Pour about ¼ cup batter for each pancake into skillet; cook 3½ to 4 minutes or until tops are covered with bubbles and edges look cooked. Turn and cook other side. Remove pancakes to a serving platter; keep warm. Repeat procedure with remaining batter, adding 1 tablespoon oil to skillet per batch. Yield: 18 (4-inch) pancakes.   Christopher Mejia

Note: These pancakes contain more sugar than most, so it's important to use lower heat to prevent them from browning on the outside before they're done inside.

Heaven's Bounty
Long Beach Catholic School Parents' Club
Long Beach, New York

Twin Mountain Blueberry Coffee Cakes

Savor the essence of fresh blueberries in these coffee cakes that are crowned with coconut and a sprinkling of brown sugar. This recipe can be cut in half easily to make just one coffee cake, but making two offers a bonus. You can keep one and give the other one to a friend.

2 cups all-purpose flour	2 large eggs, lightly beaten
1 cup sugar	1½ cups fresh blueberries
1 tablespoon baking powder	1¼ cups flaked coconut
¼ teaspoon salt	½ cup firmly packed light
½ cup shortening	brown sugar
1 cup milk	

Combine first 4 ingredients in a large bowl. Cut shortening into flour mixture with a pastry blender until crumbly.

Stir together milk and eggs. Add milk mixture to flour mixture, stirring just until moistened. Fold in blueberries. Pour batter into 2 greased 9-inch cakepans. Sprinkle with coconut and brown sugar. Bake at 375° for 23 to 25 minutes or until a wooden pick inserted in center comes out clean. Yield: 2 (9-inch) coffee cakes.

Everything But the Entrée
The Junior League of Parkersburg, West Virginia

Strawberry-Cream Cheese Coffee Cake

2¼ cups all-purpose flour
¾ cup sugar
¾ cup butter or margarine
½ teaspoon baking powder
½ teaspoon baking soda
¾ cup sour cream
1 large egg, lightly beaten

1 teaspoon almond extract
1 (8-ounce) package cream
   cheese, softened
¼ cup sugar
2 large eggs
½ cup strawberry preserves
½ cup sliced almonds

Combine flour and ¾ cup sugar in a large bowl. Cut butter into flour mixture with a pastry blender until crumbly; set aside 1 cup crumb mixture.

Add baking powder and next 4 ingredients to remaining crumb mixture; stir well. Spread dough in bottom and 2 inches up sides of a greased and floured 10-inch springform pan (dough should be about ¼ inch thick on sides).

Combine cream cheese, ¼ cup sugar, and 2 eggs; beat at medium speed with an electric mixer until smooth. Pour batter into prepared pan. Spoon preserves evenly over cream cheese mixture.

Combine reserved 1 cup crumb mixture and sliced almonds; sprinkle over preserves.

Bake at 350° for 55 minutes or until filling is almost set and crust is lightly browned. (Filling will firm up as it cools.) Run knife around edge of pan to release sides. Cool 15 minutes in pan on a wire rack; remove sides of pan. Cool completely. Yield: 1 (10-inch) coffee cake.

Carolina Thyme
The Junior League of Durham and Orange Counties, Inc.
Durham, North Carolina

Apple-Cream Cheese Coffee Cake

2½ cups all-purpose flour
¾ cup sugar
¾ cup butter or margarine
½ cup chopped pecans
½ teaspoon baking powder
½ teaspoon baking soda

¼ teaspoon salt
¾ cup sour cream
1 large egg
1 teaspoon vanilla extract
Cream Cheese Filling
Apple Filling

Combine flour and sugar in a large bowl. Cut butter into flour mixture with a pastry blender until crumbly. Reserve 1 cup flour mixture for topping; stir pecans into reserved topping, and set aside. Stir baking powder and next 5 ingredients into remaining flour mixture.

Spread mixture into bottom and 2 inches up sides of a greased and floured 9-inch springform pan. Prepare Cream Cheese Filling, and spoon over crust. Prepare Apple Filling, and spoon over cream cheese mixture. Sprinkle reserved topping mixture over Apple Filling.

Bake at 350° for 1 hour and 15 minutes or until cream cheese filling is set and apples are tender. Cool 15 minutes in pan on a wire rack. Remove sides of pan. Serve warm. Yield: 1 (9-inch) coffee cake.

Cream Cheese Filling

1 (8-ounce) package cream
   cheese, softened
1 (3-ounce) package cream
   cheese, softened
½ cup sugar

1 large egg
1 tablespoon fresh lemon
   juice
1 teaspoon vanilla extract

Beat cream cheese at medium speed with an electric mixer until creamy; gradually add sugar, beating well. Add egg, beating just until blended. Stir in lemon juice and vanilla. Yield: 1½ cups.

Apple Filling

2 baking apples, peeled and
   thinly sliced (we tested with
   Braeburn)
1 tablespoon fresh lemon
   juice

¾ cup raisins
½ cup sugar
1 tablespoon ground
   cinnamon

Combine all ingredients in a large bowl; toss well. Yield: 3¾ cups.

Meet Us in the Kitchen
The Junior League of St. Louis, Missouri

Roquefort Popovers

1½ cups milk
6 ounces Roquefort cheese,
   crumbled
1 teaspoon salt
¼ teaspoon freshly ground
   pepper
2 cups all-purpose flour
6 large eggs

Combine milk and cheese in a medium saucepan, and cook over medium heat, stirring constantly, until cheese melts. Remove from heat. Whisk in salt and pepper.

Place flour in a medium bowl. Add cheese mixture; whisk until blended (batter will be lumpy). Add eggs, 1 at a time, whisking well after each addition.

Pour batter into a popover pan coated with cooking spray. Bake at 400° for 20 minutes. Reduce heat to 350°. Bake 15 more minutes.

Remove from popover pan immediately. Pierce each popover with tip of a knife to let steam escape. Serve immediately. Yield: 1 dozen.

The Bounty of Chester County: Heritage Edition
Chester County Agricultural Development Council
West Chester, Pennsylvania

Blue Corn Muffins with Cheddar Cheese and Pine Nuts

Increasingly popular blue cornmeal can be found in the specialty section of most supermarkets. Enjoy these gourmet wonders with your favorite soup.

1¼ cups all-purpose flour
½ cup blue cornmeal
1 teaspoon baking soda
1 teaspoon baking powder
1 large egg, lightly beaten
½ cup vegetable oil
⅓ cup sugar
2 teaspoons salt
¾ cup buttermilk
¾ cup (3 ounces) shredded
   white Cheddar cheese
2 green onions, thinly sliced
½ cup pine nuts, toasted

Combine first 4 ingredients in a large bowl; make a well in center of mixture. Combine egg, oil, sugar, salt, and buttermilk; add to dry

ingredients, stirring just until moistened. Add Cheddar cheese and remaining ingredients, and stir just until blended.

Spoon batter into greased muffin pans, filling two-thirds full. Bake at 350° for 30 to 35 minutes or until lightly browned and a wooden pick inserted in center comes out clean. Yield: 1 dozen.

Settings on the Dock of the Bay
ASSISTANCE LEAGUE® of the Bay Area
Houston, Texas

Cherry Scones

Don't be alarmed by the crumbly consistency of the scone dough; you just have to knead it a little to incorporate the ingredients. Kneading the dough too much makes scones tough.

2 cups all-purpose flour
3 tablespoons light brown
   sugar
1 tablespoon baking powder
½ teaspoon baking soda
½ teaspoon salt
¼ cup butter or margarine,
   cut into pieces

1 cup dried cherries
1 teaspoon grated orange rind
1 egg yolk, lightly beaten
1 (8-ounce) container sour
   cream
1 egg white, lightly beaten

Stir together first 5 ingredients in a large bowl. Cut butter into flour mixture with a pastry blender until crumbly. Stir in cherries and orange rind. Combine egg yolk and sour cream; add to flour mixture, stirring just until dry ingredients are moistened.

Turn dough out onto a lightly floured surface, and knead lightly 4 or 5 times or just until dough holds together. Press dough into an 8-inch circle on an ungreased baking sheet. Cut dough into 8 wedges; separate wedges slightly. Brush with egg white. Bake at 400° for 10 to 12 minutes or until golden. Cool slightly on a wire rack. Serve warm. Yield: 8 scones. Amanda Bedingfield

Savor the Flavor: Delightfully Vegetarian
Portland Adventist Community Services
Portland, Oregon

Mango Date Nut Bread

Add a tropical flair to your morning breakfast with a slice of this delicious bread topped with cream cheese.

2 cups all-purpose flour	½ cup vegetable oil
1½ cups sugar	1 teaspoon vanilla extract
1 teaspoon baking soda	1 (24-ounce) jar mango slices,
½ teaspoon salt	drained and chopped
½ teaspoon ground	½ cup chopped dates
cinnamon	½ cup chopped pecans
3 large eggs, lightly beaten	

Stir together first 5 ingredients in a bowl. Combine eggs, oil, and vanilla, stirring with a wire whisk. Stir egg mixture into flour mixture until blended. Fold in mango, dates, and pecans. (Batter will be stiff.)

Spoon mixture evenly into 2 greased 8½- x 4½-inch loafpans. Bake at 350° for 50 minutes. Cool in pans on wire racks 10 minutes. Remove from pans, and cool completely on wire racks. Yield: 2 loaves.

Note: Substitute 2 cups chopped fresh mango for mango in a jar.

Cooking with Care
HospiceCare of the Piedmont, Inc.
Greenwood, South Carolina

Blueberry-Orange Bread

Use a flavored honey, such as orange blossom, in the orange glaze to complement the flavor of this sweet bread because the glaze is the crowning glory.

2 tablespoons butter or	1 cup sugar
margarine	2 cups all-purpose flour
¼ cup boiling water	1 teaspoon baking powder
4 teaspoons grated orange	¼ teaspoon baking soda
rind, divided	½ teaspoon salt
⅔ cup fresh orange juice,	1 cup fresh or frozen
divided	blueberries
1 large egg	2 tablespoons honey

Grease bottom of an 8½- x 4½-inch loafpan (do not grease sides).

Combine butter and boiling water in a bowl; stir until butter melts. Add 3 teaspoons rind and ½ cup juice. Beat egg and sugar in a large mixing bowl at medium speed with an electric mixer until blended.

Combine flour and next 3 ingredients. Add dry ingredients to egg mixture alternately with orange mixture, beating until smooth. Fold in berries. Pour into prepared pan. Bake at 350° for 35 minutes or until a wooden pick inserted in center comes out clean. Remove bread from pans immediately, and place on a wire rack.

Combine remaining 1 teaspoon rind, remaining juice, and honey; spoon glaze over loaf. Cool on wire rack. Yield: 1 loaf.   Sue Wilch

Feeding the Flock
St. Philips Episcopal Church
Topeka, Kansas

Zucchini-Cranberry Holiday Bread

3 cups all-purpose flour
1 teaspoon baking soda
½ teaspoon baking powder
1¼ teaspoons salt
2½ teaspoons ground
   cinnamon
¼ teaspoon ground nutmeg
1 cup fresh cranberries,
   coarsely chopped

1 tablespoon sugar
3 large eggs, lightly beaten
2 cups sugar
1 cup vegetable oil
1 tablespoon vanilla extract
1½ cups shredded zucchini
½ cup chopped pecans

Combine first 6 ingredients in a large bowl; set aside. Sprinkle cranberries with 1 tablespoon sugar; set aside. Combine eggs, 2 cups sugar, oil, and vanilla. Gradually add flour mixture, and stir just until blended. Fold in cranberry mixture, zucchini, and pecans. Spoon batter into 2 well-greased 8½- x 4½-inch loafpans.

Bake at 350° for 50 minutes or until a wooden pick inserted in center comes out clean. Cool in pans on wire racks 10 minutes. Remove from pans; cool on wire racks. Yield: 2 loaves.   Mary Edington

202's Totally Tempting Treasures
American Legion Auxiliary Green-Pierce Unit 202
Wichita Falls, Texas

Vidalia-Cheddar Spoonbread

1 large Vidalia onion, thinly sliced
¼ cup butter or margarine, melted
1 (8½-ounce) package corn muffin mix
1 large egg, beaten
⅓ cup milk
1 cup cream-style corn
1 (8-ounce) container sour cream
½ teaspoon salt
1 cup (4 ounces) shredded sharp Cheddar cheese, divided

Cook onion in melted butter in a large skillet over medium heat 10 minutes or until soft. Set aside.

Combine corn muffin mix and next 3 ingredients. Spoon into a greased 8-inch square pan. Stir together sour cream, salt, ½ cup cheese, and reserved onion. Spread evenly over corn mixture; sprinkle with remaining ½ cup cheese.

Bake at 425° for 30 minutes. Serve spoonbread immediately. Yield: 6 to 8 servings. Pam Pahl

Cooking with Friends
Brunswick Community Hospital
Supply, North Carolina

Lavosh

We couldn't get enough of this flaky crackerlike bread with sesame seeds. It's great paired with soups or salads, or just by itself.

3 cups all-purpose flour
¼ cup sugar
½ teaspoon salt
½ teaspoon baking soda
¼ cup sesame seeds
1 cup buttermilk
1 cup butter or margarine, melted

Combine first 5 ingredients. Add buttermilk and butter, stirring until a stiff dough forms. Shape dough into a ball. Wrap in plastic wrap; chill 8 hours. Divide dough into 16 equal portions. Shape portions into balls.

Roll 1 ball of dough paper-thin on a lightly floured surface; turn dough over, and roll again. Continue rolling and turning until dough

is a 9-inch circle, dusting lightly with flour, if necessary, to prevent sticking. Place dough circle on a large ungreased baking sheet; quickly roll into a 10-inch circle (dough tends to shrink when transferred).

Bake at 375° for 6 minutes or until lightly browned (edges will be darker than center). Remove to a wire rack, using a wide spatula. Repeat procedure with remaining portions of dough. To serve, break bread rounds into large pieces. Yield: 16 rounds.   Alice Murata

Note: The secret to crisp, flaky lavosh is rolling the dough paper-thin. Also, it's not necessary to let baking sheets cool between baking subsequent dough rounds, but baking time will be slightly reduced. Dark pans may require even less baking time.

Ofukuro No Aji: Favorite Recipes from Mama's Kitchen
Hōkūlani Cultural Exchange Committee
(Hōkūlani Elementary School)
Honolulu, Hawaii

Almost-a-Meal French Bread

½ cup butter or margarine, softened
½ cup (2 ounces) shredded Swiss cheese
10 bacon slices, cooked and crumbled
1 tablespoon chopped fresh chives

1 tablespoon prepared mustard
2 teaspoons poppy seeds
2 teaspoons fresh lemon juice
1 (16-ounce) loaf unsliced French bread (we tested with Pepperidge Farm)

Combine first 7 ingredients in a small bowl.

Slice bread crosswise into ¾-inch-thick slices, cutting to, but not through, bottom of bread. Spread butter mixture between slices.

Wrap bread in aluminum foil, sealing tightly. Bake at 350° for 20 minutes or until cheese melts and bread is thoroughly heated. Yield: 12 servings.   Tip Ryan

Breakfast in Cairo, Dinner in Rome
International School of Minnesota Foundation
Eden Prairie, Minnesota

Soft Croissants

1 (¼-ounce) envelope active dry yeast
¼ cup warm water (100° to 110°)
5 tablespoons sugar
1 teaspoon salt
¼ cup shortening
¾ cup milk
3¼ to 3¾ cups all-purpose flour
2 large eggs, lightly beaten
½ cup butter or margarine, melted
1 large egg, lightly beaten

Combine yeast and warm water in a 1-cup glass measuring cup; let stand 5 minutes.

Combine sugar, salt, shortening, and milk in a medium saucepan; cook over medium heat until smooth, stirring occasionally. Remove from heat.

Combine sugar mixture, 2 cups flour, yeast mixture, and 2 eggs in a large bowl; stir well. Gradually stir in enough of remaining flour to make a soft dough.

Turn dough out onto a lightly floured surface, and knead until smooth and elastic (about 4 minutes). Place in a well-greased bowl, turning to grease top. Cover and let rise in a warm place (85°), free from drafts, 1 hour or until doubled in bulk.

Meanwhile, combine butter and 1 egg in a small bowl; stir well. Set aside.

Punch dough down. Divide dough into 3 equal portions. Roll each portion into a 12-inch circle. Brush each circle with butter mixture, reserving any remaining mixture; cut each into 8 wedges. Roll up each wedge tightly, beginning at wide end, and seal points. Place rolls, point side down, on lightly greased baking sheets, curving into crescent shapes.

Cover and let rise in a warm place, free from drafts, 30 minutes or until doubled in bulk. Brush rolls with remaining butter mixture.

Bake at 400° for 12 minutes or until croissants are lightly browned. Cool slightly on baking sheets, and remove to wire racks to cool. Yield: 2 dozen.

Glenna Ragan

Of Books and Cooks
Woman's Book Club
Harrison, Arkansas

Fried Yeast Rolls

A specialty in Greece, these pillowy beignetlike bites of sweetened dough are best eaten warm, especially drizzled with honey. Be sure to turn them often when frying because they brown quickly.

2 cups warm milk (100° to 110°)
2 (¼-ounce) envelopes rapid-rise yeast
1 teaspoon sugar
½ teaspoon salt
3½ cups all-purpose flour
1 cup canola oil
Cinnamon sugar
Honey

Combine first 4 ingredients in a small bowl; let stand 5 minutes.

Combine yeast mixture and 2 cups flour in a large bowl; stir well. Gradually stir in remaining 1½ cups flour to make a soft dough (dough will be slightly sticky). Stir dough in bowl with a wooden spoon for 5 minutes. Cover bowl tightly with plastic wrap, and chill 8 to 24 hours.

When ready to cook, heat oil in a large heavy skillet over medium-high heat. Punch dough down in bowl. Pinch off small pieces of dough (about 1½-inch balls), and stretch dough in hands to make 2-inch squares. Fry dough, in batches, in hot oil 2 or 3 minutes or until golden, turning occasionally to maintain even browning. Drain rolls on paper towels. Lightly sprinkle rolls with cinnamon sugar; drizzle with honey. Serve warm. Yield: 2½ dozen.   Anastasia Dussin

Flavor It Greek! A Celebration of Food, Faith and Family
Philoptochos Society of Holy Trinity Greek Orthodox Church
Portland, Oregon

Light and Tasty Whole Wheat Rolls

Whole wheat never tasted as good as it does in these soft and slightly sweet rolls that are great alone or smeared with butter.

2 (¼-ounce) envelopes active dry yeast
½ cup warm water (100° to 110°)
1 cup warm milk (100° to 110°)
½ cup butter or margarine, softened
1 cup instant potato flakes
½ cup firmly packed light brown sugar
1 teaspoon salt
2 large eggs
1½ cups whole wheat flour
1 cup all-purpose flour
1 large egg
1 tablespoon water

Combine yeast and ½ cup warm water in a 1-cup glass measuring cup; let stand 5 minutes.

Combine milk and next 4 ingredients in a large bowl; beat at medium speed with an electric mixer until well blended. Add yeast mixture and 2 eggs, beating just until blended. Stir in whole wheat flour and all-purpose flour. Turn dough out onto a lightly floured surface, and knead until smooth and elastic (about 7 minutes). Place in a well-greased bowl, turning to grease top.

Cover and let rise in a warm place (85°), free from drafts, 1 hour or until doubled in bulk.

Punch dough down, and divide into 18 portions; roll each portion into a ball. Place 2 inches apart on a greased baking sheet. Combine 1 egg and 1 tablespoon water in a small bowl; stir well. Lightly brush tops of dough with egg mixture.

Cover and let rise in a warm place, free from drafts, 1 hour or until doubled in bulk. Bake at 350° for 17 minutes or until golden. Yield: 1½ dozen.

Picnics, Potlucks & Prizewinners
Indiana 4-H Foundation, Inc.
Indianapolis, Indiana

Apple Quickie Sticky Buns

This yeast dough doesn't require any kneading; just drop the dough by tablespoonfuls onto the buttery cinnamon topping, bake, and enjoy!

3¼ cups all-purpose flour
2 (¼-ounce) envelopes active
    dry yeast
¼ cup butter or margarine
¾ cup milk
½ cup water
¼ cup sugar
1 teaspoon salt
1 large egg

1½ cups chopped apple (we
    tested with Braeburn)
1 cup firmly packed light
    brown sugar
¾ cup chopped pecans
¾ cup butter or margarine
1 teaspoon ground cinnamon
1 tablespoon light corn syrup
1 tablespoon water

Combine 1½ cups flour and yeast in a large mixing bowl.

Melt ¼ cup butter in a small saucepan over medium-low heat. Add milk, ½ cup water, ¼ cup sugar, and salt; cook over medium-low heat until hot (120° to 130°). Add milk mixture to flour mixture, and beat at medium speed with an electric mixer 3 minutes. Add egg, beating well. Stir in remaining 1¾ cups flour and apple.

Cover and let rise in a warm place (85°), free from drafts, 30 minutes or until doubled in bulk.

Meanwhile, combine brown sugar and remaining 5 ingredients in a small saucepan. Cook over medium heat until butter melts, stirring often.

Pour brown sugar mixture into a greased 13- x 9-inch pan. Drop dough by 15 heaping tablespoonfuls over sugar mixture. Bake at 375° for 22 to 25 minutes or until lightly browned. Let cool 1 minute. To serve, invert pan onto a serving platter. Yield: 15 buns.

Recipes from the Heart
Littleton Regional Hospital Helping Hands
Littleton, New Hampshire

Soft Breadsticks

*These soft homemade breadsticks are the perfect foil for just about any
savory or sweet sprinkles such as rosemary, cinnamon, or sugar.*

1 (¼-ounce) envelope active
   dry yeast
1 cup warm water (100° to
   110°)
2¾ to 3 cups all-purpose flour
¼ cup vegetable oil
3 tablespoons sugar

1 teaspoon salt
Cornmeal
¼ cup butter or margarine,
   melted
Dried Italian seasoning
Garlic salt

Combine yeast and warm water in a 2-cup glass measuring cup; let
stand 5 minutes.

Combine yeast mixture, 2 cups flour, oil, sugar, and salt in a large
mixing bowl; beat at medium speed with an electric mixer until well
blended. Gradually stir in enough of remaining flour to make a soft
dough.

Turn dough out onto a lightly floured surface, and knead until
smooth and elastic (about 5 minutes). Place in a well-greased bowl,
turning to grease top.

Cover and let rise in a warm place (85°), free from drafts, 1 hour or
until doubled in bulk.

Punch dough down, and divide into 12 portions. Roll each portion
into a 9-inch strip. Place strips on greased baking sheets dusted with
cornmeal; let rise, uncovered, in a warm place, free from drafts, 25 to
30 minutes or until doubled in bulk.

Bake at 400° for 10 minutes or until lightly browned. Brush with
melted butter, and sprinkle evenly with Italian seasoning and garlic
salt. Serve warm. Yield: 12 breadsticks. Kamma Michaud

Recipes from the Heart of Maine
Friends of the Millinocket Memorial Library
Millinocket, Maine

English Muffin Loaves

Savor this bread just as you would English muffins–toasted and topped with butter and your favorite jelly.

2 cups milk	1 tablespoon sugar
½ cup water	2 teaspoons salt
5¼ to 5½ cups all-purpose flour	¼ teaspoon baking soda
2 (¼-ounce) envelopes active dry yeast	Cornmeal

Combine milk and water in a small saucepan; heat to 120° to 130°.

Combine 3 cups flour, yeast, and next 3 ingredients in a large mixing bowl. Gradually add warm milk mixture to flour mixture, beating at medium speed with an electric mixer until well blended. Gradually stir in enough of remaining flour to make a soft dough.

Spread dough evenly into 2 greased 9- x 5-inch loafpans lightly sprinkled with cornmeal. Sprinkle each loaf with cornmeal. Cover with a cloth towel, and let rise in a warm place (85°), free from drafts, 1 hour or until doubled in bulk.

Bake at 400° for 20 minutes or until loaves sound hollow when tapped. Remove loaves from pans, and let cool completely on wire racks. Yield: 2 loaves.

Patricia Keller

Cooking with Class
Timber Lake Booster Club
Timber Lake, South Dakota

Swedish Cardamom Bread

Shot with a hint of orange as well as cardamom, which lends an exotic sweet flavor, this versatile bread can be toasted for breakfast, served at dinner, or topped with your favorite cheese for dessert.

2 (¼-ounce) envelopes active
    dry yeast
⅓ cup warm water (100° to
    110°)
½ cup butter or margarine,
    softened
¾ cup sugar
3 large eggs
7 to 7½ cups all-purpose flour
1½ cups warm milk (100° to
    110°)

¼ cup sour cream
1 tablespoon grated orange
    rind
2¼ teaspoons ground
    cardamom
2 teaspoons salt
1 large egg, lightly beaten
2 teaspoons sugar

Combine yeast and warm water in a 1-cup glass measuring cup; let stand 5 minutes.

Beat butter in a large mixing bowl at medium speed with an electric mixer until creamy; gradually add ¾ cup sugar, beating well. Add 3 eggs; beat well. Stir in 2 cups flour, yeast mixture, warm milk, and next 4 ingredients. Gradually stir in enough of remaining flour to make a soft dough.

Turn dough out onto a floured surface, and knead until smooth and elastic (8 to 10 minutes). Place in a well-greased bowl, turning to grease top. Cover and let rise in a warm place (85°), free from drafts, 1 hour or until doubled in bulk.

Punch dough down; divide in half. Shape each portion into 3 (24-inch-long) ropes; place ropes on 2 lightly greased baking sheets. Braid ropes, pinching ends under. Cover and let rise in a warm place 30 more minutes or until doubled in bulk. Brush loaves gently with beaten egg. Sprinkle each loaf with 1 teaspoon sugar.

Bake at 375° for 25 to 28 minutes or until loaves are golden. Remove from pans immediately. Cool bread on wire racks. Yield: 2 loaves.

Abigail Emerson

Breakfast in Cairo, Dinner in Rome
International School of Minnesota Foundation
Eden Prairie, Minnesota

Cakes

Carrot-Pineapple Bundt Cake, page 110

Toffee Bar Cake with Praline Sauce

2 cups all-purpose flour
1 cup firmly packed dark
  brown sugar
½ cup sugar
½ cup unsalted butter,
  softened
½ teaspoon salt
4 (1.4-ounce) chocolate-
  covered toffee candy bars,
  chopped

1 cup chopped pecans
1 teaspoon baking soda
1 cup buttermilk
1 large egg, lightly beaten
1 teaspoon vanilla extract
Praline Sauce

Combine first 5 ingredients in a large mixing bowl; beat at low speed with an electric mixer until crumbly. Combine ½ cup crumb mixture, chopped toffee bars, and pecans in a medium bowl; set aside. Add soda to remaining crumb mixture. Stir together buttermilk, egg, and vanilla; add to crumb mixture, stirring just until moistened.

Spoon batter into a lightly greased 13- x 9-inch pan. Sprinkle toffee mixture on top. Bake at 350° for 35 minutes or until a wooden pick inserted in center comes out clean. Cool completely in pan on a wire rack. Cut into squares, and serve with Praline Sauce. Yield: 15 servings.

Praline Sauce

1½ cups firmly packed light
  brown sugar
⅔ cup light corn syrup

¼ cup butter or margarine
1 (5-ounce) can evaporated
  milk

Combine sugar, corn syrup, and butter in a medium saucepan. Place over medium heat; bring to a boil. Remove from heat, and cool 10 minutes or until lukewarm; whisk in milk. Serve immediately, or cover and chill. Yield: 2 cups.

Key Ingredients
Le Bonheur Club, Inc.
Memphis, Tennessee

Cranapple Walnut Cake

Sweetened whipped cream provides the finishing touch and cuts the tartness of the apples and cranberries in this moist cake.

1 cup firmly packed light brown sugar
½ cup vegetable oil
2 large eggs
1 teaspoon vanilla extract
2 cups all-purpose flour
1 teaspoon baking soda
1 teaspoon salt
1 teaspoon ground cinnamon
½ teaspoon ground nutmeg
3 cups peeled and coarsely chopped Granny Smith apple (about 2 medium)
2½ cups fresh cranberries
½ cup chopped walnuts
Sweetened whipped cream (optional)

Combine sugar and oil in a large mixing bowl; beat at medium speed with an electric mixer until well blended. Add eggs and vanilla; beat well.

Combine flour and next 4 ingredients; add to egg mixture. Beat at low speed just until blended. Stir in apple, cranberries, and walnuts (batter will be very thick). Spread batter in a greased 13- x 9-inch pan.

Bake at 350° for 40 minutes or until a wooden pick inserted in center comes out clean. Cut into squares. Serve warm or at room temperature. Top each serving with a dollop of whipped cream, if desired. Yield: 12 servings.

Florence Hirsch

A Little DAPS of This . . . A Little DAPS of That
Dallas Area Parkinsonism Society (DAPS)
Dallas, Texas

Apple Spice Cake

Three cheers for convenience products that make this tender cake a hands-down favorite and an instant success, especially when crowned with the brown sugar frosting.

1 (18.25-ounce) package spice cake mix without pudding (we tested with Duncan Hines)
4 large eggs
½ cup vegetable oil
1 cup apple juice
1 (3.4-ounce) package butterscotch instant pudding mix
Frosting

Combine first 5 ingredients in a large bowl; beat at medium speed with an electric mixer 2 minutes or until blended. Pour batter into a greased and floured 13- x 9-inch pan.

Bake at 350° for 35 to 38 minutes or until a wooden pick inserted in center comes out clean. Cool cake completely in pan on a wire rack. Spread cake with cooled Frosting. Yield: 12 servings.

Frosting

1 cup firmly packed light brown sugar
½ cup butter or margarine
½ cup evaporated milk
1 teaspoon vanilla extract

Combine first 3 ingredients in a medium saucepan over medium-high heat; bring to a boil. Boil 3 minutes, stirring constantly. Remove from heat; stir in vanilla. Cool completely. (Frosting is thin and pourable and is more like a glaze than traditional swirled frosting.) Yield: 1¼ cups.

Shirley Reinert

Cooking with Class
Timber Lake Booster Club
Timber Lake, South Dakota

Almond Cake with Plum Compote

If you want a more pronounced orange flavor in the cake, use the rind of two oranges.

1 (8-ounce) can almond paste
1 cup sugar
¾ cup butter or margarine, softened
5 large eggs
1 tablespoon grated orange rind

1½ cups sifted cake flour
¾ teaspoon baking powder
¼ teaspoon salt
Plum Compote
Whipped cream

Combine first 3 ingredients in a large mixing bowl; beat at high speed with an electric mixer until light and fluffy. Add eggs, 1 at a time, beating after each addition. Stir in orange rind.

Combine flour, baking powder, and salt. Fold dry ingredients into almond paste mixture. Pour into a greased and floured 9-inch round cakepan. Bake at 325° for 45 minutes or until a wooden pick inserted in center comes out clean. Cool in pan on a wire rack 10 minutes; remove from pan, and cool on wire rack. Cut into wedges to serve. Top each serving with Plum Compote and a dollop of whipped cream. Yield: 12 servings.

Plum Compote

½ vanilla bean
1 cup sugar
1 cup water

1 (3-inch) cinnamon stick
½ lemon
1½ pounds plums, quartered

Cut vanilla bean in half lengthwise; scrape seeds from vanilla bean into a medium saucepan. Add vanilla bean pods, sugar, and next 3 ingredients; bring to a boil. Add plums; reduce heat, and simmer, uncovered, 7 minutes or until softened. Discard bean pods, cinnamon stick, and lemon. Serve immediately, or let cool until ready to serve. Yield: 3 cups.

Treasures of the Tropics
Hibiscus Children's Center
Jensen Beach, Florida

Fuzzy Navel Cake

Two types of yogurt lend a unique flavor to this extremely moist cake that's named after the popular drink.

1 (18.25-ounce) package white cake mix (we tested with Duncan Hines)
1 (8-ounce) container low-fat orange yogurt
1 (8-ounce) container low-fat peach yogurt
⅓ cup vegetable oil
2 large eggs
1¼ cups peach liqueur, divided
1 cup orange marmalade
2 tablespoons sugar
1 (8-ounce) container frozen whipped topping, thawed
½ (8-ounce) package cream cheese, softened

Combine first 5 ingredients in a large mixing bowl. Add ¾ cup peach liqueur. Beat at high speed with an electric mixer 3 minutes. Spoon batter into 2 greased and floured 9-inch round cakepans. Bake at 350° for 35 minutes or until a wooden pick inserted in center comes out clean. Cool in pans on wire racks 10 minutes. Remove from pans, and cool completely on wire racks.

Combine marmalade, remaining ½ cup peach liqueur, and sugar in a medium saucepan. Cook over medium heat until bubbly. Let cool completely. Spread cooled mixture between cake layers.

Beat whipped topping and cream cheese with an electric mixer at high speed 3 minutes or until fluffy. Spread whipped topping mixture on top and sides of cake. Yield: 1 (9-inch) cake.

Chautauqua Celebrations
Wythe Arts Council, Ltd.
Wytheville, Virginia

Coconut-Sour Cream Cake

You're just 5 ingredients away from a decadent dessert experience! A creamy coconut filling anchors each layer of this make-ahead cake. Garnish with strawberries or other fresh berries for a dazzling finish.

1 (18.25-ounce) package
   butter-recipe cake mix
   (we tested with Pillsbury)
1 (16-ounce) container sour
   cream
2 cups sugar

4 cups sweetened flaked
   coconut
1½ cups frozen whipped
   topping, thawed
Garnish: fresh strawberries

Prepare cake mix according to package directions, using 2 (9-inch) round cakepans. Cool layers completely on wire racks. Slice each cake layer horizontally in half, using a long serrated knife.

Combine sour cream, sugar, and coconut in a bowl; stir well. Cover and chill 1½ hours. Reserve 1 cup sour cream mixture. Spread remaining sour cream mixture between cake layers.

Fold whipped topping into reserved sour cream mixture. Spread on top and sides of cake. Place cake in an airtight container. Cover and chill at least 8 hours. Garnish, if desired. Yield: 1 (9-inch) cake.

A Taste of Enchantment
The Junior League of Albuquerque, New Mexico

Holiday Eggnog Cake

You can use homemade or store-bought eggnog in this cake version of the favorite holiday drink.

2 cups all-purpose flour
1½ cups sugar
3½ teaspoons baking powder
1 teaspoon salt
1 teaspoon ground nutmeg
¼ teaspoon ground ginger
¼ cup shortening
¼ cup butter or margarine, softened

1 cup eggnog
1 teaspoon rum flavoring
3 large eggs
1½ cups whipping cream
1 teaspoon rum flavoring
½ cup sifted powdered sugar

Combine first 11 ingredients in a large mixing bowl; beat at medium speed with an electric mixer 30 seconds. Beat at high speed 3 minutes. Pour batter into 2 greased and floured 8-inch round cakepans.

Bake at 350° for 30 to 32 minutes or until a wooden pick inserted in center comes out clean. Cool in pans on wire racks 10 minutes; remove from pans, and cool on wire racks.

Beat whipping cream and 1 teaspoon rum flavoring at medium speed until foamy. Gradually add powdered sugar, beating until stiff peaks form. Spread between layers and on top and sides of cake. Store cake in refrigerator. Yield: 1 (8-inch) cake.

America Celebrates Columbus
The Junior League of Columbus, Ohio

Whiskey Cake

1 (18.25-ounce) package yellow or white cake mix
1 (3.4-ounce) package vanilla instant pudding mix
2 tablespoons whiskey
4 large eggs
1 cup milk
½ cup vegetable oil
1 cup chopped walnuts
2 tablespoons all-purpose flour
¼ cup butter or margarine
¼ cup sugar
½ cup whiskey

Combine first 6 ingredients in a large mixing bowl; beat at low speed with an electric mixer 2 minutes. Combine walnuts and flour; fold into batter. Pour batter into a greased 12-cup Bundt pan. Bake at 350° for 40 to 45 minutes or until a long wooden pick inserted in center comes out clean. Let cake cool completely in pan on a wire rack.

Combine butter and sugar in a small saucepan. Cook over medium heat, stirring constantly, until butter melts and sugar dissolves. Remove from heat, and stir in ½ cup whiskey. Remove cake from pan, and brush with glaze. Yield: 1 (10-inch) cake.   J. C. Hurlburt

Homemade with Love
Swanton-Missisquoi Valley Lions Club
Highgate Center, Vermont

Carrot-Pineapple Bundt Cake

Crushed pineapple adds just the right touch of sweetness to this traditional carrot cake that's frosted with a vanilla- and cinnamon-flavored frosting.

1 (8-ounce) can crushed
  pineapple, undrained
3 cups all-purpose flour
2 cups sugar
2 teaspoons baking soda
1½ teaspoons salt
1 teaspoon baking powder
2 teaspoons ground cinnamon
3 large eggs
1½ cups vegetable oil
2 teaspoons vanilla extract
2 cups shredded carrot
1½ cups chopped walnuts
Cream Cheese Frosting

Drain pineapple, reserving juice; set both aside.

Combine flour and next 5 ingredients.

Beat eggs, oil, vanilla, and reserved juice at medium speed with an electric mixer until smooth. Add flour mixture, beating at low speed until blended. Fold in reserved pineapple, carrot, and walnuts. Pour batter into a greased and floured 12-cup Bundt pan. Bake at 325° for 1 hour and 25 to 30 minutes or until a long wooden pick inserted in center comes out clean. Cool in pan on a wire rack 15 minutes; remove cake from pan, and cool completely on wire rack. Spoon Cream Cheese Frosting over cake, spreading to drip down sides. Yield: 1 (10-inch) cake.

Cream Cheese Frosting

1 (3-ounce) package cream
  cheese, softened
2 tablespoons butter or
  margarine, softened
1 tablespoon vanilla extract
1¼ cups sifted powdered
  sugar
1 teaspoon ground cinnamon

Beat cream cheese, butter, and vanilla at medium speed with an electric mixer until creamy. Combine powdered sugar and cinnamon. Gradually add powdered sugar mixture to cream cheese mixture, beating until smooth. Yield: 1 cup.   Sheri Hawkins

Panthers' Pantry
Children's Educational Foundation
Madera, California

Angel Pound Cake

A cross between a pound cake and angel food cake, this lighter-than-air cake is divine alone or heavenly with a topping of fresh fruit.

1 cup butter or margarine, softened
½ cup shortening
3 cups sugar
5 large eggs
3 cups all-purpose flour
1 teaspoon baking powder
¼ teaspoon salt
1 cup milk
1 teaspoon vanilla extract
1 teaspoon lemon extract

Beat butter and shortening at medium speed with an electric mixer about 2 minutes or until creamy. Gradually add sugar, beating 5 to 7 minutes. Add eggs, 1 at a time, beating just until yellow disappears. Combine flour, baking powder, and salt; add to butter mixture alternately with milk, beginning and ending with flour mixture. Beat at low speed just until blended after each addition. Stir in flavorings. Pour into a greased and floured 12-cup Bundt or 10-inch tube pan.

Bake at 350° for 1 hour and 15 minutes or until a wooden pick inserted in center comes out clean. Cool in pan on a wire rack 10 minutes; remove from pan, and let cool completely on wire rack. Yield: 1 (10-inch) cake.

Penny Booth

A Dab of This and a Dab of That
Bethlehem Baptist Church Senior Missionary
Ninety Six, South Carolina

Cranberry Sauce Cake

If mayonnaise as an ingredient seems odd, don't be alarmed; it adds flavor and moisture to this cranberry-orange cake.

3 cups all-purpose flour
1½ cups sugar
1 cup mayonnaise
1 (16-ounce) can whole-berry cranberry sauce
1 tablespoon grated orange rind
⅓ cup orange juice
1 teaspoon baking soda
1 teaspoon salt
1 teaspoon orange extract
1 cup chopped walnuts
1 cup sifted powdered sugar
2 tablespoons orange juice

Draw a circle with a 10-inch diameter on a piece of wax paper or parchment paper, using a 10-inch tube pan as a guide. Draw another circle, using inside tube as a guide. Cut out circles. Coat pan with cooking spray; place paper liner into tube pan; lightly coat circles with cooking spray. Set aside.

Combine flour and next 8 ingredients in a large bowl; beat at medium speed with an electric mixer until well blended. Fold in walnuts. Spoon batter into prepared tube pan. Bake at 350° for 55 to 57 minutes or until a wooden pick inserted in center comes out clean. Cool cake in pan on a wire rack 10 minutes; remove from pan, and peel off wax paper. Cool completely on wire rack.

Combine powdered sugar and orange juice; stir well. Spoon glaze over cooled cake, allowing it to drizzle down sides of cake. Yield: 1 (10-inch) cake.

Tucson Treasures: Recipes & Reflections
Tucson Medical Center Auxiliary
Tucson, Arizona

Orange Chiffon Cake

This spongelike cake tends to dry out quickly, so be sure to cover it after it cools.

2¼ cups sifted cake flour
1½ cups sugar
1 tablespoon baking powder
1 teaspoon salt
½ cup vegetable oil
5 egg yolks

2 tablespoons grated orange rind
¾ cup orange juice
6 egg whites
½ teaspoon cream of tartar
⅛ teaspoon salt

Combine first 4 ingredients in a large bowl. Add oil, yolks, rind, and orange juice; beat at medium speed with an electric mixer until well blended.

Beat egg whites, cream of tartar, and ⅛ teaspoon salt at high speed until soft peaks form; gently fold into batter. Pour batter into an ungreased 10-inch tube pan, spreading batter evenly in pan.

Bake at 325° for 42 to 45 minutes or until cake springs back when lightly touched. Remove from oven; invert pan, and let cool in pan 40 minutes. Loosen cake from sides of pan, using a narrow metal spatula; remove from pan. Yield: 1 (10-inch) cake.   Jane Siegrist

Mealtime and Memories
Stumptown Mennonite Church Women
Bird-in-Hand, Pennsylvania

Georgia Peach Shortcake

This shortcake is a variation of a classic shortcake, only it's chocolate. The chocolate layers are frosted with clouds of whipped cream. You can substitute canned or frozen peaches for fresh, or use strawberries.

4 large eggs, separated	1 teaspoon vanilla extract
½ cup sugar	2 tablespoons sugar
½ cup all-purpose flour	2 cups heavy whipping cream
⅓ cup cocoa	¾ cup sifted powdered sugar
¼ cup sugar	1 teaspoon vanilla extract
½ teaspoon baking soda	3 cups sliced fresh peaches,
½ teaspoon salt	well drained
⅓ cup water	

Grease bottom of 2 (9-inch) square cakepans; line with wax paper, and grease wax paper. Set pans aside.

Beat egg yolks at medium speed with an electric mixer 3 minutes. Gradually add ½ cup sugar; beat 2 minutes. Combine flour, cocoa, ¼ cup sugar, soda, and salt. Add flour mixture alternately with water, beating on low speed just until smooth. Stir in 1 teaspoon vanilla. Beat egg whites in a large mixing bowl until foamy; add 2 tablespoons sugar; beat until stiff peaks form. Fold chocolate mixture into egg white mixture.

Spread batter evenly in prepared pans. Bake at 375° for 14 to 16 minutes or until a wooden pick inserted in center comes out clean. Cool in pans on wire racks 10 minutes; remove from pans. Remove wax paper, and cool cake completely on wire racks.

Beat whipping cream until foamy; gradually add powdered sugar and 1 teaspoon vanilla, beating until soft peaks form.

Place 1 cake layer upside down on a serving plate; frost with 1 cup whipped cream. Make a border with whipped cream ½ inch high and 1 inch wide around edge of layer. Fill center with peach slices, reserving 12 peach slices for top of cake. Carefully place remaining layer, top side up, on filling. Reserve 1 cup whipped cream; gently spread remaining whipped cream on top of cake. Using reserved whipped cream, make a border around edge of top layer. Arrange reserved peach slices in center of cake. Chill 1 hour before serving. Yield: 1 (9-inch) cake.   Irene Darling

Cooking Seasoned with Love
Upsala Community Presbyterian Church
Sanford, Florida

Glazed Square Cakes

These dainty little cake squares, topped with pie filling and dusted lightly with powdered sugar, are perfect for an intimate party or baby shower. Use the leftover pie filling to top pancakes or waffles to liven up breakfast.

1 cup butter or margarine, softened
1½ cups sugar
4 large eggs
2 cups all-purpose flour

1 teaspoon vanilla extract
¾ cup blueberry or cherry pie filling
3 tablespoons powdered sugar

Beat butter and 1½ cups sugar at medium speed with an electric mixer until fluffy. Add eggs, 1 at a time, beating until blended after each addition. Stir in flour, blending well. Stir in vanilla.

Spread batter in a well-greased 15- x 10-inch jellyroll pan. Mark batter with tip of a knife into 24 squares. Drop a rounded teaspoon of filling in center of each square.

Bake at 350° for 23 minutes or until cake springs back when lightly touched. Cool in pan on a wire rack. Cut into squares, and sprinkle with powdered sugar. Yield: 2 dozen.

Past and Present Meatless Treasures
Kaneohe Seventh-day Adventist Church
Kaneohe, Hawaii

Pear Skillet Cake with Caramel-Rum Sauce

For a nostalgic treat reminiscent of times gone by, delight in a piece of this gingerbread-like cake topped with succulent pear slices and dripping with Caramel-Rum Sauce. It's good old-fashioned eating.

1 cup firmly packed dark
   brown sugar
6 tablespoons unsalted butter,
   cut into pieces
1⅓ cups all-purpose flour
1⅓ cups sugar
1¼ teaspoons baking soda
½ teaspoon salt
2 teaspoons ground cinnamon

2 large eggs
½ cup vegetable oil
1 small firm pear, unpeeled
   and coarsely grated
1 tablespoon grated fresh
   ginger
4 firm pears, peeled and cut
   into 6 wedges each
Caramel-Rum Sauce

Sprinkle brown sugar evenly in a 12-inch cast-iron skillet. Add butter, and place skillet in a 350° oven for 8 minutes or until butter melts. Remove skillet from oven, and stir brown sugar mixture until blended.

Combine flour and next 4 ingredients in a large bowl. Add eggs and oil, beating at low speed with an electric mixer until blended. Stir in grated pear and ginger; set aside.

Arrange pear wedges over brown sugar mixture in skillet in a flower pattern, putting any extra pieces in center. Spoon batter evenly over pears.

Bake at 350° for 1 hour or until a wooden pick inserted in center of cake comes out clean. Run a knife around edge of cake to loosen from pan; cool in pan on a wire rack 20 minutes. Invert cake onto a large serving plate. Serve immediately with warm Caramel-Rum Sauce. Yield: 1 (12-inch) cake.

Caramel-Rum Sauce

½ cup whipping cream
½ cup unsalted butter
½ cup sugar

½ cup firmly packed dark
   brown sugar
3 tablespoons dark rum

Combine first 4 ingredients in a medium saucepan; cook over medium heat until butter melts and sugars dissolve. Bring to a boil; cook 3 minutes or until slightly thickened. Stir in rum. Let stand 5 minutes. Yield: 1½ cups.

*Cooking with Music: Celebrating the Tastes and Traditions of the
Boston Symphony Orchestra*
Boston Symphony Association of Volunteers
Boston, Massachusetts

Strawberry Cream Cake

Cloudlike layers of whipped topping spread between the layers and on the sides of an angel food cake are dotted with sweet strawberries for a summer dessert. To easily cut cake into even layers, use a serrated knife and a gentle sawing motion.

1 (14-ounce) can sweetened
   condensed milk
⅓ cup fresh lemon juice
   (about 3 medium lemons)
1 teaspoon almond extract

1 (12-ounce) container frozen
   whipped topping, thawed
1 (8-inch) round angel food
   cake
2 pints fresh strawberries

Combine first 3 ingredients in a large bowl; stir until well blended. Fold in whipped topping. Cover and chill 10 minutes.

Cut cake horizontally into 3 layers. Reserve 5 strawberries; coarsely chop remaining strawberries and fold into whipped topping mixture. Spread between layers and on top and sides of cake. Spoon remaining filling into center of cake, and top with reserved strawberries. Yield: 1 (8-inch) cake.

At Your Service: Southern Recipes, Places and Traditions
The Junior League of Gwinnett and North Fulton Counties
Duluth, Georgia

Mexican Chocolate Soufflé Cakes

A fanned strawberry atop each little cake makes a pretty presentation for an elegant dessert. You can make the batter up to 4 hours ahead and then bake it during dinner.

1 (8-ounce) package semisweet chocolate baking squares, chopped (we tested with Baker's)
½ cup unsalted butter, cut into 1-inch pieces
1½ teaspoons instant coffee granules
⅛ teaspoon salt
6 egg yolks
¼ cup sugar
1 teaspoon ground cinnamon
1 teaspoon vanilla extract
2 egg whites
1 tablespoon sugar
Powdered sugar
Sweetened Whipped Cream
Garnishes: fresh strawberry fans, mint sprigs

Butter bottom and sides of 6 (4-inch) tart pans with removable bottoms. Set aside.

Combine chocolate and butter in a medium saucepan; cook over low heat until chocolate melts, stirring occasionally. Remove from heat. Stir in coffee granules and salt. Let cool 5 minutes.

Beat egg yolks and next 3 ingredients until thick and pale. Gradually stir 2 tablespoons chocolate mixture into yolk mixture; add to remaining chocolate mixture.

Beat egg whites at high speed with an electric mixer until foamy. Add 1 tablespoon sugar, beating until stiff peaks form and sugar dissolves (2 to 3 minutes). Fold into chocolate mixture. Pour evenly into prepared pans. Cover and chill 2 to 4 hours.

When ready to bake, uncover tart pans, and place 1 inch apart on baking sheets. Bake, uncovered, at 400° for 11 minutes or until edges are set (center will be soft but will set as it cools). Cool in pans on wire racks 5 minutes. To serve, carefully remove sides of tart pans. Sprinkle cakes with powdered sugar, and serve warm with Sweetened Whipped Cream. Garnish, if desired. Yield: 6 servings.

Sweetened Whipped Cream

½ cup whipping cream   1 tablespoon sugar

Beat cream until foamy; gradually add sugar, beating until soft peaks form. Yield: 1 cup.   Connie Smith and James Davis

Note: To make strawberry fans, slice a large strawberry about 3 or 4 times from below the stem and through the tip. Carefully spread the slices into a fan shape.

Menus & Memories
The University of Oklahoma Women's Association
Norman, Oklahoma

Key Lime Cheesecake

If you're a fan of creamy, citrusy cheesecake, look no further than this lime-infused version that can be dressed up easily with slices of fresh lime and dollops of whipped cream.

2 cups graham cracker crumbs
½ cup packed light brown
    sugar
5 tablespoons butter or
    margarine, melted
4 (8-ounce) packages cream
    cheese, softened
1⅔ cups sugar

⅓ cup sour cream
4 large eggs
1 egg yolk
⅓ cup whipping cream
1 cup all-purpose flour
1 tablespoon vanilla extract
½ cup Key lime juice

Wrap aluminum foil around the bottom and halfway up the sides of a 10-inch springform pan.

Combine first 3 ingredients in a small bowl; stir well. Firmly press mixture in prepared pan.

Beat cream cheese and 1⅔ cups sugar at medium speed with an electric mixer until creamy; add sour cream, and beat well. Add eggs and egg yolk, 1 at a time, beating after each addition. Add whipping cream and remaining 3 ingredients; beat well. Pour batter into prepared pan. Place springform pan into a larger pan; add hot water to larger pan to a depth of 1 inch.

Bake at 325° for 1 hour and 20 minutes (center will not be completely set). Run a knife around edge of pan to release sides. Cool cheesecake completely on a wire rack; cover and chill 8 hours. Remove sides of pan when ready to serve. Yield: 14 servings.

A Sunsational Encore
The Junior League of Greater Orlando, Florida

Chocolate-White Chocolate Cheesecake

Every cheesecake should be this easy and taste this velvety rich. Using a vegetable peeler makes it easy to quickly peel chocolate shavings from a bar of good quality chocolate.

28 cream-filled chocolate
    sandwich cookies
1½ cups sugar, divided
6 tablespoons unsalted butter,
    melted
5 (8-ounce) packages cream
    cheese, softened
¼ cup all-purpose flour

5 large eggs
2 egg yolks
1 teaspoon vanilla extract
8 (1-ounce) white chocolate
    baking squares, chopped
    (we tested with Ghirardelli)
¼ cup half-and-half
Garnish: chocolate curls

Position knife blade in food processor bowl; add cookies and ¼ cup sugar. Process until finely ground. Add butter; process until well blended, stopping to scrape down sides. Firmly press crumb mixture in bottom and 1 inch up sides of a greased 10-inch springform pan. Chill 1 hour.

Beat cream cheese at medium speed with a heavy-duty electric mixer until creamy. Combine remaining 1¼ cups sugar and flour. Gradually add sugar mixture to cream cheese, beating well. Add eggs and yolks, 1 at a time, beating after each addition. Stir in vanilla, white chocolate, and half-and-half. Pour mixture into prepared crust.

Bake at 325° for 1 hour and 15 minutes or until cheesecake is almost set. Turn oven off, and partially open oven door; leave cheesecake in oven 30 minutes. Let cool to room temperature in pan on a wire rack. Cover and chill at least 8 hours. Remove sides of pan when ready to serve. Garnish, if desired. Yield: 12 servings.   Lynette Earley

Our Daily Bread
First Presbyterian Church of Orlando—Weekday School
Orlando, Florida

Cookies & Candies

Lollipop Cookies, page 125

Cranberry Chip Cookies

Similar to a macaroon, these cranberry-studded delights are slightly crisp on the outside and soft in the middle. Make sure to store them in an airtight container to keep them fresh.

½ cup butter or margarine, softened
½ cup sugar
1 large egg
1 teaspoon vanilla extract
1 cup all-purpose flour
1 cup uncooked quick-cooking oats
1 teaspoon baking powder
1 cup white chocolate morsels
½ cup dried cranberries
½ cup flaked coconut

Beat first 4 ingredients at medium speed with an electric mixer until creamy.

Combine flour, oats, and baking powder. Gradually add flour mixture to butter mixture, beating at low speed until a soft dough forms. Stir in white chocolate morsels, cranberries, and coconut.

Drop dough by heaping teaspoonfuls 2 inches apart onto ungreased baking sheets. Bake at 350° for 9 to 11 minutes or until set. Cool on baking sheets 2 minutes; remove to wire racks to cool completely. Yield: 3 dozen. Kate Painter

Dixon Fixins
Dixon Ambulatory Care Center
Westminster, Maryland

Breakfast Cookies

On those days when you're in a rush, these cookies are great to grab and go when you're running out the door. A 1½-inch cookie scoop makes it easy to get a uniform-size cookie every time.

1 cup shortening	1 teaspoon baking soda
1 cup firmly packed light	1 teaspoon salt
brown sugar	2 cups uncooked regular oats
2 large eggs	2 cups crisp rice cereal
½ teaspoon vanilla extract	1 (12-ounce) package
1½ cups all-purpose flour	semisweet chocolate morsels
1 teaspoon baking powder	1 cup chopped pecans

Beat shortening and sugar at medium speed with an electric mixer until fluffy. Add eggs and vanilla, beating well.

Combine flour and next 3 ingredients in a small bowl; add to shortening mixture, mixing well. Stir in oats and remaining ingredients.

Drop dough by heaping teaspoonfuls 2 inches apart onto lightly greased baking sheets. Bake at 350° for 10 minutes or until lightly browned. Cool slightly on baking sheets; remove to wire racks to cool completely. Yield: 5½ dozen. Sandy Henning

Fine Food from the Friends
Friends of the Superior Public Library, Inc.
Superior, Wisconsin

Butterscotch-Oatmeal Cookies

¾ cup shortening
1 cup firmly packed light
   brown sugar
½ cup sugar
1 large egg
¼ cup water
1 teaspoon vanilla extract

1 cup all-purpose flour
1 teaspoon salt
½ teaspoon baking soda
3 cups uncooked quick-
   cooking oats
1 (11-ounce) package
   butterscotch morsels

Beat shortening at medium speed with an electric mixer until fluffy; gradually add sugars, beating mixture well. Add egg, water, and vanilla; beat well.

Combine flour, salt, and soda. Gradually add to shortening mixture, beating well. Stir in oats and butterscotch morsels.

Drop dough by heaping teaspoonfuls onto greased baking sheets. Bake at 350° for 12 minutes or until edges are lightly browned. Cool on baking sheets 2 minutes; remove to wire racks to cool completely. Yield: about 4 dozen.   Linda Taylor

Cross Village: A Selection of Tastes, Art, and Memories
Cross Village Community Services
Cross Village, Michigan

Lollipop Cookies

A definite kid-pleaser, these cookies are as easy to make as they are to eat. Be creative with the decorating by using your favorite candies.

1 cup butter or margarine, softened
1 cup firmly packed light brown sugar
1 cup sugar
2 large eggs
1 teaspoon vanilla extract
2 cups all-purpose flour
1 teaspoon baking powder
1 teaspoon baking soda

1 teaspoon salt
2 cups uncooked quick-cooking oats
2 cups crisp rice cereal
Wooden craft sticks
Garnishes: rainbow candy sprinkles, candy-coated peanut butter pieces, candy-coated chocolate pieces

Beat butter at medium speed with an electric mixer until creamy; gradually add sugars, beating well. Add eggs and vanilla; beat well.

Combine flour, baking powder, soda, and salt; gradually add to butter mixture, beating well. Stir in oats and cereal. Cover and chill 30 minutes.

Shape dough into 1½-inch balls. Place 3 inches apart on greased baking sheets. Press a stick into 1 end of each ball. Flatten to a 2-inch diameter. Garnish, if desired. Bake at 325° for 16 minutes or until lightly browned. Cool on baking sheets 2 minutes; remove to wire racks to cool completely. Yield: about 5 dozen.   Karen Peterman

Ofukuro No Aji: Favorite Recipes from Mama's Kitchen
Hōkūlani Cultural Exchange Committee
(Hōkūlani Elementary School)
Honolulu, Hawaii

Caramel-Filled Chocolate Cookies

The marriage of chocolate and caramel has long been a favorite, and this cookie is no exception. The caramel is hidden in the cookie and oozes out with every bite.

1 cup butter or margarine, softened
1 cup sugar
1 cup firmly packed brown sugar
2 large eggs
2 teaspoons vanilla extract
2¼ cups all-purpose flour
1 teaspoon baking soda
¾ cup cocoa
1 cup finely chopped walnuts, divided
1 tablespoon sugar
1 (9-ounce) package chocolate-coated caramels (we tested with Rolos)

Beat butter at medium speed with an electric mixer until creamy; gradually add sugars, beating well. Add eggs and vanilla; beat well.

Combine flour, soda, and cocoa; gradually add to butter mixture, beating well. Stir in ½ cup walnuts. Cover and chill dough at least 2 hours. Combine remaining ½ cup walnuts and 1 tablespoon sugar.

Divide dough into 4 equal portions. Work with 1 portion at a time, storing remaining dough in refrigerator.

Divide each portion into 12 pieces. Quickly press each piece of dough around a caramel; roll into a ball. Dip 1 side of ball in walnut mixture. Place balls, walnut sides up, 2 inches apart on ungreased baking sheets.

Bake at 375° for 8 minutes. (Cookies will look soft.) Cool 1 minute on baking sheets; remove to wire racks to cool completely. Yield: 4 dozen.   Kurtis Abbott

Business is Cookin' with FBLA
Lakeview Future Business Leaders of America
Columbus, Nebraska

Sweetie Pies

What's a sweetie pie? Think of the chewy texture and fudgy chocolate taste of brownies baked into a cookie. Have a tall glass of cold milk at hand.

2 (1-ounce) unsweetened chocolate baking squares, chopped
¾ cup semisweet chocolate morsels
½ cup butter or margarine, softened
1 cup sugar
2 large eggs
2 teaspoons vanilla extract
1½ cups all-purpose flour
1 cup semisweet chocolate morsels
½ cup white chocolate morsels
¼ cup milk chocolate morsels

Combine unsweetened chocolate and ¾ cup semisweet chocolate morsels in a heavy saucepan. Cook over low heat, stirring occasionally, until chocolate melts; cool.

Beat butter and sugar at medium speed with an electric mixer until creamy. Add eggs and vanilla; beat well. Stir in melted chocolate. Gradually stir flour into egg mixture. Stir in 1 cup semisweet chocolate morsels and white and milk chocolate morsels. Cover and chill 1 hour.

Shape dough into 1-inch balls. Place 2 inches apart on ungreased baking sheets. Flatten each cookie into a 1½-inch circle. Bake at 375° for 11 minutes. Cool slightly on baking sheets; remove to wire racks to cool completely. Yield: 3½ dozen. Joleen Kragt

Jubilee 2000 Recipe Collection
St. Alphonsus Liguori Parish—Hospitality Committee
Prospect Heights, Illinois

Macadamia Balls

These bite-sized balls are perfect to pop in your mouth while sipping a cup of coffee.

1 cup butter or margarine, softened	¾ cup uncooked quick-cooking oats
½ cup powdered sugar	1 (3½-ounce) jar macadamia nuts, chopped
1 teaspoon vanilla extract	Powdered sugar
2 cups all-purpose flour	

Beat butter at medium speed with an electric mixer until creamy. Add ½ cup powdered sugar, and beat well. Add vanilla and flour, beating well. Stir in oats and macadamia nuts. Shape into 1-inch balls. Place on ungreased baking sheets.

Bake at 375° for 12 to 14 minutes or until golden. Remove from baking sheets, and immediately roll in powdered sugar. Cool on wire racks. Yield: 3 dozen.   Robin Turner Higdon

Beyond Cotton Country
The Junior League of Morgan County
Decatur, Alabama

Sweet Koulourakia

This Greek treat has a texture similar to a shortbread cookie. Traditionally, the dough is shaped into wreaths, figure eights, or coils, and baked.

1 cup butter or margarine, softened	1 teaspoon vanilla extract
1 cup sugar	4¾ cups all-purpose flour
2 large eggs	1 tablespoon baking powder
1 large egg, separated	½ teaspoon salt
¼ cup milk	¼ cup sesame seeds

Beat butter at medium speed with an electric mixer until creamy. Add sugar, 2 eggs, egg yolk, milk, and vanilla; beat well.

Combine flour, baking powder, and salt; stir into butter mixture.

Shape dough into 1-inch balls. Roll each ball into a 5-inch rope. Fold each rope in half, and twist twice. Place twists on greased baking sheets.

Lightly beat remaining egg white; brush over twists. Sprinkle twists evenly with sesame seeds. Bake at 350° for 15 minutes. Yield: 5 dozen.

Good Food, Served Right
Traditional Arts in Upstate New York
Canton, New York

Lemon Icebox Cookies

1 cup shortening
½ cup sugar
½ cup firmly packed light
  brown sugar
1 large egg, beaten
1 tablespoon grated lemon
  rind

2 tablespoons lemon juice
2 cups all-purpose flour
¾ teaspoon baking soda
½ teaspoon salt
1 cup chopped pecans

Beat shortening and sugars at medium speed with an electric mixer until fluffy. Add egg, lemon rind, and lemon juice, beating well.

Combine flour, soda, and salt; add to shortening mixture, beating well. Stir in pecans. Divide dough into 3 equal portions; roll each into a 3-inch log. Wrap in plastic wrap; freeze until firm.

Cut each log (while still frozen) into ¼-inch slices, using a sharp knife. Place on ungreased baking sheets. Bake at 325° for 12 minutes. Cool 2 minutes on baking sheets. Remove to wire racks to cool completely. Yield: about 3 dozen.   Frances Jones

St. Andrew's Cooks Again
Presbyterian Women of St. Andrew
Beaumont, Texas

Sugar Cookies

Lemon adds a surprising tang to this traditional sugar cookie dough recipe.

⅔ cup butter or margarine,
   softened
¾ cup sugar
1 large egg
4 teaspoons milk
½ teaspoon vanilla extract

½ teaspoon lemon extract
2 cups all-purpose flour
1½ teaspoons baking powder
¼ teaspoon salt
Sugar

Beat butter and ¾ cup sugar at medium speed with an electric mixer until creamy, beating well. Add egg; beat well. Add milk, vanilla, and lemon extract; beat well.

Combine flour, baking powder, and salt; stir into butter mixture. Cover and chill 1 hour.

Divide dough into 4 equal portions. Work with 1 portion of dough at a time, storing remaining portion in refrigerator. Roll each portion to ⅛-inch thickness on a lightly floured surface. Cut with a 2½-inch cookie cutter; place on ungreased baking sheets. Sprinkle with sugar.

Bake at 375° for 10 minutes or until edges are lightly browned. Cool 1 minute on baking sheets; remove to wire racks, and let cool completely. Yield: 2 dozen.
           Verna Heidebrecht

Glen Haven Community Cookbook 1999
Glen Haven Area Volunteer Fire Department
Glen Haven, Colorado

Sweet Ravioli

We were won over by this lemon-infused sugar cookie dough that's cut into squares and filled with preserves, then sealed to resemble ravioli. They are as fun to make as they are to eat. The dough chills overnight, making this a good cookie to make ahead.

1 cup butter or margarine, softened	3 cups all-purpose flour
⅔ cup sugar	¼ teaspoon baking soda
1 large egg	⅛ teaspoon salt
1 teaspoon grated lemon rind	⅓ cup seedless raspberry preserves
1½ teaspoons vanilla extract	Sifted powdered sugar
¼ teaspoon almond extract	

Beat butter at medium speed with an electric mixer until creamy; gradually add sugar, beating mixture well. Add egg and next 3 ingredients; beat well.

Combine flour, baking soda, and salt; add to butter mixture, beating at low speed until blended. Divide dough in half; roll each portion between 2 sheets of wax paper into a 12-inch square. Chill overnight.

Remove 1 portion of dough, storing remaining portion in refrigerator. Remove top piece of wax paper, and cut dough into 64 (1½-inch) squares. Transfer 32 squares to a lightly greased baking sheet. Spoon ¼ teaspoon raspberry preserves into center of each of the 32 squares.

Cut a small "x" in center of remaining 32 squares. Place squares on top of filled squares. Gently press a fork around edges to seal. Bake at 350° for 10 minutes or until edges are golden. Immediately remove to wire racks to cool. Lightly sprinkle with powdered sugar. Repeat procedure with remaining portion of dough. Yield: 5⅓ dozen.

The Dining Car
The Service League of Denison, Texas

Fudge Puddles

If you love the familiar peanut butter cookie with a chocolate kiss in the middle, then you'll love these. Same idea, but the peanut butter dough is baked in a miniature muffin pan, then filled with a creamy chocolate filling.

½ cup butter or margarine, softened
½ cup creamy peanut butter
½ cup sugar
½ cup firmly packed light brown sugar
1 large egg
½ teaspoon vanilla extract
1¼ cups all-purpose flour
¾ teaspoon baking soda
½ teaspoon salt
Fudge Filling
Chopped peanuts

Beat butter and peanut butter at medium speed with an electric mixer until creamy; gradually add sugars, beating well. Add egg and vanilla; beat well.

Combine flour, soda, and salt; gradually add to butter mixture. Cover and chill dough 1 hour.

Shape dough into 1-inch balls. Press into lightly greased miniature (1¾-inch) muffin pans.

Bake at 325° for 16 minutes. Immediately make indentations in center of each by lightly pressing with the back of a melon ball cutter.

Cool in pan 5 minutes; remove to wire racks to cool completely. Spoon Fudge Filling into centers. Sprinkle with chopped peanuts. Yield: 3 dozen.

Fudge Filling

1 cup milk chocolate morsels
1 cup semisweet chocolate morsels
1 (14-ounce) can sweetened condensed milk
1 teaspoon vanilla extract

Melt chocolate morsels in a heavy saucepan over low heat, stirring until smooth. Remove from heat; stir in milk and vanilla. Yield: 2 cups.   Jacqueline D. Brinkley and Brenda Tanner

Walking with Christ
First Baptist Church
Mount Airy, North Carolina

Chocolate-Cream Cheese Squares

The beauty of this recipe is that you can use any cake mix flavor to create a different taste treat.

1 (18.25-ounce) package Swiss chocolate cake mix (we tested with Duncan Hines)
½ cup butter or margarine, melted
1 large egg, lightly beaten
1 cup chopped pecans

1 (8-ounce) package cream cheese, softened
2 large eggs
1 teaspoon vanilla extract
1 (16-ounce) package powdered sugar

Combine cake mix, butter, and beaten egg in a medium bowl. Stir in pecans. Press mixture into a lightly greased 13- x 9-inch pan.

Beat cream cheese, 2 eggs, and vanilla at medium speed with an electric mixer until blended; gradually add powdered sugar, beating 2 minutes or until smooth. Spoon cream cheese mixture over cake mix mixture, spreading to edges. Bake at 325° for 45 minutes or until lightly browned. Cool completely in pan on a wire rack; cut into squares. Yield: 3 dozen.

From Black Tie to Blackeyed Peas: Savannah's Savory Secrets
St. Joseph's Foundation of Savannah, Inc.
Savannah, Georgia

Chocolate Truffles

The sky is the limit when it comes to coatings for this decadent chocolate candy. Think sprinkles, nuts, coconut, and small candies, to name a few.

⅔ cup heavy whipping cream
3 tablespoons unsalted butter, cut into pieces
2 tablespoons sugar
1 tablespoon hazelnut liqueur

2 (4-ounce) packages German chocolate baking squares, broken into pieces
Unsweetened cocoa
Ground hazelnuts

Combine first 3 ingredients in a medium saucepan over medium heat. Bring to a boil, stirring constantly. Remove from heat; add liqueur and chocolate pieces. Stir until chocolate mixture is smooth. Cover and chill at least 3 hours or until firm enough to handle. Shape into 1-inch balls, and roll in cocoa or ground hazelnuts. Store in refrigerator. Yield: 2 dozen.   Earlene Smith

V.C.O.S. Sharing Our Best
Volusia County Orchid Society, Inc.
DeLand, Florida

Microwave Divinity

Don't save this recipe for a rainy day. Instead, for best results, try it on a sunny day when the humidity's low.

4 cups sugar
1 cup light corn syrup
¾ cup water
¼ teaspoon salt

3 egg whites
1 teaspoon vanilla extract
½ cup chopped pecans

Combine first 4 ingredients in a 4-quart microwave-safe bowl. Microwave at HIGH 20 minutes or until hard ball stage (when mixture forms a hard yet pliable ball when dropped into cold water or a candy thermometer registers 250°), stirring every 3 minutes.

Beat egg whites in a large mixing bowl at high speed with an electric mixer until soft peaks form. Pour hot sugar mixture in a heavy stream over beaten egg whites, beating constantly at high speed. Add vanilla, and continue beating just until mixture holds its shape (about 7 minutes). Stir in chopped pecans.

Working quickly, drop divinity by rounded teaspoonfuls onto wax paper, and let cool. Peel from wax paper, and store in an airtight container. Yield: about 4 dozen (2¼ pounds).   Bob Rooney

Note: We tested this recipe in an 1100-watt microwave. If the wattage of your microwave oven is different, your cook time may change accordingly.

Divine Offerings: Recipes and Hints for the Kitchen
St. Charles Presbyterian Women
St. Charles, Missouri

Opera Creams

Similar to a praline, this creamy candy is loaded with nuts.

2 cups sugar	⅛ teaspoon salt
¾ cup whipping cream	1 teaspoon vanilla extract
1 cup half-and-half	1½ cups chopped pecans
2 tablespoons light corn syrup	

Combine first 5 ingredients in a 4-quart heavy saucepan. Bring to a boil over medium heat, stirring gently. Cook, stirring often, over medium heat until candy thermometer registers 240° (soft ball stage). Remove from heat; stir in vanilla and pecans. Beat with a wooden spoon just until mixture begins to thicken. Working rapidly, drop by tablespoonfuls onto wax paper; let stand until firm. Yield: about 2 dozen (1¼ pounds).   Eleanor Christensen

Fine Food from the Friends
Friends of the Superior Public Library, Inc.
Superior, Wisconsin

Macadamia-Almond Brittle

The microwave makes it a breeze to whip up this brittle.

1 cup sugar
¾ cup chopped macadamia
   nuts
¾ cup chopped almonds
½ cup light corn syrup

1 tablespoon butter or
   margarine, softened
2 teaspoons vanilla extract
1 teaspoon baking soda

Combine first 4 ingredients in a 4-quart glass bowl. Microwave, uncovered, at HIGH 6 minutes (mixture should be bubbly). Quickly stir in butter and vanilla; microwave at HIGH 2 minutes or until hard crack stage (when mixture separates into threads that are hard and brittle when dropped into cold water or a candy thermometer registers 300°). Quickly add baking soda, stirring until mixture is foamy.

Working rapidly, pour mixture into a buttered 15- x 10-inch jellyroll pan, spreading thinly. Let cool completely. Break into pieces. Store in an airtight container. Yield: 1 pound.   Joyce Ogle

Note: We tested this recipe in an 1100-watt microwave oven. If the wattage of your microwave oven is different, your cook time may change accordingly.

Lake Waccamaw United Methodist Church Cookbook
Lake Waccamaw United Methodist Church
Lake Waccamaw, North Carolina

Desserts

Chocolate Pears in Raspberry Sauce, page 138

Chocolate Pears in Raspberry Sauce

The ingredients for this beautiful dessert can be prepared ahead and assembled just before serving.

Raspberry Sauce
Chocolate Sauce
6 firm ripe pears

3 cups water
3 tablespoons lemon juice
½ large vanilla bean, split

Prepare Raspberry Sauce and Chocolate Sauce; cover and chill.

Slice ¼ inch from bottom of each pear, allowing pears to stand. Peel pears, leaving stem ends intact; core from bottom.

Bring water, lemon juice, and vanilla bean to a boil in a heavy saucepan over medium heat. Stand pears in liquid. Cover, reduce heat, and simmer 20 minutes or until pears are tender. Remove pears from liquid, and cool; discard cooking liquid.

Spoon chilled Raspberry Sauce evenly on each of 6 dessert plates. Stand pears in Raspberry Sauce, and drizzle pears evenly with chilled Chocolate Sauce. Yield: 6 servings.

Raspberry Sauce

1 (14-ounce) package frozen
  unsweetened raspberries,
  thawed

2½ tablespoons sugar
½ teaspoon cornstarch

Combine raspberries and sugar in a saucepan. Cook over medium-low heat 4 minutes or until sugar dissolves, stirring constantly. Pour mixture through a wire-mesh strainer into a bowl, discarding pulp and seeds. Return liquid to saucepan; whisk in cornstarch. Bring to a boil over medium heat. Boil 1 minute or until slightly thickened. Pour into a bowl; cover and chill. Yield: ¾ cup.

Chocolate Sauce

2½ tablespoons sugar
2½ tablespoons cocoa
2 tablespoons water

2 tablespoons light corn syrup
½ teaspoon vanilla extract

Combine sugar and cocoa in a saucepan. Stir in water and corn syrup until smooth. Bring to a boil over medium heat. Boil 1 minute or until slightly thickened. Remove from heat, and stir in vanilla. Pour into a bowl; cover and chill. Yield: ⅓ cup.

Always in Season
The Junior League of Salt Lake City, Utah

Chocolate Cheese Ball

A unique addition to any dessert table, this rich and creamy ball of chocolate and cream cheese can be rolled in your favorite nuts or even chocolate sprinkles for the true chocoholic. It'll disappear in a hurry at any party.

1 (8-ounce) package cream cheese, softened
¼ cup butter or margarine, softened
¾ cup powdered sugar
2 tablespoons light brown sugar

3 tablespoons cocoa
1 tablespoon coffee liqueur
¼ cup semisweet chocolate mini-morsels
¼ cup finely chopped pecans

Beat cream cheese and butter at medium speed with an electric mixer until fluffy. Stir in sugars, cocoa, and liqueur; fold in chocolate morsels. Cover and chill 2 hours or until firm.

Shape mixture into a ball, and roll in pecans. Serve with graham crackers or fruit. Yield: 1 (4-inch) cheese ball.

Ropin' the Flavors of Texas
The Junior League of Victoria, Texas

Chocolate-Raspberry Supremes

Chocolate and raspberry make a happy pairing of flavors in these gooey squares.

1 cup all-purpose flour
¼ cup sifted powdered sugar
½ cup butter or margarine
1 (3-ounce) package cream
   cheese, softened
2 tablespoons milk
1 cup white chocolate morsels,
   melted

½ cup raspberry jam
4 (1-ounce) semisweet
   chocolate baking squares,
   coarsely chopped
2 tablespoons shortening

Combine flour and powdered sugar in a medium bowl; cut in butter with a pastry blender until mixture is crumbly. Press mixture into an ungreased 9-inch square pan. Bake at 375° for 17 minutes or until lightly browned.

Beat cream cheese and milk in a small bowl until smooth; add melted white chocolate morsels, and blend well.

Drop cream cheese mixture by tablespoonfuls over the baked crust; carefully spread over crust. Spread jam over cream cheese layer; chill 15 minutes or until mixture is set.

Melt semisweet chocolate and shortening in a small saucepan over low heat, stirring often. Spread over jam layer. Cool completely; cut into squares. Store, covered, in the refrigerator. Yield: 16 servings.

A Sunsational Encore
The Junior League of Greater Orlando, Florida

Lime Flans

*Looking for the perfect dessert with a Mexican-inspired meal? Try this
rich custard with a burst of cooling lime to tame the heat of a fiery meal.*

¾ cup sugar	2½ teaspoons vanilla extract
3 large eggs, lightly beaten	2 cups heavy whipping cream
5 egg yolks, lightly beaten	1½ cups milk
⅔ cup sugar	1 tablespoon grated lime rind
¼ teaspoon salt	Garnish: lime slices

Sprinkle ¾ cup sugar in a large heavy skillet. Cook over medium
heat, stirring constantly with a wooden spoon, until sugar melts and
turns light brown. Quickly pour hot caramel into 8 (6-ounce) custard
cups or ramekins, tilting each cup to coat bottom evenly. Place cups in
a large roasting pan; set aside.

Combine eggs, egg yolks, and next 3 ingredients in a large bowl. Set
aside.

Cook whipping cream and milk in a heavy saucepan over medium-
high heat to 180° or until tiny bubbles form around edge (do not boil).
Remove from heat.

Gradually add hot milk to egg mixture, stirring constantly with a wire
whisk. Pour egg mixture over syrup in prepared custard cups. Sprinkle
with lime rind. Add hot water to roasting pan to a depth of 1 inch.
Bake, uncovered, at 325° for 43 to 45 minutes or until a knife inserted
near center comes out clean.

Remove cups from pan; cool completely on a wire rack. Cover and
chill at least 8 hours. Loosen edges of flans with a small sharp knife,
and invert onto rimmed serving plates, letting melted caramel drizzle
over top. Garnish, if desired. Yield: 8 servings.

Ropin' the Flavors of Texas
The Junior League of Victoria, Texas

Raspberry Crème Brûlée

Smooth and silky with a caramelized sugar top, this popular dessert sparkles with fresh raspberries that add another dimension of sweetness.

2 cups fresh raspberries
3 cups half-and-half
½ cup sugar
3 large eggs

4 egg yolks
1 teaspoon vanilla extract
⅓ cup firmly packed light
   brown sugar

Spoon raspberries evenly into 8 (4-ounce) ramekins or custard cups.

Combine half-and-half and next 4 ingredients, stirring with a wire whisk until smooth. Pour evenly over berries; place dishes in a large roasting pan. Add hot water to pan to a depth of ½ inch.

Bake, uncovered, at 300° for 50 to 60 minutes or until almost set. Remove custards from water, and cool on a wire rack. Cover and chill at least 8 hours.

Sprinkle 2 teaspoons brown sugar evenly over each custard; place custards on a baking sheet. Broil 5½ inches from heat 2 minutes or just until sugar melts. Let stand 5 minutes to allow sugar to harden. Yield: 8 servings.

Splendor in the Bluegrass
The Junior League of Louisville, Kentucky

Chocolate Bread Pudding with Godiva Cream

Godiva, as you know, is synonymous with all things chocolate. The chocolate liqueur-laced whipped topping adds a sinfully rich touch to this bread pudding.

5 cups diced white bread
1 cup semisweet chocolate
   morsels
3 cups milk
3 tablespoons Godiva liqueur
   or crème de cacao
3 egg yolks
⅓ cup sugar

½ teaspoon ground
   cinnamon
¼ teaspoon salt
1 teaspoon vanilla extract
1 cup whipping cream
2 tablespoons Godiva liqueur
   or crème de cacao

Combine bread and chocolate morsels in a greased 11- x 7-inch baking dish. Stir together milk and next 6 ingredients; pour milk mixture over bread mixture. Let stand 15 minutes. Bake at 350° for 1 hour or until set and puffy.

Beat whipping cream until foamy; gradually add 2 tablespoons liqueur, beating until soft peaks form. Serve over warm pudding. Yield: 6 servings.

At Your Service: Southern Recipes, Places and Traditions
The Junior League of Gwinnett and North Fulton Counties
Duluth, Georgia

Bread and Butter Pudding with Raspberry Sauce

Unlike traditional bread puddings, this one sports a custard layer on the bottom and is bathed in a sweet raspberry sauce.

12 (½-inch-thick) slices French bread	1 cup whipping cream
¼ cup butter, softened	1 cup sugar
6 large eggs, lightly beaten	2 teaspoons vanilla extract
3 egg yolks, lightly beaten	⅛ teaspoon ground nutmeg
4 cups milk	¼ teaspoon salt
	Raspberry Sauce

Spread each bread slice evenly with butter; place slices, buttered side up, in a greased 13- x 9- inch baking dish.

Combine eggs, egg yolks, and next 6 ingredients in a large bowl. Pour egg mixture evenly over bread slices. Let stand 20 minutes. Place in a large roasting pan. Add hot water to pan to a depth of 1 inch.

Bake at 350° for 50 minutes or until a knife inserted in center of pudding comes out clean. Let stand 5 minutes. Serve with Raspberry Sauce. Yield: 12 servings.

Raspberry Sauce

1 (10-ounce) package frozen raspberries, thawed	¼ cup sugar
	1½ tablespoons cherry liqueur

Process raspberries in a food processor until pureed. Press raspberries through a wire-mesh strainer, using the back of a spoon to squeeze out juice. Discard pulp and seeds. Add sugar and liqueur to puree; stir until sugar dissolves. Yield: ¾ cup.   Barbi Smith

Divine Offerings: Recipes and Hints for the Kitchen
St. Charles Presbyterian Women
St. Charles, Missouri

Strawberry Soufflé with Sliced Strawberries

Top off this dessert deliciously with a dollop of sweetened whipped cream.

3 tablespoons sugar
6 cups fresh strawberries, hulled and divided
3 tablespoons sugar
1 tablespoon cornstarch

¾ teaspoon grated orange rind
1 tablespoon sugar
4 egg whites
3 tablespoons sugar

Lightly grease a 6-cup soufflé dish; dust with 3 tablespoons sugar to coat, shaking out loose sugar.

Process 3 cups strawberries, 3 tablespoons sugar, and cornstarch in a food processor until coarsely pureed. Spoon into a medium saucepan. Cook over medium heat, stirring constantly, 3 minutes or until mixture comes to a boil and thickens. Stir in orange rind. Cool completely.

Slice remaining strawberries, and place in a medium bowl. Stir in 1 tablespoon sugar. Set aside.

Beat egg whites at high speed with an electric mixer until foamy. Add 3 tablespoons sugar, 1 tablespoon at a time, beating until stiff peaks form and sugar dissolves (2 to 4 minutes). Fold in pureed strawberries, one-third at a time. Spoon into prepared dish.

Bake at 400° for 18 minutes or until puffed and golden brown. Serve with reserved sliced strawberries. Yield: 8 servings.

Note: If you're in a hurry, put saucepan in a bowl of ice water to cool the pureed strawberry mixture more quickly.

Meet Us in the Kitchen
The Junior League of St. Louis, Missouri

Lemon Meringue Torte

This variation of lemon pie is fabulous! The meringue bottom cushions a layer of whipped cream that's topped with a lemon filling and more whipped cream!

3 egg whites	4 egg yolks
¾ teaspoon lemon juice	2 tablespoons grated lemon
⅛ teaspoon cream of tartar	rind
⅛ teaspoon salt	¼ cup fresh lemon juice
1½ cups sugar, divided	1½ cups whipping cream

Beat first 4 ingredients at high speed with an electric mixer until foamy. Add 1 cup sugar, 1 tablespoon at a time, beating until stiff peaks form and sugar dissolves (2 to 4 minutes). Spread meringue in a lightly greased 9-inch springform pan. Bake at 275° for 40 minutes. Turn oven off, and cool in oven 2 to 8 hours.

Beat egg yolks until thick and pale. Gradually beat in remaining ½ cup sugar; stir in lemon rind and juice. Place in top of a double boiler; bring water to a boil. Reduce heat to low; cook, stirring constantly with a wire whisk, until mixture begins to thicken and thermometer registers 160°. Cook 3 minutes, stirring constantly. Remove from heat; cool completely. (Mixture will be very thick.)

Beat whipping cream until soft peaks form. Spread half of whipped cream over meringue.

Spoon small dollops of lemon mixture (about 1 heaping tablespoon each) on top of whipped cream. Gently spread dollops to within ½ inch of edges of torte. Spread remaining whipped cream over lemon mixture, sealing to edges of pan. Cover and chill at least 8 hours. Yield: 6 servings.

From Black Tie to Blackeyed Peas: Savannah's Savory Secrets
St. Joseph's Foundation of Savannah, Inc.
Savannah, Georgia

Lemon Trifle

This tangy, refreshing treat adorned with the fruits of summer will have everyone going back for seconds.

1 (14-ounce) can sweetened condensed milk
1 (8-ounce) container lemon yogurt
1 tablespoon grated lemon rind
1 (8-ounce) container whipped topping, thawed
1 (1-pound) angel food cake, cut into bite-size pieces

⅓ cup fresh lemon juice (about 1½ lemons)
2 cups sliced fresh strawberries
1 cup fresh blueberries
1 cup fresh raspberries
½ cup flaked coconut, lightly toasted

Combine first 3 ingredients; fold in whipped topping. Toss cake pieces with lemon juice. Layer one-third of cake pieces and one-third of whipped topping mixture in a 6-quart trifle bowl. Top with sliced strawberries.

Layer half each of remaining cake, whipped topping mixture, blueberries, and raspberries. Repeat layers once. Sprinkle with coconut. Cover and chill at least 8 hours. Yield: 8 to 10 servings.

Sweet Pickin's
The Junior League of Fayetteville, North Carolina

Chocolate Mocha Truffle

A chocolaty version of your typical trifle, this decadent coffee-flavored dessert is definitely worthy of seconds.

1 (22.5-ounce) package brownie mix
4 teaspoons instant coffee granules
¼ cup warm water
2 (3.9-ounce) packages white chocolate instant pudding mix

1¾ cups milk
1 (12-ounce) container frozen whipped topping, thawed
6 (1.4-ounce) chocolate-covered toffee candy bars, crushed (we tested with Skor)

Bake brownie mix according to package directions. Cool in pan on a wire rack; cut into bite-size squares.

Dissolve coffee granules in warm water. Combine pudding and milk; beat at low speed with an electric mixer 2 minutes. Fold in coffee and whipped topping; set aside.

Place half of brownie squares in a 12-cup trifle bowl or a large glass bowl. Spoon half of pudding mixture over brownie squares; sprinkle with half of crushed candy. Repeat layers, ending with candy. Cover and chill at least 3 hours. Yield: 12 to 14 servings.   Tisa Kosbab

Bless This Food: A Collection of Prayers & Recipes
Steel Lake Presbyterian Church—Women's Ministries
Federal Way, Washington

Frozen Fruit Cups

If you want to serve these ice creamlike cups for a holiday dessert, use red and green maraschino cherries for a festive look. They'll freeze well for up to a month so you can serve them as needed until it's time to make more.

1 (10-ounce) jar maraschino
  cherries, drained
1 (11-ounce) can mandarin
  oranges in light syrup,
  drained
1 (8-ounce) package cream
  cheese, softened

½ cup sugar
1 (8-ounce) can crushed
  pineapple, drained
½ cup chopped pecans
1 (8-ounce) container frozen
  whipped topping, thawed

Slice 11 cherries in half, and reserve for garnish. Chop remaining cherries; set aside. Slice 11 orange segments in half, and reserve for garnish. Coarsely chop remaining oranges; set aside.

Beat cream cheese and sugar at medium speed with an electric mixer until creamy. Stir in chopped cherries, pineapple, and pecans. Fold in chopped oranges and whipped topping.

Spoon cream cheese mixture evenly into 22 muffin cups with foil (not paper) liners. Garnish with reserved cherry and orange segment halves. Freeze until firm. Remove from freezer 10 minutes before serving. Yield: 22 servings.

Deborah Trouse

The Western New York Federal Court Centennial Cookbook
U.S. District Court, Western District of New York
Buffalo, New York

Decadent Ice Cream Cake Dessert

This eye-catching dessert that received our highest rating will have you feeling nothing but guilty pleasure as it passes your lips.

2¼ cups crumbled macaroons, divided

3 cups chocolate ice cream, softened

4 (1.4-ounce) chocolate-covered toffee candy bars, coarsely chopped (we tested with Skor)

¼ cup chocolate syrup, divided

3 tablespoons coffee liqueur, divided

3 cups vanilla ice cream, slightly softened

1 (1.4-ounce) chocolate-covered toffee candy bar, coarsely chopped

Press 1¼ cups crumbled macaroons into an 8-inch springform pan. Spread chocolate ice cream evenly over macaroons, and sprinkle with 4 chopped candy bars. Drizzle with 3 tablespoons chocolate syrup and 2 tablespoons liqueur. Freeze 30 minutes.

Spread remaining 1 cup crumbled macaroons over top. Layer vanilla ice cream, 1 chopped candy bar, remaining 1 tablespoon chocolate syrup, and remaining 1 tablespoon liqueur over macaroon layer. Cover and freeze at least 8 hours.

Place on a serving plate; remove sides of pan. Yield: 6 to 8 servings.

Note: Freeze the candy bars ahead and they'll be easy to break with a meat mallet. Substitute chocolate or vanilla wafers for macaroons, or use other flavors of ice cream, if desired.

Savor the Moment
The Junior League of Boca Raton, Florida

Kiwifruit Sorbet

Enjoy this refreshing dessert year-round. Use either green or the now-popular yellow kiwifruit for an interesting color change.

1 cup sugar
½ cup water
2 pounds kiwifruit, peeled and
   sliced (about 13 kiwifruit)

Raspberry Sauce
Garnish: kiwifruit slices

Combine sugar and water in a small saucepan; bring to a boil. Reduce heat, and simmer, uncovered, 2 to 3 minutes or until sugar melts, stirring occasionally. Remove from heat, and cool completely.

Process 2 pounds kiwifruit in a food processor until smooth. Reserve 1 cup kiwifruit puree. Pour remaining kiwifruit puree through a wire-mesh strainer into a bowl, discarding pulp. Add reserved kiwifruit puree and syrup. Pour kiwifruit mixture into freezer container of a hand-turned or electric freezer. Freeze according to manufacturer's instructions. Spoon mixture into an airtight container, and freeze until firm. Serve with Raspberry Sauce. Garnish, if desired. Yield: 3½ cups.

Raspberry Sauce

1 (10-ounce) package frozen
   raspberries, thawed
¼ cup sugar

2 tablespoons seedless
   raspberry jam

Process all ingredients in a blender or food processor until smooth. Pour mixture through a wire-mesh strainer into a bowl, discarding pulp and seeds. Yield: 1 cup.

More Enchanted Eating from the West Shore
Friends of the Symphony
Muskegon, Michigan

Cranberry Ice

This dessert is a cross between ice cream and slushy ice, but it's firm enough to cut. It's the perfect holiday dessert when you're looking for something that's not too sweet.

4 cups fresh or frozen
   cranberries, thawed
4 cups water

2 cups sugar
1 tablespoon fresh lemon juice
⅔ cup whipping cream

Combine cranberries and water in a large saucepan. Bring to a boil over high heat; boil 7 minutes or until skins pop. Press cranberry mixture through a wire-mesh strainer into a large saucepan, discarding skins. Add sugar. Bring mixture to a boil over high heat; boil 1 minute or until sugar dissolves, stirring constantly. Cool completely. Add lemon juice; stir in whipping cream. Pour mixture into a 9- x 5-inch loafpan. Cover and freeze at least 4 hours or until firm. To serve, cut into slices, and serve immediately. Yield: 10 servings.

Faithfully Charleston
St. Michael's Episcopal Church
Charleston, South Carolina

Lemon Ice Cream

5½ cups heavy whipping
   cream
5½ cups milk
4 cups sugar

1 tablespoon grated lemon rind
2 teaspoons lemon extract
2 cups fresh lemon juice
   (about 8 large lemons)

Pour all ingredients into freezer container of a 5-quart hand-turned or electric freezer. Freeze according to manufacturer's instructions.
Pack freezer with additional ice and rock salt, and let stand 1 hour before serving. Yield: 5 quarts.   Jim Watkins

Bread from the Brook
The Church at Brook Hills
Birmingham, Alabama

Eggs and Cheese

Tomato, Cheese, and Herb Tart, page 160

Judy's Seafood Quiche

Two types of cheese encase a rich crab and shrimp filling in this quiche that's great to serve at a brunch.

3 (1-ounce) slices Swiss cheese
1 unbaked (9-inch) deep-dish pastry shell
½ cup fresh lump crabmeat, drained
½ cup chopped cooked shrimp
½ cup sliced fresh mushrooms

3 large eggs, lightly beaten
1 cup half-and-half
3 tablespoons all-purpose flour
1½ teaspoons garlic powder
¾ teaspoon salt
¼ teaspoon pepper
¼ cup (1 ounce) shredded Cheddar cheese

Place Swiss cheese in pastry shell.

Combine crabmeat, shrimp, and mushrooms; sprinkle evenly over cheese. Combine eggs and next 5 ingredients in a medium bowl; stir well with a wire whisk. Pour over crabmeat mixture. Sprinkle with Cheddar cheese.

Bake at 350° for 50 minutes or until set. Let stand 10 minutes before serving. Yield: 6 servings.   Laura Kelley

Ragin Cajun Cookbook
Beacon Club of University of Louisiana at Lafayette
Lafayette, Louisiana

Vegetable Quiche

This beautiful and flavorful tart can be enjoyed in any season and is always good to have in your recipe repertoire for those unexpected lunch guests.

1 (10-ounce) package frozen chopped spinach
½ cup chopped green onions
½ (8-ounce) package sliced fresh mushrooms
1 garlic clove, minced
2 tablespoons butter or margarine, melted
3 large eggs, lightly beaten
¾ cup half-and-half
1 teaspoon salt

1 teaspoon dried basil
½ teaspoon celery salt
1½ cups (6 ounces) shredded Swiss cheese
1 unbaked 9-inch pastry shell
2 tomatoes, sliced
1 tablespoon freshly shredded Parmesan cheese
1 tablespoon fine, dry breadcrumbs (store-bought)

Cook spinach according to package directions; drain spinach in a colander, pressing with paper towels to remove excess moisture; set aside.

Cook green onions, mushrooms, and garlic in butter in a large skillet over medium-high heat, stirring constantly, until tender.

Combine eggs and next 4 ingredients. Layer onion mixture, spinach, and Swiss cheese in pastry shell. Pour egg mixture into shell. Arrange tomato slices around outer edge of pastry shell. Bake at 425° for 15 minutes. Reduce oven temperature to 350°, and bake 20 more minutes. Combine Parmesan cheese and breadcrumbs. Sprinkle cheese mixture over tomatoes, and bake 5 more minutes. Let stand 5 minutes before serving. Yield: 6 servings.   Ruth Gardner

Savor the Flavor: Delightfully Vegetarian
Portland Adventist Community Services
Portland, Oregon

Apple-Cheese Quiches

This quiche recipe traces its history back to the late 1970s, where it was a featured dish at an apple festival in Virginia. Contributor Brenda Gonzales counts it as one of her all-time favorites.

2 cups (8 ounces) shredded Swiss cheese
½ pound ground pork sausage, cooked and well drained
2 cups peeled, thinly sliced Granny Smith apples (about 3 apples)
1 (4.25-ounce) can sliced mushrooms, drained

2 unbaked (9-inch) deep-dish pastry shells
4 large eggs
1 tablespoon all-purpose flour
1 teaspoon salt
1 cup milk
1 cup evaporated milk
1½ tablespoons butter or margarine, melted

Divide and layer first 4 ingredients in pastry shells.

Combine eggs and remaining 5 ingredients in a medium bowl, whisking well. Pour mixture evenly over layered ingredients.

Bake at 375° for 30 minutes. Let stand 5 to 10 minutes before serving. Yield: 12 servings.

Brenda Gonzales

Forget Me Not: Recipes and Stories to Remember
Hospice and Palliative Care of Greensboro, North Carolina

Silvio's Omelet

½ cup chopped onion
1 cup peeled and shredded baking potato (raw)
3 tablespoons olive oil
⅓ cup chopped green bell pepper
⅓ cup chopped red bell pepper
⅓ cup chopped yellow bell pepper

1 (6-ounce) package sliced ham, diced
6 large eggs, lightly beaten
½ cup (2 ounces) shredded Cheddar cheese
¼ teaspoon salt
¼ teaspoon pepper

Cook onion and potato in hot oil in a 10-inch ovenproof skillet over medium-high heat until tender. Add bell peppers and ham, cooking until peppers are soft.

Reduce heat to low, and add eggs to skillet. As mixture starts to cook, gently lift edges with a spatula, and tilt pan so uncooked portion flows underneath. Cook 10 minutes or until done, continuing to tilt pan to allow uncooked portion to set. Sprinkle omelet with cheese, salt, and pepper; broil 3 inches from heat 3 minutes or until golden. Yield: 3 servings.

Unis Scola

V.C.O.S. Sharing Our Best
Volusia County Orchid Society, Inc.
DeLand, Florida

Fresh Blueberry Strata

We were won over by this strata that showcases fresh blueberries and puffs up beautifully when baked. There is syrup in the strata already, but drizzling each piece with extra syrup really complements the flavor.

10 white bread slices, crusts trimmed	9 large eggs, lightly beaten
½ (8 ounce) package cream cheese, cubed	1½ cups milk
1 cup fresh blueberries	½ cup half-and-half
	¼ cup maple syrup
	Maple syrup

Cut bread into cubes. Place two-thirds of bread cubes in a greased 13- x 9-inch pan. Sprinkle evenly with cream cheese and blueberries. Top with remaining bread cubes.

Combine eggs, milk, half-and-half, and ¼ cup maple syrup in a large bowl; stir well with a wire whisk. Pour mixture over layers; press down lightly with a spatula to submerge bread cubes. Cover and chill 8 hours.

Uncover and bake at 325° for 1 hour or until set and golden around the edges. Let stand 10 minutes before serving. Serve with warm maple syrup. Yield: 6 to 8 servings.

Art Fare: A Commemorative Celebration of Art & Food
The Toledo Museum of Art Aides
Toledo, Ohio

Spinach Strata

You can relax and enjoy your morning when you serve this make-ahead dish to your family or weekend guests. With just a few ingredients and minimal prep time, a savory spinach-and-cheese strata will be ready for baking after chilling overnight.

10 white bread slices, cut into
  1-inch cubes (we tested with
  Pepperidge Farm Hearty
  White Bread)
1 (10-ounce) package frozen
  chopped spinach, thawed
  and drained
2 cups (8 ounces) shredded
  sharp Cheddar cheese

4 large eggs
1 (10¾-ounce) can cream of
  chicken soup, undiluted
1 cup water
½ teaspoon salt
¼ teaspoon ground nutmeg
¼ teaspoon pepper

Place half of bread cubes in a lightly greased 13- x 9-inch baking dish. Spread spinach evenly over bread. Sprinkle with 1 cup cheese. Top with remaining bread cubes and cheese.

Whisk together eggs and remaining 5 ingredients until smooth; pour evenly over bread mixture. Cover and chill at least 4 hours.

Bake, uncovered, at 350° for 40 minutes or until mixture is set and lightly browned. Yield: 6 servings.   Laura Mahrenholz

Jubilee 2000 Recipe Collection
St. Alphonsus Liguori Parish—Hospitality Committee
Prospect Heights, Illinois

Strata Oscar

6 ounces fresh asparagus
12 to 14 white bread slices,
   crusts trimmed
1 pound fresh lump crabmeat,
   drained
2 tablespoons finely chopped
   onion
½ cup mayonnaise
1¾ cups (7 ounces)
   shredded Gruyère or
   Swiss cheese

¼ cup grated Parmesan cheese
10 large eggs
2 cups milk
2 teaspoons Dijon mustard
½ teaspoon white
   Worcestershire sauce
1½ teaspoons salt
½ teaspoon pepper

Snap off tough ends of asparagus; cut asparagus diagonally into 1-inch pieces; set aside.

Arrange half of bread slices in a greased 13- x 9-inch baking dish. Combine crabmeat, asparagus, onion, and mayonnaise. Spread mixture over bread slices. Combine cheeses, and sprinkle 1½ cups cheese mixture over crabmeat mixture. Top with remaining bread slices.

Whisk together eggs and remaining 5 ingredients. Pour mixture evenly over bread. Cover and chill at least 2 hours.

Bake, uncovered, at 350° for 25 to 30 minutes or until puffed and lightly browned. Sprinkle remaining cheese over strata; bake 10 more minutes or until cheese melts. Let stand 10 minutes before serving. Yield: 8 servings.

Savor the Moment
The Junior League of Boca Raton, Florida

Tomato, Cheese, and Herb Tart

A slice of this cheesy tomato tart and a simple green salad make an ideal light summer supper.

2 firm tomatoes, cut into
  ¼-inch slices
1¼ cups all-purpose flour
¼ teaspoon salt
½ cup butter or margarine,
  cut into 1-inch pieces
3 tablespoons ice water
8 ounces Gruyère cheese, cut
  into ¼-inch-thick slices

1 tablespoon chopped fresh
  basil
1 tablespoon chopped fresh
  thyme
1 tablespoon chopped fresh
  oregano
3 tablespoons grated
  Parmesan cheese

Drain tomato slices on paper towels 45 minutes.

Pulse flour and salt in a food processor 3 or 4 times or until combined. Add butter, and pulse 5 or 6 times or until crumbly. With processor running, gradually add 3 tablespoons water, and process until dough forms a ball and leaves sides of bowl, adding more water, if necessary. Shape dough into a disk. Cover and chill 30 minutes.

Roll pastry to ⅛-inch thickness on a lightly floured surface. Fit into an 11-inch tart pan with removable bottom; trim off excess pastry along edges. Prick bottom and sides of pastry with a fork; freeze 15 minutes. Bake at 425° for 15 minutes or until golden brown. Cool completely on a wire rack.

Reduce oven temperature to 375°. Line pastry with cheese slices. Arrange tomato slices evenly over cheese. Sprinkle with herbs and Parmesan cheese. Bake at 375° for 25 minutes. Remove to a wire rack. Let stand 10 minutes before serving. Yield: 1 (11-inch) tart.

Splendor in the Bluegrass
The Junior League of Louisville, Kentucky

Wild Rice Country Tart

Wild rice is known for its nutty flavor and slightly crunchy texture, which shine through in this rustic tart. It's perfect for breakfast or with a bowl of soup for a light lunch.

½ (15-ounce) package
   refrigerated piecrusts
2 cups (8 ounces) shredded
   Swiss cheese, divided
1 (4.5-ounce) jar sliced
   mushrooms, drained
½ cup cooked wild rice
⅓ cup finely chopped red bell
   pepper

¼ cup sliced green onions
3 large eggs
1 (8-ounce) container sour
   cream
1 tablespoon country-style
   Dijon mustard
½ teaspoon salt
⅛ teaspoon pepper
12 pecan halves

Firmly press dough in bottom and up sides of a 9-inch tart pan with removable bottom. Bake at 425° for 10 minutes or until lightly browned. Remove from oven, and cool on a wire rack. Sprinkle crust with 1 cup cheese.

Combine mushrooms and next 3 ingredients. Spread mushroom mixture evenly over cheese layer. Whisk together eggs and next 4 ingredients. Pour egg mixture over mushroom layer. Sprinkle with remaining 1 cup cheese. Arrange pecan halves on tart. Bake at 400° for 45 minutes or until a knife inserted in center comes out clean. Let stand 10 minutes before serving. Yield: 6 to 8 servings.

Past and Present Meatless Treasures
Kaneohe Seventh-day Adventist Church
Kaneohe, Hawaii

Eggs Olé with Red Pepper Cream Sauce

Serve warm corn or flour tortillas with this light and fluffy Mexican dish. Use any leftover red pepper sauce to toss with pasta for a light supper.

½ cup all-purpose flour
1 teaspoon baking powder
1 teaspoon salt
10 large eggs
4 cups (16 ounces) shredded
  Monterey Jack cheese
2 cups small-curd cottage
  cheese

½ cup butter or margarine,
  melted
1 (4.5-ounce) can chopped
  green chiles, drained
Red Pepper Cream Sauce
2 tablespoons chopped fresh
  chives
Garnish: jalapeño slices

Combine first 3 ingredients; set aside. Whisk eggs; gradually add flour mixture, cheeses, and butter. Stir in green chiles. Pour egg mixture into a lightly greased 13- x 9-inch baking dish. Bake at 350° for 35 to 37 minutes or until lightly browned.

While casserole bakes, prepare Red Pepper Cream Sauce; keep warm. When ready to serve, pour about ⅓ cup sauce onto each of 8 serving plates. Cut the casserole into squares, and place on sauce. Sprinkle with chopped fresh chives, and garnish, if desired. Yield: 8 servings.

Red Pepper Cream Sauce

1 cup chopped red bell
  pepper
¼ cup thinly sliced green
  onions
¼ cup butter or margarine,
  melted
5 tablespoons all-purpose
  flour

1¾ cups milk
1 tablespoon fresh lemon
  juice
¼ teaspoon salt
¼ teaspoon ground white
  pepper

Sauté bell pepper and green onions in butter in a medium saucepan over medium heat 2 minutes or until soft. Stir in flour; reduce heat, and cook over low heat 1 minute, stirring constantly.

Remove from heat; gradually stir in milk and lemon juice. Cook over medium heat until thickened, stirring constantly. Stir in salt and pepper. Process in blender until pureed. Yield: 3 cups.

Art Fare: A Commemorative Celebration of Art & Food
The Toledo Museum of Art Aides
Toledo, Ohio

The Ultimate Grilled Cheese

Three kinds of cheese sandwiched between two slices of perfectly golden brown sourdough just beg to be eaten with a bowl of your favorite soup.

¾ cup mayonnaise
1 (3-ounce) package cream cheese, softened
1 cup (4 ounces) shredded Cheddar cheese
1 cup (4 ounces) shredded mozzarella cheese

½ teaspoon garlic powder
⅛ teaspoon seasoned salt
10 (½-inch) slices sourdough bread
2 tablespoons butter or margarine, softened

Beat mayonnaise and cream cheese at medium speed with an electric mixer until light and fluffy. Stir in Cheddar cheese and next 3 ingredients. Spread each of 5 bread slices evenly with cheese mixture.

Top with remaining bread slices.

Spread butter on both sides of sandwiches. Cook in batches in skillet over medium heat until lightly browned on both sides. Serve immediately. Yield: 5 sandwiches.   Sylvia Autrey

Cooking with the Original Search Engine
Fort Worth Public Library All Staff Association
Fort Worth, Texas

Croissant Bake

Start a new holiday tradition this year by serving this cheese- and bacon-studded treat for breakfast. One croissant equals one serving because it's extremely rich and buttery.

4 croissants
4 ounces sliced mozzarella
   cheese (about 6 slices)
2 cups (8 ounces) shredded
   Gruyère cheese
½ pound bacon (8 slices),
   cooked and crumbled
6 large eggs

1 cup milk
¼ teaspoon salt
¼ teaspoon ground nutmeg
¼ teaspoon pepper
½ cup grated Parmesan
   cheese
Garnish: fresh parsley sprigs

Slice croissants in half lengthwise. Place bottom halves, cut sides up, in an 11- x 7-inch baking dish. Top evenly with mozzarella cheese. Sprinkle with Gruyère cheese and bacon.

Combine eggs and next 4 ingredients in a bowl. Pour half of egg mixture over croissants and cheese. Place remaining croissant halves on top, cut sides down. Pour remaining egg mixture over croissants. Sprinkle with Parmesan cheese.

Bake at 350° for 30 minutes or until set. Cover with aluminum foil during baking, if necessary, to prevent excessive browning. Garnish, if desired. Serve immediately. Yield: 4 servings.

Carolina Thyme
The Junior League of Durham and Orange Counties, Inc.
Durham, North Carolina

Blue Knoll Cheesy Apple-Egg Bake

All you need to accompany a slice of this cheesy egg concoction is a toasted bagel and a medley of fruit.

2 cups peeled and sliced
   Granny Smith apples
2 tablespoons cinnamon sugar
6 bacon slices, cooked and
   crumbled
2 cups (8 ounces) shredded
   Cheddar cheese

2 cups milk
6 large eggs
2 cups biscuit mix
   Maple syrup

Layer first 4 ingredients in a lightly greased 13- x 9-inch baking dish. Whisk together milk and eggs in a bowl until blended. Add biscuit mix, and whisk until smooth. Pour egg mixture over layers. Bake at 375° for 30 minutes or until set. Serve with warm maple syrup. Yield: 6 to 8 servings. Mary and Gil Carlson

Vintage Virginia: A History of Good Taste
The Virginia Dietetic Association
Centreville, Virginia

Sausage Soufflé

This scrumptious soufflé billows over the top of the baking dish, so hurry it out to your guests so they can enjoy the fleeting presentation!

1 **pound mild ground pork sausage**
5 **large eggs**
2 **cups milk**
2 **cups half-and-half**
1 **cup (4 ounces) shredded Cheddar cheese**
1 **teaspoon paprika**

1 **teaspoon Worcestershire sauce**
1 **teaspoon garlic salt**
1 **teaspoon dry mustard**
12 **white bread slices, crusts trimmed**
Butter or margarine, softened

Cook sausage in a small skillet, stirring until it crumbles and is no longer pink; drain.

Combine eggs and next 7 ingredients. Stir in sausage.

Spread 1 side of bread slices lightly with butter; cut into small pieces. Line bottom of a greased 13- x 9-inch baking dish with bread, buttered side up. Pour egg mixture over bread. Bake at 350° for 1 hour or until puffed and golden. Serve immediately. Yield: 6 to 8 servings.

Cooking with Care
HospiceCare of the Piedmont, Inc.
Greenwood, South Carolina

Suisse Eggs

"Suisse" in the title is for the creamy Swiss cheese sauce that's poured over the poached egg and English muffin combo made famous in France. If you don't have the time to poach the eggs, fried eggs work just as well.

8   large eggs
2   tablespoons butter or margarine
2   tablespoons all-purpose flour
¼   teaspoon dry mustard
¼   teaspoon Worcestershire sauce
1½   cups milk

¼   teaspoon salt
½   cup (2 ounces) shredded Swiss cheese
4   English muffins, split and toasted
¼   teaspoon paprika
2   teaspoons chopped fresh chives

Lightly grease a large skillet; add water to a depth of 2 inches. Bring to a boil; reduce heat, and maintain a light simmer. Working in batches to poach 4 eggs at a time, break eggs, 1 at a time, into a cup; slip egg into water, holding cup as close as possible to surface of water. Simmer 5 minutes or until done. Remove eggs with a slotted spoon; trim edges of eggs, if desired. Set aside.

Melt butter in a small heavy saucepan over low heat; whisk in flour and mustard until smooth. Cook 1 minute, whisking constantly. Gradually whisk in Worcestershire sauce and milk. Cook over medium heat, whisking constantly, until mixture is thickened and bubbly. Stir in salt. Remove from heat; add cheese, stirring until cheese melts and sauce is smooth. Place 1 egg on each muffin half, and drizzle 2 tablespoons sauce over each egg. Sprinkle with paprika and chives. Yield: 4 servings.

Judy and Davis Egle

Menus & Memories
The University of Oklahoma Women's Association
Norman, Oklahoma

Green Eggs and Ham

A term made popular by Dr. Seuss, green eggs and ham aren't just for children. Our version puts an ethnic spin on the traditional deviled eggs by using avocado and lime juice in the filling and topping it off with browned bits of ham.

6 ounces thinly sliced country ham
12 hard-cooked eggs, peeled
1 ripe avocado, peeled and mashed
2 tablespoons finely chopped onion

2 tablespoons mayonnaise
2 tablespoons fresh lime juice
1 teaspoon hot sauce
1 garlic clove, minced
1 small tomato, peeled, seeded, and finely chopped

Cook ham in a large nonstick skillet over medium-high heat 2 to 3 minutes on each side or until lightly browned and crisp. Drain and finely chop; set aside.

Cut eggs in half lengthwise, and carefully remove yolks. Mash yolks; add avocado and next 5 ingredients to yolk; stir well. Add tomato, and stir well.

Spoon yolk mixture into egg white halves. Sprinkle with chopped ham. Yield: 2 dozen.

Christy Jones

Cooking for Good
West End Charities
Dallas, Texas

Fish & Shellfish

Lowcountry Shrimp Boil, page 181

Citrus Halibut

1 tablespoon olive oil
1 garlic clove, minced
¼ cup chopped onion
4 (5- to 6-ounce) halibut steaks
  (¾ inch thick)
½ teaspoon salt
¼ cup fresh orange juice
1 tablespoon fresh lemon
  juice
2 tablespoons chopped fresh
  parsley
½ teaspoon grated orange
  rind

Heat oil in a large skillet over medium-high heat. Add garlic and onion; sauté 2 minutes or until tender. Sprinkle halibut steaks with salt. Place halibut steaks in a lightly greased 13- x 9-inch baking dish. Spoon onion mixture evenly over steaks.

Combine orange juice and lemon juice; drizzle over steaks. Sprinkle with parsley and orange rind. Cover and bake at 400° for 15 to 17 minutes or until fish flakes with a fork. Spoon juices over fish; serve immediately. Yield: 4 servings.   Wanda Crow

Note: Grate the orange before you juice it.

Bless This Food: A Collection of Prayers & Recipes
Steel Lake Presbyterian Church—Women's Ministries
Federal Way, Washington

Gourmet Grouper Fillets

¾ cup freshly grated
  Parmesan cheese
½ cup butter or margarine,
  softened
3 tablespoons mayonnaise
3 tablespoons chopped green
  onions
2 teaspoons chopped fresh
  chives
6 (8-ounce) grouper or other
  mild whitefish fillets (1 inch
  thick)
¼ cup lemon juice
½ teaspoon salt
½ teaspoon pepper
Garnishes: lemon slices,
  chopped fresh chives

Combine first 5 ingredients in a small bowl. Place fish on a lightly greased rack in a broiler pan. Drizzle with lemon juice; sprinkle with salt and pepper. Broil 5½ inches from heat 15 to 20 minutes or until fish flakes with a fork. Spread fish with cheese mixture. Broil 4 to 5 more minutes or until lightly browned and bubbly; transfer fillets to serving plates. Garnish, if desired. Yield: 6 servings.

At Your Service: Southern Recipes, Places and Traditions
The Junior League of Gwinnett and North Fulton Counties
Duluth, Georgia

Grouper Sautéed with Tomatoes, Pine Nuts, and Goat Cheese

A lean, white saltwater fish, grouper is mild-flavored with a meaty texture that goes from simple to sublime in this dressed-up dish. Tomatoes add color, while pine nuts and goat cheese contribute crunch and creaminess to make this dish one of our favorites.

1 tablespoon vegetable oil
¼ cup all-purpose flour
4 (6- to 8-ounce) grouper
    fillets (1 inch thick)
4 garlic cloves, minced
¼ cup chopped fresh basil
¼ cup pine nuts, toasted
4 plum tomatoes, chopped
¼ cup dry sherry

2 tablespoons fresh lemon
    juice
¼ teaspoon salt
¼ teaspoon freshly ground
    pepper
½ cup crumbled goat cheese
6 green onions, cut into
    ¼-inch pieces

Heat oil in a large skillet over medium-high heat until hot. Place flour in a shallow dish. Dip fillets in flour to lightly coat. Cook in hot oil 5 minutes on each side or until golden brown. Remove to a platter, and keep warm.

Add garlic to hot oil. Reduce heat, and cook 1 minute, stirring constantly. Add basil and next 4 ingredients. Cook over high heat 2 minutes. Return grouper to skillet. Season with salt and pepper. Cook until thoroughly heated.

Place 1 fillet on each of 4 serving plates. Spoon tomato mixture evenly over fillets. Sprinkle with cheese and green onions. Yield: 4 servings.

Entirely Entertaining in the Bonnet House Style
Bonnet House Alliance
Ft. Lauderdale, Florida

Sautéed Whitefish with Sun-Dried Tomato-Basil Mayonnaise

Be sure to store this flavor-packed mayonnaise, covered, in the fridge because it tends to discolor if left out. The mayonnaise also is great spread on a sandwich or as a topping for chicken.

1 cup all-purpose flour	1 cup peanut oil
1 teaspoon salt	Sun-Dried Tomato-Basil
½ teaspoon pepper, divided	Mayonnaise
4 (8-ounce) grouper or	
whitefish fillets (about	
1 inch thick)	

Combine first 3 ingredients in a shallow dish. Dredge fillets in flour mixture.

Heat peanut oil in a large skillet over medium-high heat until hot. Fry fillets 5 minutes on each side until golden. Drain on paper towels. Serve immediately with Sun-Dried Tomato-Basil Mayonnaise. Yield: 4 servings.

Sun-Dried Tomato-Basil Mayonnaise

¾ cup mayonnaise	1 tablespoon lemon juice
8 dried tomatoes in oil,	1 teaspoon minced garlic
finely chopped	¼ teaspoon salt
3 tablespoons chopped fresh	¼ teaspoon pepper
basil	

Stir together all ingredients in a bowl. Cover and chill. Yield: 1 cup.

Art Fare: A Commemorative Celebration of Art & Food
The Toledo Museum of Art Aides
Toledo, Ohio

Red Snapper Fillets with Avocado Sauce

Cornstarch may seem like an unusual ingredient when it comes to dredging the fish, but it makes a delicate coating once pan-fried. The accompanying sauce is smooth in texture, flavorful, and can be used with other fish as well as chicken.

2 ripe avocados, peeled and coarsely chopped (about 1½ cups)
3 tablespoons fresh lime juice (about 2 limes)
1½ teaspoons salt
1 teaspoon ground white pepper
2 tablespoons mayonnaise
2 tablespoons sour cream
½ teaspoon hot sauce
2 garlic cloves, minced
¾ cup cornstarch
½ teaspoon salt
½ teaspoon dried tarragon
½ teaspoon ground black pepper
6 (6- to 8-ounce) red snapper fillets (1½ inches thick)
3 tablespoons olive oil
Garnish: lime slices

Process first 8 ingredients in a blender until smooth, stopping to scrape down sides.

Combine cornstarch and next 3 ingredients in a shallow dish; dredge fish in cornstarch mixture, shaking off excess. Heat oil in a large skillet; add fish, and cook 3 to 4 minutes on each side or until fish flakes with a fork. Serve with avocado sauce. Garnish, if desired. Yield: 6 servings.

Seasons of Santa Fe
Kitchen Angels
Santa Fe, New Mexico

Grilled Swordfish with Orange and Tomato Salsa

¾ cup teriyaki sauce
½ cup dry sherry
4 garlic cloves, minced
2 teaspoons minced fresh
 ginger

1 teaspoon sesame oil
6 (5- to 6-ounce) swordfish
 steaks (1 inch thick)
Orange and Tomato Salsa

Combine first 5 ingredients in a medium saucepan. Bring to a boil; cook 1 minute, stirring constantly. Remove from heat; cool completely. Pour marinade into a shallow dish or heavy-duty zip-top plastic bag; add swordfish steaks. Cover or seal, and marinate in refrigerator 1½ hours, turning occasionally. Remove steaks from marinade, discarding marinade.

While fish marinates, prepare Orange and Tomato Salsa; cover and chill.

Coat food rack with cooking spray; place on grill over medium-high heat (350° to 400°). Place swordfish on rack, and grill, covered with grill lid, about 7 minutes on each side or until fish flakes with a fork. Serve with salsa. Yield: 6 servings.

Orange and Tomato Salsa

3 large oranges, peeled and
 chopped
2 garlic cloves, minced
1½ cups seeded and chopped
 tomato
⅓ cup chopped onion
¼ cup chopped fresh parsley
2 tablespoons fresh orange
 juice

2 teaspoons balsamic vinegar
1 teaspoon minced fresh
 ginger
½ teaspoon salt
¼ teaspoon ground black
 pepper
⅛ teaspoon ground red
 pepper

Combine all ingredients. Cover and chill at least 1 hour. Yield: 4 cups.

Oh My Stars! Recipes That Shine
The Junior League of Roanoke Valley, Virginia

Swordfish with Cilantro Paste

The cilantro paste is similar to pesto in texture. It provides a surprising bite to this mild fish.

2 cups fresh cilantro sprigs
   (about 2 small bunches)
¼ cup olive oil
2 garlic cloves, minced
2 tablespoons pine nuts
1 tablespoon fresh lime juice
½ teaspoon salt
1 teaspoon curry powder

1 teaspoon ground cumin
½ teaspoon ground ginger
½ teaspoon salt
½ teaspoon pepper
½ teaspoon chili powder
4 (8-ounce) swordfish steaks
   (1½ inches thick)
2 tablespoons olive oil

Place first 6 ingredients in a blender; process until smooth.

Combine curry powder and next 5 ingredients in a small bowl; rub spice mixture evenly over both sides of swordfish steaks.

Heat 2 tablespoons oil in a large skillet over medium-high heat until hot; add steaks, and cook 4 to 5 minutes on each side or until fish flakes with a fork. Serve with cilantro paste. Yield: 4 servings.

Cooking with Music: Celebrating the Tastes and Traditions of the
Boston Symphony Orchestra
Boston Symphony Association of Volunteers
Boston, Massachusetts

Pan-Seared Salmon with Orange-Ginger Couscous

Soy sauce and brown sugar work together to form a sweet, caramelized crust on the salmon. Couscous flavored with orange and ginger complements the fish.

¼ cup firmly packed light
  brown sugar
¼ cup soy sauce

1 tablespoon Dijon mustard
4 (6-ounce) salmon steaks
Orange-Ginger Couscous

Combine first 3 ingredients in a large heavy-duty zip-top plastic bag; add salmon. Marinate in refrigerator 2 hours, turning occasionally. Remove salmon, and discard marinade.

Cook salmon in a lightly greased skillet over medium-high heat 4 minutes on each side or until fish flakes with a fork. Serve with Orange-Ginger Couscous. Yield: 4 servings.

Orange-Ginger Couscous

2 cups orange juice
⅓ cup dried cranberries
1½ teaspoons butter or
  margarine
1 teaspoon grated orange rind
1 teaspoon minced fresh
  ginger

½ teaspoon salt
¼ teaspoon ground
  cinnamon
1 (10-ounce) package couscous
¼ cup sliced almonds,
  toasted

Combine first 7 ingredients in a medium saucepan. Bring to a boil over medium heat. Remove from heat. Stir in couscous. Cover and let stand 5 minutes. Fluff with a fork. Stir in almonds. Yield: 4 cups.

Carolina Thyme
The Junior League of Durham and Orange Counties, Inc.
Durham, North Carolina

Mango Salmon

Make the salsa ahead so that it can chill while the fish marinates.

¼ cup chopped fresh mint
¼ cup chopped fresh cilantro
2 teaspoons fresh lime juice
1 teaspoon chili oil
¼ teaspoon salt

¼ teaspoon pepper
1 (2-pound) salmon fillet
Mango Salsa
Hot cooked rice

Combine first 6 ingredients in a heavy-duty zip-top plastic bag. Add salmon; seal bag securely, and marinate in refrigerator 1 hour, turning occasionally.

Remove salmon from marinade, and place salmon on a 30- x 12-inch sheet of aluminum foil; bring edges of foil up, but do not seal. Pour marinade over salmon. Fold foil over fish; crimp edges to seal.

Grill salmon, covered with grill lid, over medium-high heat (350° to 400°) about 10 minutes or until salmon flakes with a fork. Slice salmon into individual servings, and place on individual serving plates; spoon Mango Salsa to side of salmon. Serve with rice. Yield: 4 to 6 servings.

Mango Salsa

3 mangoes, chopped
¼ cup chopped fresh mint
¼ cup chopped fresh cilantro
1 tablespoon fresh lime juice

½ cup pineapple tidbits in
  juice, undrained
¼ teaspoon salt
¼ teaspoon pepper

Combine all ingredients in a bowl. Cover and chill at least 1 hour. Yield: 4½ cups.

More Enchanted Eating from the West Shore
Friends of the Symphony
Muskegon, Michigan

Grilled Tuna Steaks with Cantaloupe Salsa

Salsa comes in many varieties and flavors. This one showcases fresh chunks of melon with a kick of heat from the jalapeño peppers. Be sure to pick a melon that yields to slight pressure when touched for optimum ripeness.

¾ **cup coarsely chopped cantaloupe**
¼ **cup chopped onion**
2 **tablespoons chopped fresh cilantro**
1 **tablespoon fresh lime juice**
2 **teaspoons olive oil**
1 **teaspoon seeded and minced jalapeño pepper**

¼ **teaspoon salt**
⅛ **teaspoon pepper**
2 **(1-inch-thick) tuna steaks, (about ¾ pound)**
2 **teaspoons olive oil**
⅛ **teaspoon salt**
⅛ **teaspoon pepper**

Combine first 8 ingredients in a small bowl. Cover and let stand 15 minutes.

Brush both sides of tuna with oil; sprinkle with salt and pepper.

Coat grill rack with cooking spray; place rack on grill over medium-high heat (350° to 400°). Place tuna on rack, and grill, covered with grill lid, 5 minutes on each side or until fish flakes with a fork. Serve salsa over tuna. Yield: 2 servings.

Meet Us in the Kitchen
The Junior League of St. Louis, Missouri

Sand Island Clams and Angel Hair Pasta

1 cup chopped onion (about 1 medium)
2 tablespoons chopped fresh parsley
4 garlic cloves, minced
¼ cup olive oil
1 (14-ounce) can chicken broth
1 tablespoon all-purpose flour
½ cup dry white wine
3 (6.75-ounce) cans minced clams, drained
1 teaspoon salt
1 teaspoon pepper
1 (16-ounce) package angel hair pasta
5 tablespoons olive oil
½ cup freshly grated Parmesan cheese

Sauté onion, parsley, and garlic in ¼ cup hot oil over medium-high heat 4 minutes or until almost tender. Whisk together broth and flour in a small bowl until smooth; add to onion mixture. Cook 5 minutes, stirring often. Add wine, and cook 5 minutes or until sauce is reduced by half. Stir in clams, salt, and pepper; cook 5 minutes or until thoroughly heated. Keep warm.

Cook pasta according to package directions; drain. Add 5 tablespoons oil and Parmesan cheese to pasta; toss well. Divide pasta evenly among serving bowls; spoon sauce over pasta. Yield: 8 servings.

Entertaining Thoughts . . .
The Junior League of the Lehigh Valley
Bethlehem, Pennsylvania

Angel Hair Pasta with Scallops, Asparagus, and Cilantro Cream

A creamy sauce of white wine, whipping cream, and cilantro bathes buttery sea scallops and perfectly tender asparagus with rich flavor.

6 ounces uncooked dried angel hair pasta
1 pound fresh asparagus, cut into 1-inch pieces
1¼ pounds sea scallops
1 tablespoon butter or margarine
1 large shallot, minced

½ cup dry white wine
½ cup bottled clam juice
1 cup whipping cream, divided
½ teaspoon salt
½ teaspoon pepper
¼ cup chopped fresh cilantro

Cook pasta according to package directions; drain well. Set aside, and keep warm.

Meanwhile, cook asparagus in a small amount of boiling water 4 minutes or until crisp-tender; drain. Set aside.

Rinse scallops, and pat dry.

Melt butter in a large saucepan over medium-high heat. Add shallot, and sauté 2 minutes. Add wine and clam juice; bring to a boil. Add ½ cup whipping cream, scallops, salt, and pepper. Cover, reduce heat, and simmer 3 minutes. Transfer scallops to a plate, using a slotted spoon. Cover and keep warm.

Bring scallop liquid to a boil. Add remaining ½ cup cream, and return to a boil. Cook, stirring often, until sauce thickens and reduces to 1½ cups. Stir in asparagus and scallops. Cook over low heat just until thoroughly heated.

Toss with pasta and cilantro. Serve immediately. Yield: 4 servings.

An Acquired Taste
Winchester Thurston School
Pittsburgh, Pennsylvania

Lowcountry Shrimp Boil

Here's a simple, old-fashioned recipe that needs only garlic butter and cocktail sauce to make it extraordinary. Be sure to cover the table with newspaper, and let everyone peel their own shrimp. Collect shrimp peelings and corn cobs in newspaper for easy cleanup.

4 ears fresh corn
3 quarts water
2 to 3 celery ribs
1 (3-ounce) package boil-in-bag shrimp and crab boil (we tested with Zatarain's)
½ teaspoon salt

1 pound smoked sausage, cut into 2-inch pieces
2 pounds new potatoes
2 pounds unpeeled, medium-size fresh shrimp
Dash of hot sauce

Remove husks and silks from corn; cut ears in half.

Bring water to a boil in a large Dutch oven; add celery and next 4 ingredients. Cook over medium heat 15 minutes. Add corn, and cook 7 minutes or until vegetables are tender. Add shrimp and hot sauce; cook 4 minutes or until shrimp turn pink. Drain, discarding celery and seafood seasoning bag. Place shrimp, corn, sausage, and potatoes in a large bowl. Yield: 4 servings.

Note: Serve with lemon slices, and cocktail sauce, tartar sauce, or garlic butter.

At Your Service: Southern Recipes, Places and Traditions
The Junior League of Gwinnett and North Fulton Counties
Duluth, Georgia

Martini Shrimp

¼ cup olive oil
2 pounds peeled and deveined medium-size fresh shrimp
1 tablespoon minced shallot
2 large garlic cloves, minced
¼ cup extra-dry vermouth
¼ cup vodka or gin

½ cup dried tomato strips
⅛ teaspoon ground red pepper
1 cup heavy whipping cream
½ teaspoon salt
⅛ teaspoon ground white pepper

Heat oil in a large skillet over medium-high heat. Add shrimp; sauté 3 to 5 minutes; remove shrimp. Add shallot and garlic; sauté 3 minutes. Stir in vermouth and next 3 ingredients; cook 3 minutes or until sauce begins to thicken. Stir in cream, salt, and white pepper; cook 3 minutes. Return shrimp to skillet; cook 1 minute. Yield: 3 servings.

Settings on the Dock of the Bay
ASSISTANCE LEAGUE® of the Bay Area
Houston, Texas

Fired-Up Shrimp

1 pound unpeeled, jumbo fresh shrimp
3 tablespoons olive oil
2 tablespoons grated lemon rind
¼ teaspoon ground red pepper
2 teaspoons chopped fresh thyme

1 tablespoon chopped fresh parsley
6 to 8 (12-inch) wooden skewers
5 ounces thinly sliced pancetta, cut in half
2 tablespoons fresh lemon juice

Peel shrimp; devein, leaving tails on. Whisk together oil and next 4 ingredients; add shrimp. Chill 2 hours. While shrimp marinates, soak wooden skewers in water at least 30 minutes. Wrap each shrimp in 1 slice pancetta; thread shrimp onto skewers. Grill shrimp, covered with grill lid, over medium-high heat (350° to 400°) 3 minutes on each side. Drizzle with juice. Serve immediately. Yield: 4 to 6 servings.

Key Ingredients
Le Bonheur Club, Inc.
Memphis, Tennessee

Shrimp Casserole

Elegance reigns in this creamy casserole that boasts fresh asparagus, mushrooms, and artichoke hearts, and is topped with Parmesan cheese. Crusty bread is a must to soak up and savor all of the decadent cream sauce.

4½ cups water
1½ pounds unpeeled, large
     fresh shrimp
1 pound fresh asparagus
1 (14-ounce) can quartered
     artichoke hearts, drained
     and chopped
6 tablespoons butter or
     margarine, divided
1 (8-ounce) package sliced
     fresh mushrooms
¼ cup all-purpose flour
¾ cup whipping cream

¾ cup milk
¼ cup dry sherry
1 tablespoon Worcestershire
     sauce
¾ teaspoon salt
¼ teaspoon ground black
     pepper
⅛ teaspoon ground red
     pepper
¼ cup freshly grated
     Parmesan cheese
Paprika
Hot cooked rice

Bring water to a boil; add shrimp, and cook 3 to 5 minutes or just until shrimp turn pink. Drain and rinse with cold water. Peel shrimp, and devein, if desired.

Snap off tough ends of asparagus. Cut asparagus into 1-inch pieces. Arrange asparagus in a steamer basket over boiling water. Cover and steam 8 minutes or until crisp-tender.

Arrange asparagus, artichokes, and shrimp in a lightly greased 2-quart baking dish. Melt 2 tablespoons butter in a large skillet over medium heat; add mushrooms, and sauté until tender. Arrange mushrooms over shrimp.

Melt remaining ¼ cup butter in a heavy saucepan over low heat; whisk in flour until smooth. Cook 1 minute, whisking constantly. Gradually whisk in cream and milk; cook over medium heat, whisking constantly, until mixture is thickened and bubbly. Stir in sherry, Worcestershire sauce, salt, and peppers. Pour mixture over mushrooms. Sprinkle with Parmesan cheese and paprika. Bake, uncovered, at 375° for 20 minutes. Let stand 5 minutes before serving. Serve with rice. Yield: 6 servings.

Forget Me Not: Recipes and Stories to Remember
Hospice and Palliative Care of Greensboro, North Carolina

Carnival Loaf

The juice of the oysters and scalloped spinach mixture soaks into the bread while cooking, making this a soft sandwich for eating with a knife and fork.

1 (10-ounce) package frozen
   chopped spinach
¼ cup olive oil
¼ cup butter or margarine,
   softened
1 garlic clove, minced
1 (10-inch) round loaf Italian
   or Tuscan bread
3 large eggs
¾ cup mayonnaise
6 bacon slices, cooked and
   crumbled

½ teaspoon salt
¼ teaspoon freshly ground
   pepper
⅛ teaspoon ground mace
1 pint fresh oysters, rinsed
   and drained
2 tomatoes, sliced
½ cup freshly grated
   Parmesan cheese

Cook spinach according to package directions, adding olive oil to water; drain.

Combine butter and garlic in a small bowl; stir with a wooden spoon until well blended.

Slice off top of bread loaf; scoop out center, leaving a ½-inch shell. Process soft center of bread in a blender or food processor to make fine breadcrumbs.

Combine eggs and mayonnaise in a small bowl; stir with a wire whisk. Stir in spinach, bacon, and next 3 ingredients.

Spread the inside and top of bread round with butter mixture. Pat oysters dry with paper towels. Arrange oysters on bottom of bread loaf. Layer half each of spinach mixture, tomato slices, breadcrumbs, and cheese; repeat layers, ending with cheese. Replace top of bread loaf; wrap loaf in aluminum foil, and place on a baking sheet. Bake at 350° for 45 minutes or until cheese melts. Cut into 6 wedges. Yield: 6 servings.

From Black Tie to Blackeyed Peas: Savannah's Savory Secrets
St. Joseph's Foundation of Savannah, Inc.
Savannah, Georgia

Tuna at Its Best

Substitute slivered almonds for potato chips to add extra crunch to this casserole.

6 ounces uncooked medium egg noodles

1 (6-ounce) can chunk tuna in spring water, drained and flaked

1 (4-ounce) jar sliced mushrooms, drained

½ cup frozen sweet peas, thawed

½ cup (2 ounces) shredded Monterey Jack cheese

1 (10¾-ounce) can cream of mushroom soup, undiluted

½ cup milk

½ cup mayonnaise

½ teaspoon salt

¼ teaspoon onion powder

⅛ teaspoon pepper

¾ cup crushed potato chips

Cook noodles according to package directions; drain. Combine noodles, tuna, and next 3 ingredients. Combine soup and next 5 ingredients; stir into noodle mixture.

Spoon tuna mixture into a lightly greased 11- x 7-inch baking dish. Sprinkle with potato chips. Bake, uncovered, at 350° for 40 minutes or until hot. Yield: 4 servings.

Specialties of the Haus
TCM International, Inc.
Indianapolis, Indiana

Ultimate Seafood

6 cups water
2½ pounds unpeeled,
   medium-size fresh shrimp
¼ teaspoon salt
⅛ teaspoon pepper
2 tablespoons butter or
   margarine
2 tablespoons all-purpose
   flour
2 cups heavy whipping cream
2 tablespoons lemon juice
2 tablespoons dry sherry
1 tablespoon Worcestershire
   sauce

1 tablespoon ketchup
½ teaspoon dry mustard
½ teaspoon curry powder
½ teaspoon paprika
2 (14-ounce) cans artichoke
   heart quarters, drained
1 pound fresh lump crabmeat,
   drained
1½ cups (6 ounces) shredded
   Cheddar cheese
½ teaspoon paprika
Hot cooked rice

Bring water to a boil; add shrimp, and cook 3 to 5 minutes or just until shrimp turn pink. Drain and rinse with cold water. Peel shrimp, and devein, if desired. Sprinkle shrimp with salt and pepper; set aside.

Melt butter in a heavy saucepan over low heat; whisk in flour until smooth. Cook 1 minute, whisking constantly. Gradually whisk in cream and next 7 ingredients; cook over medium heat, whisking constantly, until mixture is thickened and bubbly.

Layer artichoke, crabmeat, and shrimp in an ungreased 13- x 9-inch baking dish. Pour sauce over layers; sprinkle with cheese and paprika.

Bake, uncovered, at 375° for 15 minutes. Serve over rice. Yield: 8 servings.

From Black Tie to Blackeyed Peas: Savannah's Savory Secrets
St. Joseph's Foundation of Savannah, Inc.
Savannah, Georgia

Meats

Orange-Honey Pork Tenderloin, page 201

"Smoked" Brisket

Bacon contributes a smoky flavor to this melt-in-your-mouth brisket, and spicy tomatoes with green chiles add a touch of heat.

2 bacon slices, chopped
1 (2-pound) boneless beef
  brisket
2 large onions, sliced
2 garlic cloves, minced
1 (10-ounce) can diced
  tomatoes and green chiles
  (we tested with Rotel)
1 cup dry red wine or water

2 tablespoons fresh lemon
  juice
1 tablespoon Worcestershire
  sauce
2 bay leaves
1 teaspoon dried thyme
¾ teaspoon salt
¼ teaspoon pepper

Cook bacon in a large ovenproof Dutch oven over medium heat 2 minutes, stirring often. Remove bacon, reserving drippings in pan. Add brisket, and cook 5 minutes on each side. Transfer brisket to a platter.

Add onion to Dutch oven; cook 5 minutes, stirring often. Add garlic; cook 1 minute. Add bacon, tomatoes and green chiles, and remaining 7 ingredients.

Return brisket to Dutch oven; bring to a boil. Remove from heat. Bake, covered, at 350° for 3 hours. Discard bay leaves before serving. To serve, slice brisket diagonally across the grain into thin slices. Yield: 4 servings.

Sedonia Perrodin

Ragin Cajun Cookbook
Beacon Club of University of Louisiana at Lafayette
Lafayette, Louisiana

Beef Tenderloin Stuffed with Goat Cheese

An intimate dinner for two is the perfect occasion to serve this elegant tenderloin with its peppery coating and creamy goat cheese filling.

1 (¾-pound) beef tenderloin, trimmed
5 ounces crumbled goat cheese
¾ cup loosely packed fresh baby spinach leaves
2 garlic cloves, minced

¾ teaspoon salt
½ teaspoon black pepper
2 tablespoons black peppercorns, coarsely crushed

Slice tenderloin lengthwise to, but not through, the center, leaving 1 long side connected. Open tenderloin out flat.

Combine goat cheese and next 4 ingredients in a small bowl. Spread goat cheese mixture over tenderloin. Fold 1 side of tenderloin back over; tie tenderloin at 2-inch intervals with string. Roll tenderloin in crushed peppercorns, pressing lightly.

Place tenderloin on a lightly greased rack in a shallow roasting pan. Bake, uncovered, at 425° for 15 minutes. Reduce oven temperature to 325°. Bake 45 more minutes or until a meat thermometer inserted into thickest portion registers 145° (medium rare) or 160° (medium). Let stand 10 minutes before slicing. Yield: 2 servings.

Austin Entertains
The Junior League of Austin, Texas

Classic Beef Tenderloin

There's no need to marinate this succulent beef tenderloin. The high heat seals in the juices for truly "classic" results. Line the roasting pan with aluminum foil for easy cleanup.

3 tablespoons Dijon mustard
2 tablespoons butter or margarine, softened
2 teaspoons salt

4 teaspoons mixed peppercorns, ground
1 (2-pound) beef tenderloin, trimmed

Combine first 4 ingredients; spread butter mixture over beef. Place beef on a rack in a roasting pan. Bake at 450° for 45 minutes or until a meat thermometer inserted into thickest portion registers 145° (medium rare) or 160° (medium). Let stand 10 minutes before slicing. Yield: 4 to 6 servings.

Splendor in the Bluegrass
The Junior League of Louisville, Kentucky

Steak Diane

Classically, Steak Diane would be prepared at the table by a captain in a grand hotel dining room, but this version can be prepared easily right in your own kitchen. This recipe embodies all the flavors of the traditional dish—thinly sliced tenderloin steaks, shallots, mustard, and a splash each of brandy and sherry.

6 (4- to 6-ounce) beef tenderloin steaks (1 inch thick)
1 tablespoon coarsely ground pepper
1 tablespoon butter
¾ cup finely chopped shallots
½ cup beef broth

½ cup heavy whipping cream
¼ cup dry white wine
¼ cup white wine vinegar
1 tablespoon Dijon mustard
2 teaspoons dry mustard
½ teaspoon salt
1 tablespoon butter
2 tablespoons dry sherry
2 tablespoons brandy

Sprinkle both sides of steaks with pepper. Melt 1 tablespoon butter in a large nonstick skillet over medium-high heat. Add shallots; sauté

1½ minutes or until shallots are tender. Add beef broth and next 6 ingredients. Bring to a boil; cook, stirring constantly, until liquid is reduced by half. Pour sauce into a bowl; set aside.

Wipe skillet with paper towels. Melt 1 tablespoon butter in skillet over medium-high heat. Add steaks, and cook 6 minutes on each side or to desired degree of doneness. Transfer to a platter; keep warm. Add sherry and brandy to skillet; bring to a boil. Stir in cream sauce. Pour over steaks. Serve immediately. Yield: 6 servings.

Las Vegas: Glitter to Gourmet
The Junior League of Las Vegas, Nevada

Bavarian Pot Roast

This slightly sweet pot roast makes an abundance of beer-spiked gravy, perfect for topping mashed potatoes or popovers.

1 (3-pound) boneless chuck roast, trimmed	1 tablespoon white vinegar
2 tablespoons vegetable oil	2 teaspoons salt
1¼ cups water	1 teaspoon ground cinnamon
¾ cup beer	1 bay leaf
1 (8-ounce) can tomato sauce	½ teaspoon ground ginger
½ cup chopped onion	½ teaspoon pepper
2 tablespoons sugar	¼ cup cornstarch
	¼ cup water

Brown roast on all sides in hot oil in a Dutch oven. Add 1¼ cups water and next 10 ingredients. Cover, reduce heat, and simmer 2½ to 3 hours or until roast is tender. Remove roast to a serving platter. Discard bay leaf.

Combine cornstarch and ¼ cup water. Stir cornstarch mixture slowly into pan juices. Cook, stirring constantly, over medium heat until thickened. Yield: 8 to 10 servings. Susan Oogjen

The Western New York Federal Court Centennial Cookbook
U.S. District Court, Western District of New York
Buffalo, New York

Teriyaki Finger Steaks

Enjoy these soy sauce-laced bits of meat right off the skewer or as a hearty addition to a salad.

2 **pounds boneless top sirloin steak**	2 **tablespoons minced onion**
½ **cup soy sauce**	1 **tablespoon vegetable oil**
¼ **cup rice wine vinegar**	1 **garlic clove, minced**
2 **tablespoons light brown sugar**	½ **teaspoon ground ginger**
	⅛ **teaspoon pepper**
	8 **(12-inch) wooden skewers**

Trim fat from steak, and slice steak across the grain lengthwise into ½-inch strips; place in a large bowl. Combine soy sauce and next 7 ingredients in a small bowl; pour over meat, and toss well to coat. Cover and marinate in refrigerator 8 hours.

Soak wooden skewers in water 30 minutes.

Thread meat onto wooden skewers; discard any remaining marinade. Grill skewers, covered with grill lid, over medium-high heat (350° to 400°) 7 minutes or to desired degree of doneness. Yield: 6 to 8 servings.   Joyce Ogle

Lake Waccamaw United Methodist Church Cookbook
Lake Waccamaw United Methodist Church
Lake Waccamaw, North Carolina

Braised Short Ribs of Beef

Use the juices leftover from cooking these succulent ribs to make a gravy for the ribs or mashed potatoes.

3 tablespoons all-purpose flour
2 teaspoons salt
½ teaspoon freshly ground pepper
¼ teaspoon dried rosemary
3 pounds lean beef short ribs, trimmed

3 tablespoons vegetable oil, divided
½ cup chopped onion
½ cup chopped celery
1½ cups beef consommé
3 tablespoons all-purpose flour
¼ cup water

Combine first 4 ingredients. Dredge ribs in flour mixture. Set aside. Heat 1 tablespoon oil in a large skillet over medium-high heat; add onion and celery. Sauté 5 minutes or until tender. Transfer vegetables to a Dutch oven.

Cook ribs, in batches, in remaining 2 tablespoons oil 7 to 8 minutes on each side or until browned. Place ribs in a Dutch oven. Drain pan juices from skillet.

Add beef consommé to rib mixture. Cover and bake at 300° for 3 hours or until tender.

Combine 3 tablespoons flour and water in a medium saucepan, stirring until smooth; gradually stir in pan juices from skillet. Cook, stirring constantly, over medium-high heat until thick and bubbly. Serve gravy with ribs and vegetables. Yield: 4 servings.   Susie McKinney

Our Daily Bread
First Presbyterian Church of Orlando—Weekday School
Orlando, Florida

Upside-Down Meat Loaf

½ cup firmly packed light
  brown sugar
½ cup ketchup
2 pounds lean ground beef
2 large eggs, lightly beaten
1 small onion, chopped

¾ cup crushed saltine
  crackers (about 27 crackers)
¾ cup milk
1 teaspoon salt
½ teaspoon pepper
¼ teaspoon ground ginger

Press brown sugar in bottom of a 9- x 5-inch loafpan. Spread ketchup over sugar. Combine ground beef and remaining 7 ingredients in a large bowl, and stir well. Shape beef mixture into a loaf, and place in prepared pan. Bake, uncovered, at 350° for 2 hours. Let stand 10 minutes. Drain pan juices, if necessary; invert meat loaf onto a serving plate. Yield: 6 servings.   Bill Hoffmann

Embden Centennial Cookbook
St. John Lutheran Church
Wheatland, North Dakota

Cajun Meat Loaf

Take traditional meat loaf to new heights with the addition of thyme, cumin, and ground red pepper that lend Cajun flair.

2 tablespoons olive oil
½ large onion, chopped
½ cup chopped green bell
  pepper
1 teaspoon salt
¾ teaspoon ground red
  pepper
½ teaspoon freshly ground
  black pepper
½ teaspoon dried thyme

¼ teaspoon ground cumin
1 pound lean ground beef
1 large egg, lightly beaten
2 tablespoons ketchup
½ cup fine, dry breadcrumbs
  (store-bought)
1 teaspoon Worcestershire
  sauce
¼ cup ketchup

Heat oil in a medium skillet over medium-high heat. Add onion and bell pepper; sauté 8 to 10 minutes. Stir in salt and next 4 ingredients.
Combine beef, egg, 2 tablespoons ketchup, breadcrumbs, Worcestershire sauce, and sautéed vegetables; mix well. Shape meat

mixture into a 5- x 3-inch loaf on a lightly greased rack in a broiler pan lined with aluminum foil. Bake, uncovered, at 350° for 30 minutes. Spread ¼ cup ketchup over top, and bake 15 more minutes. Let stand 10 minutes before slicing. Yield: 2 to 4 servings.

Oh My Stars! Recipes That Shine
The Junior League of Roanoke Valley, Virginia

Veal with Spinach and Mustard Sauce

1½ **pounds thinly sliced veal
  cutlets (about 12)**
½ **cup all-purpose flour**
2 **teaspoons Creole seasoning**
¼ **teaspoon salt**
6 **tablespoons olive oil**
1¼ **cups half-and-half**
3 **tablespoons Creole mustard**
2 **tablespoons sour cream**

¼ **teaspoon salt**
1 **tablespoon butter or
  margarine**
2 **teaspoons Creole seasoning**
1 **teaspoon sesame seeds,
  toasted**
½ **cup chicken broth**
2 **(6-ounce) packages fresh
  baby spinach**

Place veal between 2 sheets of heavy-duty plastic wrap, and flatten to ⅛-inch thickness, using a meat mallet or rolling pin. Pat veal dry with paper towels. Combine flour, 2 teaspoons Creole seasoning, and ¼ teaspoon salt; dredge veal in flour mixture.

Sauté veal, in 3 batches in hot oil, in a large nonstick skillet over medium-high heat 1½ to 2 minutes on each side or until browned, using about 2 tablespoons olive oil for each batch. Transfer veal to a platter, and keep warm.

Stir together half-and-half and next 3 ingredients in a small saucepan; cook over medium heat 8 minutes or until thoroughly heated, stirring occasionally.

Melt butter in large skillet over medium heat. Add 2 teaspoons Creole seasoning and sesame seeds; cook 1 minute. Gradually add chicken broth. Add spinach, in batches; cover and cook 7 minutes or until liquid is almost absorbed. Serve veal over spinach mixture. Spoon sauce over veal. Yield: 6 servings.

Las Vegas: Glitter to Gourmet
The Junior League of Las Vegas, Nevada

Goose Pond Farm Citrus Lamb

The essence of orange brings out the rich flavors of this specialty dish.
For your convenience, ask your butcher to debone the lamb.

2 teaspoons grated orange
   rind
2 garlic cloves, minced
¼ cup chopped green onions
¼ cup chopped fresh parsley
¾ teaspoon crushed fresh
   rosemary
3 tablespoons olive oil
1 (4-pound) boneless leg of
   lamb or shoulder roast

1 teaspoon salt
½ teaspoon pepper
1¾ cups orange juice
¼ cup cornstarch
¼ teaspoon dried basil
Garnish: orange slices, cut in
   half

Combine first 6 ingredients. Spread mixture over unrolled roast. Sprinkle with salt and pepper. Reroll roast, and secure with heavy string at 2- to 3-inch intervals. Place in a 13- x 9-inch roasting pan. Bake at 325° for 2 to 2½ hours or until a meat thermometer inserted in center of roast registers 160° (medium). Remove roast from pan, and keep warm.

Combine orange juice and cornstarch, stirring with a wire whisk. Place pan over low heat. Stir orange juice mixture and basil into pan drippings. Cook, stirring constantly, over medium heat until thickened and bubbly. Serve over sliced lamb. Garnish, if desired. Yield: 8 to 10 servings.

Laura Bingham Ritch

Beyond Cotton Country
The Junior League of Morgan County
Decatur, Alabama

Hazelnut and Mustard Lamb Chops

Two types of mustard are preferable to coat these succulent chops for the best flavor, but if you have only one, that's fine. Just use 4 tablespoons of it.

2 tablespoons coarse-grained Dijon mustard
2 tablespoons Dijon mustard
2 tablespoons dry white wine
½ cup ground hazelnuts
¼ cup soft breadcrumbs (homemade)
2 tablespoons chopped fresh parsley

1½ teaspoons minced garlic
4 (2- to 3-ounce) lamb loin chops
1 teaspoon freshly ground pepper
2 tablespoons olive oil
1½ tablespoons butter or margarine, melted

Stir together first 3 ingredients in a shallow dish; set aside. Stir together hazelnuts, breadcrumbs, parsley, and garlic in a shallow dish; set aside.

Sprinkle lamb chops evenly with pepper. Heat oil in a large skillet over medium-high heat until hot. Add chops; cook 2 minutes on each side or until browned. Remove chops from skillet, using tongs, and dip in mustard mixture. Dredge all sides in breadcrumb mixture, pressing well.

Place chops in a lightly greased shallow roasting pan; drizzle with melted butter. Bake at 375° for 20 minutes or to desired degree of doneness. Yield: 2 servings.

Oh My Stars! Recipes That Shine
The Junior League of Roanoke Valley, Virginia

Athenian Moussaka (Athinaikos Moussaka)

We thought this Greek family favorite was the best we've ever had, so we gave it our top rating! Be sure to use a large lasagna pan because the moussaka won't fit in a 13- x 9-inch pan—there's just too much!

2 large eggplants (about 4 pounds)
1 tablespoon salt
½ cup olive oil, divided
2 tablespoons olive oil
2 medium onions, chopped
2½ pounds ground lamb or ground beef
2 teaspoons salt
2 (6-ounce) cans tomato paste
1¼ cups dry red wine
1 (3-inch) cinnamon stick
2 garlic cloves, minced

¼ cup chopped fresh parsley
3 tablespoons fine, dry breadcrumbs (store-bought)
1 cup freshly grated Parmesan cheese
⅓ cup butter or margarine
½ cup all-purpose flour
4 cups milk
1 teaspoon salt
¼ teaspoon ground nutmeg
1 cup freshly grated Parmesan cheese, divided
6 large eggs, lightly beaten

Peel eggplants, if desired, and cut lengthwise into ¼-inch-thick slices. To extract bitterness, sprinkle 1½ teaspoons salt on each side of slices; let stand 30 minutes. Rinse and pat dry with paper towels. Brush 1 side of eggplant slices with ¼ cup olive oil; place on 2 lightly greased baking sheets, brushed side up. Bake at 425° for 15 minutes. Turn slices, brush with ¼ cup olive oil, and bake 15 more minutes or until tender; set aside.

Heat 2 tablespoons olive oil in a large nonstick skillet over medium-high heat until hot. Add onion and ground lamb; cook lamb, stirring until it crumbles and is no longer pink. Drain well. Add 2 teaspoons salt and next 4 ingredients. Cover, reduce heat, and simmer 30 minutes. Discard cinnamon stick. Stir in parsley, breadcrumbs, and 1 cup Parmesan cheese; set aside.

Melt butter in a large heavy saucepan over low heat; add flour, stirring until smooth. Cook, stirring constantly, 1 minute. Gradually add milk; cook, stirring constantly, over medium heat until thickened and bubbly. Stir in 1 teaspoon salt, nutmeg, and ½ cup Parmesan cheese.

Gradually stir about 1 cup white sauce into eggs; add to remaining white sauce, stirring constantly.

Layer half of eggplant slices in a lightly greased 15- x 10-inch baking dish. Spoon meat sauce over eggplant, and top with remaining eggplant slices. Pour white sauce evenly over eggplant. Bake, uncovered, at 350° for 45 minutes. Sprinkle with remaining ½ cup Parmesan cheese; bake 10 more minutes. Let stand 10 minutes before serving. Yield: 10 to 12 servings.   Kathy Phoutrides

Flavor It Greek! A Celebration of Food, Faith and Family
Philoptochos Society of Holy Trinity Greek Orthodox Church
Portland, Oregon

Pork with Gingered Caramelized Onions

You may find caramelized onions addictive, especially in this recipe with an exotic ginger accent. Try them with other meats or poultry or atop mashed potatoes.

2 (¾-pound) pork tenderloins, cut into 1-inch slices	1 tablespoon minced fresh ginger
½ teaspoon salt	1 (8-ounce) package fresh mushrooms, cut in half
⅛ teaspoon pepper	⅓ cup sweetened dried cranberries
2 tablespoons butter or margarine	3 tablespoons apricot preserves
2 onions, sliced (about 2 cups)	

Sprinkle pork with salt and pepper. Melt butter in a large skillet over medium heat; add pork, and cook 3 minutes on each side or until golden. Remove from skillet; cover and keep warm.

Add onion to pan; cook over medium heat 20 minutes or until onion is browned and tender, stirring often. Add ginger and mushrooms; cook 2 more minutes.

Reduce heat to low; stir in cranberries and preserves. Return pork to skillet; cook until glazed and thoroughly heated. Yield: 4 servings.

Breakfast in Cairo, Dinner in Rome
International School of Minnesota Foundation
Eden Prairie, Minnesota

Pungent Pork Loin Roast

The enticing aroma of fresh sage, rosemary, and apples will fill your kitchen as you prepare this dish that makes a lovely holiday meal.

2 tablespoons chopped fresh sage
2 tablespoons chopped fresh rosemary
1½ tablespoons kosher salt
1 tablespoon black peppercorns

1 tablespoon fennel seeds
1 tablespoon olive oil
10 garlic cloves
1 (5-pound) boneless center-cut pork loin roast
Apple Bread Dressing

Process first 7 ingredients in a food processor until mixture forms a paste.

Trim excess fat from pork. Make 4 or 5 slits in top of roast, and fill each with 1 teaspoon paste mixture; spread remaining paste over top of roast. Place on a rack in a roasting pan.

Bake at 325° for 1½ hours or until a meat thermometer inserted into thickest portion registers 160°. Let stand 10 minutes before slicing. Serve with Apple Bread Dressing. Yield: 10 servings.

Apple Bread Dressing

¼ cup butter or margarine
½ cup chopped onion
3 cups chopped Granny Smith apple
2 tablespoons sugar
1 teaspoon salt

1 teaspoon chopped fresh sage
¼ teaspoon dried thyme
⅛ teaspoon pepper
4 cups cubed white bread
¼ cup chopped fresh parsley
2 tablespoons apple juice

Melt butter in a large skillet over medium-high heat; add onion, and sauté until tender. Stir in apple and next 5 ingredients. Cover and cook over medium-low heat 8 to 9 minutes or until apple is soft. Combine apple mixture, cubed bread, parsley, and juice in a large bowl; toss gently. Spoon into a lightly greased 11- x 7-inch baking dish. Cover and bake at 325° for 1 hour. Yield: about 6 cups.

Twice Treasured Recipes
The Bargain Box, Inc.
Hilton Head Island, South Carolina

Orange-Honey Pork Tenderloin

4 garlic cloves, minced
4 tablespoons chopped fresh
  thyme
3 tablespoons grated orange
  rind
1 teaspoon pepper
2 (14-ounce) pork tenderloins

2 cups fresh orange juice
½ cup rice vinegar
Vegetable oil
½ cup honey, divided
Hot cooked rice
Garnish: orange slices

Combine first 4 ingredients; rub mixture evenly over tenderloins. Place tenderloins in a large heavy-duty zip-top plastic bag. Combine orange juice and vinegar. Pour orange juice mixture over tenderloins. Seal bag securely; marinate pork in refrigerator 8 hours, turning bag occasionally.

Brush a 13- x 9-inch pan with oil. Heat pan at 425° for 4 minutes. Remove from heat. Remove tenderloins from marinade, reserving marinade. Place tenderloins in prepared pan. Drizzle 2 tablespoons honey over each tenderloin. Bake at 425° for 10 minutes. Remove tenderloins from oven, and drizzle with remaining ¼ cup honey. Bake 14 more minutes or until a meat thermometer inserted into thickest portion of tenderloin registers 160°. Transfer tenderloins to a platter, and cover loosely with aluminum foil. Let stand 5 minutes before slicing.

Pour reserved marinade in a medium saucepan, and bring to a boil. Boil marinade 17 minutes or until reduced to 1 cup. Slice tenderloins, and serve with rice and orange sauce. Garnish, if desired. Yield: 8 servings.

Vickie Gasparovic

Cooking with Class
Forest Hills Elementary School PTO
Lake Oswego, Oregon

Pork Medaillons

Succulent pieces of pork tenderloin drenched in a white wine-mustard sauce are served with colorful peppers for a stunning presentation.

1 (1-pound) pork tenderloin
2 teaspoons olive oil
¼ cup sliced green onions
⅔ cup dry white wine
1 cup beef consommé
3 tablespoons butter or
   margarine, divided

3 tablespoons Dijon mustard
⅛ teaspoon sugar
1 red bell pepper, cut into thin
   strips
1 yellow bell pepper, cut into
   thin strips
1 teaspoon balsamic vinegar

Cut tenderloin into ½-inch slices.

Heat oil in a large skillet over medium heat until hot. Add pork and green onions; cook pork 4 minutes on each side or until browned. Add wine; simmer 3 minutes or until pork is done. Remove pork from skillet; set aside, and keep warm.

Add consommé to drippings in skillet; bring to a boil. Cook 4 minutes or until reduced to ½ cup. Add 2 tablespoons butter, mustard, and sugar; stir until butter melts and mixture is smooth. Pour over pork; set aside, and keep warm.

Melt remaining 1 tablespoon butter in skillet over medium-high heat. Add bell peppers; cook, stirring constantly, 3 minutes or until crisp-tender. Stir in vinegar. Spoon around pork. Yield: 4 servings.

To Your Health: Recipes for Healthy Living from Lahey Clinic
Lahey Clinic
Burlington, Massachusetts

Pork and Red Onion Kabobs

Bite-size pieces of pork tenderloin and red onion wedges marinate in an Asian-inspired soy sauce-ginger marinade. These make a wonderful make-ahead entrée. Just thread the flavor-packed meat and onions onto skewers, grill, and, in less than 30 minutes, dinner is ready.

⅓ cup vegetable oil
¼ cup dry red wine
3 tablespoons red wine vinegar
3 tablespoons soy sauce
1 tablespoon chopped garlic
1 tablespoon minced fresh ginger

1½ teaspoons sugar
1½ pounds pork tenderloin, cut into bite-size pieces
1 large red onion, cut into small wedges
12 (8-inch) wooden skewers

Combine first 7 ingredients in a large heavy-duty zip-top plastic bag. Add pork and onion wedges. Seal bag; marinate in refrigerator 8 hours, turning occasionally.

Soak wooden skewers in water 30 minutes.

Remove pork from marinade, discarding marinade. Thread pork and onion alternately onto skewers.

Grill kabobs, covered with grill lid, over medium-high heat (350° to 400°) 8 minutes on each side or until pork is done. Yield: 4 to 6 servings.

Meet Us in the Kitchen
The Junior League of St. Louis, Missouri

Pesto Pork Chops

A palate-pleasing surprise awaits as you cut into these pesto-stuffed pork chops that boast a spicy outer coating and a jalapeño glaze that will set your taste buds tingling.

¼ cup crumbled feta cheese
2 tablespoons pine nuts, toasted
2 tablespoons pesto sauce
4 (1¼-inch-thick) bone-in pork loin chops, trimmed and cut with pockets

Spicy Rub
Jalapeño Pesto Glaze

Combine first 3 ingredients. Spoon about 2 tablespoons mixture into each pocket of pork chops; secure openings with wooden picks. Rub Spicy Rub evenly on both sides of pork chops.

Coat grill rack with cooking spray; place pork chops on grill rack. Grill, covered with grill lid, over medium-high heat (350° to 400°) 9 minutes on each side or to desired degree of doneness, brushing occasionally with Jalapeño Pesto Glaze. Yield: 4 servings.

Spicy Rub

2 teaspoons minced garlic
1 teaspoon freshly ground black pepper
½ teaspoon salt
½ teaspoon ground red pepper

½ teaspoon celery seeds
½ teaspoon fennel seeds
¼ teaspoon ground cumin
¼ teaspoon dried thyme

Combine all ingredients in a bowl. Yield: about 2 tablespoons.

Jalapeño Pesto Glaze

2 tablespoons jalapeño pepper jelly

2½ tablespoons pesto sauce
1 tablespoon balsamic vinegar

Combine all ingredients in a saucepan. Cook over medium-low heat until thoroughly heated, stirring occasionally. Yield: about ⅓ cup.

First Impressions: Dining with Distinction
The Junior League of Waterloo-Cedar Falls
Waterloo, Iowa

Sweet-and-Sour Spareribs

Simmered in a pineapple- and soy-infused sauce, these fall-off-the-bone tender ribs will have you begging for seconds.

4 **pounds spareribs**	⅔ **cup white vinegar**
1 **teaspoon salt**	½ **cup ketchup**
1 **teaspoon pepper**	½ **cup water**
1 **(8-ounce) can crushed pineapple in juice, undrained**	¼ **cup chopped green bell pepper**
⅔ **cup firmly packed light brown sugar**	2 **tablespoons cornstarch**
	2 **tablespoons soy sauce**
	2 **teaspoons dry mustard**

Cut ribs into serving-size pieces; place ribs, meat side up, in a large pan. Bake at 450° for 30 minutes or until lightly browned; drain. Sprinkle with salt and pepper.

Combine pineapple and remaining 8 ingredients in a small saucepan. Cook, stirring constantly, over medium heat 2 minutes or until thickened. Pour over ribs, and bake at 350° for 1½ hours. Yield: 6 to 8 servings.

Brenda Lanche

Cooking with the Original Search Engine
Fort Worth Public Library All Staff Association
Fort Worth, Texas

Sour Cream Pork Chops

Sometimes the simplest dishes taste the best, especially when it comes to comfort food like these tender pork chops smothered in sour cream gravy and served over rice.

8 (½- to ¾-inch-thick) boneless pork loin chops
1 teaspoon salt, divided
½ teaspoon ground sage
½ teaspoon pepper
2 teaspoons vegetable oil
2 onions, thinly sliced
1 (10½-ounce) can beef consommé
1 (8-ounce) container sour cream
3 tablespoons all-purpose flour
Hot cooked rice

Sprinkle pork chops with ½ teaspoon salt, sage, and pepper. Brown chops in hot oil in a nonstick skillet over medium-high heat. Add onion and consommé. Cover, reduce heat, and simmer 30 minutes.

Combine sour cream, flour, and remaining ½ teaspoon salt in a small bowl. Remove pork chops from skillet; stir in sour cream mixture. Return chops to skillet; simmer, uncovered, until thoroughly heated. Serve over rice. Yield: 8 servings.

Faithfully Charleston
St. Michael's Episcopal Church
Charleston, South Carolina

Pasta, Rice & Grains

Traditional Hoppin' John, page 218

Herbed Shrimp and Pasta

The captivating flavors of fresh shrimp, vegetables, and herbs shine through in this colorful pasta dish that's perfect for springtime.

10 ounces uncooked dried angel hair pasta
6 garlic cloves, minced
2 large shallots, minced
2 tablespoons olive oil
1 red bell pepper, cut into thin strips
2 small yellow squash, quartered and thinly sliced
1 pound fresh asparagus, cut into 2-inch pieces
1 (8-ounce) package sliced fresh mushrooms

1 pound medium-size, fresh shrimp, peeled and deveined
2 plum tomatoes, chopped
½ cup chopped fresh parsley
¼ cup chopped fresh basil
1 tablespoon chopped fresh thyme
1 teaspoon salt
½ teaspoon pepper
1 cup grated Parmesan cheese, divided

Cook pasta according to package directions; drain and set aside.

Sauté garlic and shallots in hot oil in a large skillet over medium-high heat until tender. Add bell pepper and next 3 ingredients. Sauté 7 minutes or until crisp-tender. Add shrimp. Cook over medium-high heat 3 to 5 minutes or until shrimp turn pink.

Stir in tomato and next 5 ingredients. Cook just until thoroughly heated.

Combine tomato mixture, ½ cup Parmesan cheese, and pasta in a large bowl. Sprinkle remaining ½ cup cheese over pasta mixture. Yield: 6 servings.

Tapestry: A Weaving of Food, Culture and Tradition
The Junior Welfare League of Rock Hill, South Carolina

Grape, Blue Cheese, and Walnut Pasta

Depending on how strong your blue cheese is, you can use more or less to suit your taste. This is a great chilled salad for a brunch or luncheon.

8 ounces uncooked dried bow tie pasta
3 cups red seedless grapes, halved
½ cup chopped green onions
1 (4-ounce) package crumbled blue cheese
1 garlic clove, minced
¼ teaspoon salt
¼ teaspoon pepper
1 cup mayonnaise
2 tablespoons fresh lemon juice
¾ cup chopped walnuts, toasted

Cook pasta according to package directions; drain. Rinse pasta with cold water, and drain. Combine pasta, grapes, and next 5 ingredients in a large bowl.

Whisk together mayonnaise and lemon juice; add to pasta mixture. Cover and chill at least 2 hours. Add walnuts, tossing well. Yield: 6 to 8 servings.

Creating a Stir
The Lexington Medical Society Auxiliary
Lexington, Kentucky

White Tie Pasta

16 ounces uncooked dried
  bow tie pasta
¼ cup chopped onion
1 garlic clove, minced
3 tablespoons unsalted butter
1 tablespoon olive oil
1 (8-ounce) package sliced
  fresh mushrooms
6 ounces prosciutto, coarsely
  chopped
1 (14-ounce) can quartered
  artichoke hearts, drained
2 tablespoons pine nuts
2 tablespoons drained capers
1½ cups heavy whipping
  cream
1 teaspoon pepper
¼ cup (1 ounce) shredded
  6-cheese blend (we tested
  with Sargento)

Cook pasta according to package directions in a large Dutch oven. Drain and return to pan. Cover and keep warm.

Cook onion and garlic in butter and hot olive oil in a large skillet over medium heat 3 minutes or until tender. Add mushrooms, and cook 5 minutes. Stir in prosciutto and artichokes; cook 3 minutes or until thoroughly heated. Add vegetable mixture, pine nuts, and capers to pasta.

Pour cream into a large skillet; add pepper. Bring to a boil over medium-high heat, stirring often; cook until reduced to 1 cup. Pour cream mixture over pasta mixture; add cheese, and toss well. Serve immediately. Yield: 6 to 8 servings.   Eddie and Terri Betcher

Look Who Came to Dinner
The Junior Auxiliary of Amory, Mississippi

White Lasagna

A white sauce peppered with mushrooms is the base for this creamy chicken and cheese lasagna.

8 ounces uncooked dried lasagna noodles
2 tablespoons butter or margarine
1 (8-ounce) package sliced fresh mushrooms
½ cup dry white wine
½ teaspoon dried tarragon
¼ cup butter or margarine
½ cup all-purpose flour
1½ teaspoons salt
¼ teaspoon ground white pepper
¼ teaspoon ground nutmeg
2 cups half-and-half
2 cups chicken broth
5 cups shredded cooked chicken
3 (5-ounce) packages Swiss cheese, shredded

Cook lasagna noodles according to package directions; drain well. Set aside.

Melt 2 tablespoons butter in a large skillet over medium-high heat; sauté mushrooms 3 minutes or until lightly browned. Add wine and tarragon to skillet; cook over medium-high heat 3 minutes or until liquid evaporates.

Melt ¼ cup butter in a large saucepan over medium heat; add flour and next 3 ingredients, stirring until smooth. Cook, stirring constantly, 1 minute. Gradually add half-and-half and broth; cook, stirring constantly, over medium-high heat until mixture is thickened and bubbly. Stir in mushroom mixture.

Spread ½ cup white sauce in a greased 13- x 9-inch baking dish. Layer half of lasagna noodles over sauce; arrange half of chicken evenly over noodles. Spoon half of remaining white sauce evenly over chicken; sprinkle with half of cheese, and place remaining noodles over cheese. Repeat layers with remaining chicken, white sauce, and cheese. Cover and bake at 350° for 1 hour or until bubbly. Let stand 10 minutes before serving. Yield: 8 servings.

First Impressions: Dining with Distinction
The Junior League of Waterloo-Cedar Falls
Waterloo, Iowa

Kirby's Linguine with Artichokes

We fell in love with this creamy shrimp and pasta dish that we thought couldn't get any better—until we topped it with Parmesan cheese and bacon.

¼ cup olive oil
½ cup butter or margarine
1 tablespoon all-purpose flour
1 cup chicken broth
6 garlic cloves, crushed
4 teaspoons lemon juice
1 tablespoon chopped fresh parsley
1 (14-ounce) can quartered artichoke hearts, drained
1 (8-ounce) package sliced fresh mushrooms

2 tablespoons freshly grated Parmesan cheese
8 ounces uncooked linguine
Freshly grated Parmesan cheese
½ teaspoon freshly ground pepper
1 (1-pound) package bacon, cooked and crumbled

Heat olive oil and butter in a heavy saucepan over medium heat until butter melts. Whisk in flour, and cook, stirring constantly, 3 minutes. Stir in chicken broth; cook 1 minute over medium heat. Add garlic, lemon juice, and parsley; cook 5 minutes. Add artichoke hearts, mushrooms, and 2 tablespoons cheese; simmer 10 minutes.

Cook linguine according to package directions; drain well. Pour sauce over linguine. Sprinkle with additional Parmesan cheese, pepper, and bacon. Yield: 4 to 6 servings.   Harriett Rodgers

V.C.O.S. Sharing Our Best
Volusia County Orchid Society, Inc.
DeLand, Florida

Springtime Orzo

Enjoy this simple side dish alongside grilled lamb for a celebratory spring dinner.

1 cup uncooked orzo
1 tablespoon butter or margarine
½ cup chopped green onions
¼ cup chopped green bell pepper
1 cup chopped cooked ham
½ cup half-and-half
½ teaspoon lemon pepper

½ teaspoon salt
2 tablespoons freshly grated Parmesan cheese
2 tablespoons chopped fresh parsley
1 (10-ounce) package frozen petite sweet peas, thawed and drained

Cook orzo according to package directions; drain well, and keep orzo warm.

Melt butter in a saucepan over medium-high heat. Add green onions, bell pepper, and ham. Cook until green onions are tender, stirring often. Stir in half-and-half, lemon pepper, and salt; cook over medium heat 5 minutes. Stir in cheese, parsley, and orzo. Cook until mixture is thoroughly heated, stirring often. Gently stir in peas; serve immediately. Yield: 4 servings.

Forget Me Not: Recipes and Stories to Remember
Hospice and Palliative Care of Greensboro, North Carolina

Brie-Tomato Pasta

Brie is a very soft cheese and melts easily when tossed with hot pasta such as in this simple meatless dish.

2 (8-ounce) rounds Brie
16 ounces uncooked dried
    penne pasta
⅓ cup olive oil, divided
3 garlic cloves, minced
5 plum tomatoes, seeded and
    chopped

2 cups chopped green onions
1 cup chopped fresh basil
2 teaspoons kosher salt
½ teaspoon pepper
½ teaspoon dried crushed red
    pepper
½ cup pine nuts, toasted

Remove and discard rind from Brie; cut cheese into ½-inch pieces.

Cook pasta according to package directions; drain. Transfer pasta to a large bowl; gently stir in cheese. Cover and let stand 3 minutes.

Heat ¼ cup oil in a small nonstick skillet. Add garlic, and sauté 2 minutes. Pour over pasta mixture. Add remaining olive oil, tomato, and next 5 ingredients, tossing gently. Sprinkle with pine nuts. Yield: 8 servings.

Kathy Cary

Look Who's Cooking in Louisville
Pitt Academy
Louisville, Kentucky

Greek Penne Pasta

All the enticing flavors of Mediterranean cuisine sparkle in this simple dish. Using baby spinach eliminates the need to remove the stems, making assembly even easier.

16 ounces uncooked dried
    penne pasta
5 garlic cloves, minced
1 tablespoon olive oil
4 cups chopped fresh spinach
2 (4½-ounce) cans sliced ripe
    olives, drained

4 large plum tomatoes, chopped
4 ounces feta cheese, crumbled
½ cup cottage cheese
1 tablespoon olive oil
½ teaspoon salt
¾ teaspoon pepper
2 tablespoons pine nuts

Cook pasta according to package directions; drain and set aside.

Sauté garlic in 1 tablespoon hot olive oil in a large nonstick skillet over medium-high heat 30 seconds. Stir in spinach, olives, and tomato. Cook 10 minutes, stirring occasionally.

Combine feta cheese and cottage cheese.

Toss pasta and 1 tablespoon oil in a large bowl. Stir in spinach mixture and cheese mixture. Season with salt and pepper. Sprinkle with pine nuts. Serve immediately. Yield: 8 servings.

Entertaining Thoughts . . .
The Junior League of the Lehigh Valley
Bethlehem, Pennsylvania

Spaghetti and Cheese

Spaghetti noodles and Monterey Jack cheese add a delightfully different twist to old-time macaroni and cheese.

7 ounces spaghetti, cooked and drained
3 cups (12 ounces) shredded Monterey Jack cheese
1 tablespoon all-purpose flour
1 teaspoon salt
½ teaspoon dry mustard
⅛ teaspoon pepper
2½ cups milk, divided
2 large eggs, lightly beaten
2 tablespoons butter or margarine
Paprika

Place half of cooked spaghetti in a lightly greased 13- x 9-inch baking dish; sprinkle with half of cheese. Repeat layers.

Combine flour, salt, dry mustard, and pepper in a small bowl. Add 1 tablespoon milk; stir to make a paste. Add beaten eggs and remaining milk to flour mixture, stirring well with a wire whisk; pour over spaghetti mixture. Dot with butter, and sprinkle with paprika. Bake at 350° for 45 minutes or until set. Let stand 5 minutes before serving. Yield: 6 to 8 servings.

Specialties of the Haus
TCM International, Inc.
Indianapolis, Indiana

Layered Ziti with Asparagus and Prosciutto

Entice your guests with this delectable make-ahead pasta dish that's full of tender asparagus, green peas, prosciutto, and two cheeses baked in a creamy white sauce. Feel free to substitute the pasta you have on hand, such as bow tie or penne.

12 ounces uncooked dried ziti
3 tablespoons olive oil
1 pound fresh asparagus, cut into 1-inch pieces
1½ cups frozen sweet peas, thawed
1 cup thinly sliced onion
2 garlic cloves, minced
¼ teaspoon dried crushed red pepper
½ cup dry white wine
1½ cups chicken broth

½ cup heavy whipping cream
½ teaspoon salt
1 teaspoon freshly ground black pepper
¼ pound thinly sliced prosciutto, minced
2 cups (8 ounces) shredded mozzarella cheese
¼ cup grated Parmesan cheese
⅔ cup soft breadcrumbs

Cook pasta according to package directions; drain and set aside.

Heat oil in a large skillet over medium heat until hot. Add asparagus and next 3 ingredients; cook 7 minutes, stirring often. Add crushed red pepper; cook 4 minutes. Add wine; cook 3 minutes or until vegetables are tender. Add chicken broth and cream. Cook 10 minutes or until reduced by one-third. Stir in salt and black pepper. Add pasta, and toss well.

Layer half of pasta mixture, half of prosciutto, half of mozzarella cheese, and half of Parmesan cheese in a greased 13- x 9-inch baking dish. Repeat layers; sprinkle with breadcrumbs.

Bake at 350° for 25 minutes or until golden and cheese melts. Let stand 10 minutes before serving. Yield: 6 servings.

Meet Us in the Kitchen
The Junior League of St. Louis, Missouri

Chicken, Andouille, and Shrimp Jambalaya

A Louisiana original, this jambalaya is supereasy because it cooks all in one pan for easy serving and cleanup.

1 pound unpeeled, large fresh shrimp
1 large bay leaf
1½ teaspoons salt
1 teaspoon dried thyme
¾ teaspoon ground white pepper
¼ teaspoon ground red pepper
¼ teaspoon freshly ground black pepper
2 tablespoons unsalted butter
8 ounces andouille sausage, chopped

12 ounces skinned and boned chicken breast halves, cut into bite-size pieces
1 medium onion, chopped
1 cup chopped celery
1 large green bell pepper, chopped
2 garlic cloves, minced
1 (8-ounce) can tomato sauce
1 (14.5-ounce) can diced tomatoes, undrained
3 cups chicken broth
1½ cups uncooked long-grain rice

Peel shrimp, and devein, if desired. Cut shrimp in half crosswise; set aside.

Combine bay leaf and next 5 ingredients in a small bowl; stir well.

Melt butter in a large Dutch oven over medium heat. Add sausage; cook, stirring constantly, 3 minutes. Add chicken; cook, stirring constantly, 5 minutes or until browned. Add spice mixture, onion, celery, bell pepper, and garlic; cook, stirring constantly, 6 minutes or until vegetables are tender. Stir in tomato sauce; cook 1 minute. Remove from heat. Stir in shrimp, tomatoes, broth, and rice. Spoon into a greased 13- x 9-inch baking dish.

Bake, uncovered, at 350° for 1½ hours or until liquid is almost absorbed and rice is tender. Discard bay leaf. Stir jambalaya before serving. Serve immediately. Yield: 6 servings.

Secret Ingredients
The Junior League of Alexandria, Louisiana

Soubise

Soubise, (pronounced soo beez*), is a white sauce with cooked onions and cream, and sometimes rice. In this recipe, the rice can be molded into small ramekins and turned out onto serving plates for a beautiful presentation.*

2 tablespoons butter or
  margarine
¾ cup chopped onion
¾ cup uncooked long-grain
  rice
⅔ cup chicken broth
⅔ cup water
¼ cup dry white wine

½ teaspoon salt
1 bay leaf
¼ cup heavy whipping cream
2 tablespoons freshly grated
  Parmesan cheese
Garnish: chopped fresh
  parsley

Melt butter in a medium saucepan over medium-low heat. Add onion; cook 3 minutes or until soft. Stir in rice. Cook, stirring constantly, over medium heat 1 minute. Add chicken broth and next 4 ingredients. Bring to a boil; cover, reduce heat, and simmer 20 minutes or until liquid is absorbed. Discard bay leaf.

Fold in whipping cream and Parmesan cheese. If desired, spoon mixture into 4 lightly greased 6-ounce ramekins. Firmly pack mixture into ramekins, and immediately invert onto individual serving plates. Garnish, if desired. Yield: 4 servings.

California Fresh Harvest: A Seasonal Journey through Northern California
The Junior League of Oakland-East Bay
Lafayette, California

Traditional Hoppin' John

4 bacon slices, diced
⅓ cup diced carrot
½ cup finely chopped celery
¼ cup finely chopped onion
2 cups fresh or frozen black-
  eyed peas, thawed
1 garlic clove, peeled
2¾ cups water

1 bay leaf
½ teaspoon salt
¼ teaspoon dried crushed red
  pepper
2 cups cooked long-grain rice
Garnishes: shredded Cheddar
  cheese, chopped green
  onions

Cook bacon in a medium saucepan until crisp; add carrot, celery, and onion, and sauté 1 minute. Add peas and next 5 ingredients.

Bring to a boil; reduce heat, and simmer, uncovered, 35 to 40 minutes or until peas are tender. Discard bay leaf.

Spoon pea mixture over rice on a serving platter. Garnish, if desired. Yield: 4 servings.

Cooking with Care
HospiceCare of the Piedmont, Inc.
Greenwood, South Carolina

Brown Rice with Nuts and Raisins

½ cup golden raisins
½ cup dry white wine
¼ cup butter or margarine, divided
¼ cup chopped onion
2 cups uncooked instant brown rice
1 (14-ounce) can chicken broth
¼ cup water
½ teaspoon salt
¼ teaspoon pepper
¾ cup slivered almonds, toasted
½ cup chopped fresh mint or fresh cilantro
Garnishes: fresh mint sprigs or fresh cilantro sprigs

Combine raisins and wine in a small bowl.

Melt 2 tablespoons butter in a medium skillet over low heat. Add onion; cook, stirring constantly, over medium-high heat until tender. Add rice; cook, stirring constantly, 3 minutes or until lightly browned. Add broth, water, salt, and pepper; bring to a boil. Cover, reduce heat, and simmer 10 minutes or until liquid is absorbed. Remove from heat; add remaining butter, stirring until butter melts. Drain raisins, discarding liquid; stir raisins into rice mixture. Add almonds and mint, stirring well. Garnish, if desired. Yield: 4 servings.

Everything But the Entrée
The Junior League of Parkersburg, West Virginia

Wild Rice with Cherries and Apricots

The perfect blend of sweet and crunchy unite in this gorgeous looking side dish that's perfect for those cold fall evenings, especially when served alongside roast pork.

1 (16-ounce) package frozen pearl onions
2 tablespoons butter or margarine
6½ cups chicken broth
3 tablespoons chopped fresh thyme, divided
1¼ cups uncooked wild rice
1¼ cups uncooked long-grain rice

¼ cup butter or margarine
1 (7-ounce) package dried apricots, coarsely chopped
1 (6-ounce) package dried cherries
1 cup raisins
1 cup chopped pecans, toasted
½ teaspoon salt
¼ teaspoon pepper

Sauté onions in 2 tablespoons butter in a large nonstick skillet over medium-high heat 15 minutes or until browned; set aside.

Combine broth and 1 tablespoon thyme in a large saucepan; bring to a boil. Stir in wild rice. Return to a boil; cover, reduce heat, and simmer 30 minutes. Stir in long-grain rice; cover and simmer 22 minutes or until liquid is absorbed and rice is tender. Remove from heat.

Stir in onions, remaining 2 tablespoons thyme, ¼ cup butter, and remaining ingredients; stir until butter melts. Yield: 8 to 10 servings.

A Taste of Enchantment
The Junior League of Albuquerque, New Mexico

Roasted Garlic and Mushroom Risotto

When making risotto, the broth is usually added in batches to allow for maximum absorption. But this version adds the broth all at once, which is easier and saves time.

2 large garlic bulbs
¼ cup olive oil, divided
¾ ounce dried porcini
    mushrooms
12 ounces mixed fresh wild
    mushrooms, sliced (we
    tested with crimini, oyster,
    and shiitake)
½ teaspoon salt
¼ teaspoon pepper
1 cup chopped shallots

2 tablespoons chopped fresh
    thyme or 2 teaspoons dried
    thyme
1½ cups uncooked Arborio rice
½ cup dry white wine
3½ to 4 cups low-sodium
    chicken broth
2 cups thinly sliced fresh baby
    spinach leaves
⅓ cup freshly grated
    Parmesan cheese

Cut tops off garlic, leaving bulbs intact. Place garlic bulbs on a piece of aluminum foil, cut side up; drizzle with 2 tablespoons oil. Wrap in foil, and bake at 400° for 1 hour. Remove from oven, and cool. Discard outermost layer of papery skin from garlic. Scoop out soft garlic pulp with a small spoon; chop garlic, and set aside.

Add hot water to porcini mushrooms to cover; allow to stand 30 minutes or until soft. Drain well, and coarsely chop.

Heat 1 tablespoon oil in a large nonstick skillet over medium-high heat. Add fresh mushrooms, and sauté 7 minutes or until lightly browned and juices evaporate. Add porcini mushrooms, salt, and pepper; cook, stirring constantly, 1 minute.

Heat remaining 1 tablespoon oil in a large saucepan over medium-high heat. Add shallots and thyme; sauté 4 minutes or until tender. Add rice and wine; cook until liquid is almost evaporated. Stir in garlic and 3½ cups broth; bring to a boil. Reduce heat, and simmer 20 minutes or until rice is tender and mixture is creamy, stirring occasionally and adding additional broth as necessary. Add mushroom mixture and spinach. Cook 1 minute or until spinach wilts; stir in cheese. Yield: 6 to 8 servings.

Secret Ingredients
The Junior League of Alexandria, Louisiana

Vegetable Risotto

5 cups vegetable broth,
  divided
5 tablespoons unsalted butter,
  divided
1 small onion, minced
⅔ cup chopped zucchini
⅔ cup chopped carrot

⅔ cup chopped broccoli
2 cups uncooked Arborio rice
1 cup dry white wine
¾ teaspoon salt
¾ teaspoon pepper
1 cup freshly grated Parmesan
  cheese, divided

Bring broth to a simmer in a large saucepan (do not boil). Keep warm over low heat.

Melt 4 tablespoons butter in a large skillet over medium-high heat. Add onion and next 3 ingredients; sauté 2 to 3 minutes or until vegetables are tender. Add rice; sauté, stirring constantly, 1 minute. Reduce heat to medium; add wine and 1 cup broth, and cook, stirring constantly, until liquid is absorbed. Repeat procedure with remaining broth, 1 cup at a time, until liquid is absorbed (about 15 minutes). Stir in salt, pepper, remaining butter, and ⅓ cup Parmesan cheese.

Spoon onto serving plates; sprinkle with remaining cheese. Serve immediately. Yield: 4 to 6 servings.

The Kosher Palette
Joseph Kushner Hebrew Academy
Livingston, New Jersey

Nutty Mint Bulgur

This healthy side dish has an intoxicating mint aroma and a variety of nuts that makes this dish extraspecial.

1½ cups water
¾ teaspoon salt
1 cup uncooked bulgur wheat
2 tablespoons pine nuts, toasted
3 tablespoons chopped
  almonds, toasted

3 tablespoons chopped
  walnuts, toasted
2 green onions, sliced
1 tablespoon minced fresh
  mint

Bring water and salt to a boil in a medium saucepan. Stir in bulgur. Cover, reduce heat, and simmer 10 minutes or until tender. Stir in toasted pine nuts and remaining ingredients. Serve immediately. Yield: 4 servings.   Elisha Swajian

Look What's Cooking . . .
Temple Sinai Sisterhood
Cranston, Rhode Island

Tabbouleh

A healthy alternative to cream-based salads, this Middle Eastern salad makes use of fresh herbs and can be eaten plain or stuffed into a pita for an easy sandwich.

½ cup uncooked bulgur wheat	2 garlic cloves, minced
½ cup boiling water	2 tablespoons olive oil
6 tomatoes, chopped	⅓ cup fresh lemon juice (about
8 green onions, chopped	3 lemons)
1 cup minced fresh parsley	1 teaspoon salt
½ cup minced fresh mint	½ teaspoon pepper

Place bulgur in a small bowl; stir in boiling water. Cover and let stand 20 minutes. Drain well.

Combine tomato and next 4 ingredients in a large bowl. Add olive oil; stir gently. Add bulgur to tomato mixture. Stir in lemon juice, salt, and pepper. Toss gently. Yield: 6 servings.   Michelle Bisceglia

The Heart of Pittsburgh
Sacred Heart Elementary School PTG
Pittsburgh, Pennsylvania

Green Chile and Cheese Polenta

Green chiles, garlic, corn, and fresh cilantro harmonize with polenta and melted Monterey Jack cheese. Couple this dish with pork, chicken, or beef.

¾ cup yellow cornmeal
2 cups milk
1 cup water
3 garlic cloves, minced
1½ teaspoons garlic salt
1 teaspoon salt
½ cup grated Parmesan
  cheese
¼ teaspoon pepper

1 (7-ounce) can whole green
  chiles, drained and sliced
1 (15-ounce) can sweet whole
  kernel corn, drained
⅔ cup chopped fresh cilantro
2 cups (8 ounces) shredded
  Monterey Jack cheese
½ cup heavy whipping cream

Combine first 6 ingredients in a saucepan. Bring to a simmer over medium heat; simmer, whisking constantly, 12 minutes or until mixture is thickened. Stir in Parmesan cheese and pepper.

Layer half each of cornmeal mixture, green chiles, corn, cilantro, Monterey Jack cheese, and whipping cream in a greased 8- x 8-inch baking dish; repeat layers with remaining ingredients. Bake, uncovered, at 400° for 25 minutes or until lightly browned. Let stand 10 minutes before serving. Yield: 9 servings.

Splendor in the Bluegrass
The Junior League of Louisville, Kentucky

Pies & Pastries

Frozen Peanut Butter Pie with Hot Fudge Sauce, page 231

Tennessee Apple Pie

6 cups peeled, sliced Granny
  Smith apples (about 5
  medium)
⅔ cup sugar
¼ cup firmly packed light
  brown sugar
½ cup orange juice
½ cup water

1 (15-ounce) package
  refrigerated piecrusts
1 egg white, lightly beaten
¼ teaspoon ground cinnamon
¼ teaspoon ground nutmeg
2 tablespoons butter or
  margarine
2 teaspoons sugar

Combine first 5 ingredients in a large skillet; bring to a boil. Cover, reduce heat to medium, and cook 10 to 15 minutes or until apple is tender. Remove apple with a slotted spoon, reserving syrup in skillet; set apple aside.

Bring syrup to a boil; cook until syrup is reduced to ½ cup, stirring often.

Fit 1 piecrust into a 9-inch pieplate according to package directions. Brush pastry with egg white. Arrange apple in piecrust; pour syrup over apple. Sprinkle with cinnamon and nutmeg; dot with butter. Roll remaining piecrust to press out fold lines. Place piecrust over filling; trim off excess pastry along edges. Fold edges under, and crimp. Brush top with remaining egg white. Sprinkle lightly with 2 teaspoons sugar. Bake at 425° for 40 minutes or until golden, shielding edges with aluminum foil after 20 minutes to prevent excessive browning. Yield: 8 servings.
                                                              Mary A. Turner

Future Generations
Robertson County Family and Community Education Clubs
County Extension Office
Springfield, Tennessee

Swedish Apple Pie

8 Granny Smith apples,
  peeled and sliced
1 tablespoon sugar
1 teaspoon ground cinnamon
¼ teaspoon ground nutmeg

1 cup sugar
1 cup all-purpose flour
1 large egg, beaten
¾ cup butter or margarine,
  melted

Grease bottom of a 9-inch pieplate; fill with apple slices. Sprinkle 1 tablespoon sugar, cinnamon, and nutmeg over apple. Combine 1 cup sugar and flour; stir in egg and butter (mixture will be thick). Spread batter over apple. Bake at 350° for 30 minutes. Increase temperature to 400°, and bake 10 minutes or until golden. Serve warm with vanilla ice cream. Yield: 8 servings.   Sharon St. Onge

Dixon Fixins
Dixon Ambulatory Care Center
Westminster, Maryland

Cranberry Surprise Pie

Serve this cranberry treat cobbler style by spooning it into bowls and topping it with ice cream or whipped cream. The surprise comes from the macaroon crust that forms on top and the addition of blueberries and coconut to the filling.

3 cups fresh or frozen coarsely chopped cranberries	⅓ cup flaked coconut
½ cup fresh or frozen blueberries	1½ cups sugar
½ cup chopped pecans or sliced almonds	1 large egg
	½ cup all-purpose flour
	6 tablespoons butter or margarine, melted

Combine cranberries and blueberries. Spoon cranberry mixture into a lightly greased 9-inch pieplate. Combine pecans and coconut, and sprinkle over cranberry mixture. Top with 1 cup sugar.

Beat egg and remaining ½ cup sugar at medium speed with an electric mixer until blended. Add flour and butter; beat at low speed until blended. Spread batter evenly over pie filling. Bake at 325° for 1 hour or until golden. Cool completely on a wire rack. Yield: 8 servings.

Cooking with Music: Celebrating the Tastes and Traditions of the Boston Symphony Orchestra
Boston Symphony Association of Volunteers
Boston, Massachusetts

Blueberry Pie with Crème Chantilly

Succulent blueberries abound in this pie that's topped with an almond-flavored cream.

4 cups fresh blueberries,
  divided
¾ cup sugar
½ cup water
2 tablespoons cornstarch
2 tablespoons water
1 tablespoon butter or
  margarine

¼ cup orange liqueur
¼ cup slivered almonds,
  toasted
1 baked 9-inch deep-dish
  pastry shell
Crème Chantilly

Process 1 cup blueberries, sugar, and ½ cup water in a blender until smooth. Pour blueberry mixture into a medium saucepan.

Combine cornstarch and 2 tablespoons water in a small bowl; gradually stir into blueberry mixture. Cook, stirring constantly, over medium heat 3 minutes or until thickened. Stir in butter, orange liqueur, almonds, and remaining blueberries. Pour into prepared pastry shell; cool on a wire rack. Cover and chill at least 8 hours. Top with Crème Chantilly before serving. Yield: 8 servings.

Crème Chantilly

1 cup heavy whipping cream
2 tablespoons sugar

¼ teaspoon almond extract

Combine all ingredients in a small chilled mixing bowl. Beat at high speed with an electric mixer until stiff peaks form. Yield: 2 cups.

Jean Shook

Plate & Palette: A Collection of Fine Art and Food
Beaufort County Arts Council
Washington, North Carolina

Sour Cream Lemon Pie

This creamy and refreshing version of Lemon Icebox Pie is a true showstopper, especially when decorated with lemon slices and fresh mint sprigs.

1 cup sugar
1 tablespoon grated lemon
  rind
⅓ cup fresh lemon juice
3 tablespoons cornstarch
1 cup half-and-half
1 tablespoon all-purpose flour
¼ cup butter or margarine
1 (8-ounce) container sour
  cream

1 baked 9-inch pastry shell
1 cup heavy whipping cream
2 tablespoons powdered sugar
½ teaspoon almond extract
½ cup sour cream
Garnishes: fresh mint sprigs,
  lemon rind strips, lemon
  slices

Combine first 6 ingredients in a large saucepan, stirring until smooth. Bring to a boil; cook, stirring constantly, over medium heat 1 minute or until mixture thickens. Add butter; cook, stirring constantly, 1 minute. Remove from heat, and let cool. Fold in 8 ounces sour cream. Pour into prepared pastry shell. Cover and chill 8 hours.

Beat whipping cream until foamy; gradually add powdered sugar and almond extract, beating until soft peaks form. Fold in ½ cup sour cream. Gently spread whipped cream mixture evenly over pie. Cover and chill 2 hours. Garnish, if desired. Yield: 8 servings.

Twice Treasured Recipes
The Bargain Box, Inc.
Hilton Head Island, South Carolina

Peach Cream Pie

1 unbaked 9-inch pastry shell
3 cups peeled, sliced fresh
  peaches
¾ cup sugar

¼ cup all-purpose flour
¼ teaspoon salt
1 cup heavy whipping cream

Line pastry shell with aluminum foil; fill with pie weights or dried beans. Bake at 375° for 10 minutes. Remove weights and foil.

Combine peaches and next 3 ingredients; toss gently. Pour peach mixture into pastry shell; pour whipping cream over peach mixture. Bake at 375° for 45 minutes, shielding edges with aluminum foil, if necessary, to prevent excessive browning. Remove to a wire rack. Let cool completely. Yield: 8 servings.   Jane Harper

Cooking Up Memories
St. Paul's Episcopal Church
Chattanooga, Tennessee

Magic Margarita Pie

The pretzel crust is reminiscent of the salted rim of a frozen margarita!

1¼ cups finely crushed
  pretzels
10 tablespoons butter, melted
¼ cup sugar
1 (14-ounce) can sweetened
  condensed milk
⅓ cup frozen limeade
  concentrate, thawed

¼ cup tequila
2 tablespoons orange liqueur
1 cup whipping cream,
  whipped
Garnish: whipped cream, lime
  or orange slices, fresh mint
  sprigs

Combine crushed pretzels, butter, and sugar in a small bowl; press into bottom and up sides of a lightly greased 9-inch pieplate.

Combine condensed milk and next 3 ingredients in a bowl; mix well. Fold in 1 cup whipped cream. Pour into prepared pieplate; cover and freeze until firm. Garnish, if desired. Yield: 8 servings.

Sweet Pickin's
The Junior League of Fayetteville, North Carolina

Frozen Peanut Butter Pie with Hot Fudge Sauce

Anything drenched in fudge sauce is bound to be good, especially when it contains peanut butter and peanuts and is encased in a chocolate crust.

1½ cups chocolate wafer
    crumbs (about 30 wafers)
6 tablespoons butter, melted
1 (8-ounce) package cream
    cheese, softened
1 cup chunky peanut butter

¾ cup sugar
1 tablespoon vanilla extract
1½ cups whipping cream
Hot Fudge Sauce
Garnish: chopped miniature
    peanut butter cups

Combine wafer crumbs and butter; lightly press crumb mixture into bottom and up sides of a lightly greased 9-inch pieplate. Chill.

Combine cream cheese and next 3 ingredients in a mixing bowl. Beat at medium speed with an electric mixer until smooth.

Beat cream until soft peaks form. Fold whipped cream, one-fourth at a time, into cream cheese mixture. Spoon filling into prepared pieplate. Cover and freeze 2 hours or until firm. Let stand 30 minutes before serving. Drizzle about ¼ cup Hot Fudge Sauce over pie; serve remaining sauce with pie. Garnish, if desired. Yield: 8 servings.

Hot Fudge Sauce

½ cup sugar
½ cup whipping cream
¼ cup butter

2 (1-ounce) unsweetened
    chocolate squares, chopped
½ teaspoon vanilla extract

Combine sugar and whipping cream in a saucepan; bring to a boil, stirring constantly. Reduce heat, and simmer 6 minutes (do not stir). Remove from heat; add butter and chocolate, and stir until blended. Stir in vanilla. Yield: 1¼ cups.

Start Your Ovens: Cooking the Way It Ought'a Be
The Junior League of Bristol, TN/VA
Bristol, Virginia

Pat's Peanut Butter Ice Cream Pie

Peanut butter and chopped peanuts are sandwiched between two layers of vanilla ice cream, creating a frozen treat that's worth the wait.

½ cup light corn syrup
⅓ cup creamy peanut butter
4 cups vanilla ice cream,
   softened

1 (6-ounce) graham cracker
   crust
⅔ cup chopped unsalted
   peanuts

Stir together corn syrup and peanut butter; set aside.

Spoon 2 cups ice cream into crust; drizzle half of corn syrup mixture over ice cream, and sprinkle with ⅓ cup peanuts. Cover and freeze 1 hour. Repeat layers. Cover and freeze at least 4 hours. Yield: 6 servings.

Galyn Metcalf

Cooking with Class
Forest Hills Elementary School PTO
Lake Oswego, Oregon

Frozen Strawberry Yogurt Pie

In the mood for pie but not lots of fuss? Make this pie anytime with the help of its four convenience ingredients.

3½ cups frozen whipped
   topping, thawed
2 (8-ounce) containers
   strawberry yogurt
1 (10-ounce) package frozen
   sliced strawberries in syrup,
   thawed

1 (6-ounce) graham cracker
   crust

Stir together whipped topping and yogurt in a medium bowl. Gently fold in strawberries. Spoon mixture into crust.

Cover loosely, and freeze 4 hours or until set. Let stand at room temperature 10 minutes before serving. Yield: 6 servings.

Past and Present Meatless Treasures
Kaneohe Seventh-day Adventist Church
Kaneohe, Hawaii

Bavarian Rhubarb Tart

A cakelike crust absorbs the gooey sweetness of the caramelized rhubarb for a treat worthy of seconds. Use fresh rhubarb stalks that are firm for the best texture.

1¼ cups all-purpose flour
1 teaspoon baking powder
1 teaspoon sugar
½ teaspoon salt
½ cup butter or margarine
2 tablespoons milk
1 large egg, well beaten

4 cups chopped fresh rhubarb
2¼ cups sugar
1½ tablespoons all-purpose flour
1 teaspoon ground cinnamon
5 tablespoons butter or margarine

Combine first 4 ingredients; cut in ½ cup butter with a pastry blender until crumbly. Combine milk and egg; add to flour mixture. Stir with a fork until dry ingredients are moistened. Press into a greased 13- x 9-inch pan.

Combine rhubarb and 1½ cups sugar; spoon over crust. Combine remaining ¾ cup sugar, 1½ tablespoons flour, and cinnamon; cut in 5 tablespoons butter with a pastry blender until crumbly. Sprinkle over rhubarb mixture. Bake at 350° for 40 minutes or until crust is lightly browned and rhubarb is tender. Remove from oven, and cool completely on a wire rack. Yield: 12 servings.   Kathy Howard

Breakfast in Cairo, Dinner in Rome
International School of Minnesota Foundation
Eden Prairie, Minnesota

Swirled Pumpkin Tart

Add a dollop of whipped cream and a sprinkling of nutmeg and cinnamon as a finishing touch to this creamy tart.

1 cup graham cracker crumbs	¾ cup sugar
¼ cup ground almonds	2 large eggs
¼ cup sugar	1 cup canned mashed
6 tablespoons butter or	pumpkin
margarine, melted	1½ teaspoons pumpkin pie
1 (8-ounce) package cream	spice
cheese, softened	

Combine first 4 ingredients in a bowl, stirring until blended. Press mixture into bottom and up sides of a 9-inch pieplate; chill.

Beat cream cheese and ¾ cup sugar at medium speed with an electric mixer until smooth. Add eggs, 1 at a time, beating until blended after each addition. Reserve ½ cup batter. Stir pumpkin and pumpkin pie spice into remaining batter. Pour into prepared crust; spoon reserved ½ cup batter over pumpkin mixture. Swirl gently with a knife.

Bake at 350° for 40 to 50 minutes or until tart is almost set. Cool completely in pan on a wire rack. Cover and chill at least 8 hours. Yield: 8 servings.

Everything But the Entrée
The Junior League of Parkersburg, West Virginia

Lemon-Curd Pastry with Mixed Berries

Make a statement with this spectacular dessert that features puff pastry topped with lemon curd and an assortment of fresh berries. It makes a stunning presentation of summer's best berries.

½ (17¼-ounce) package frozen puff pastry, thawed
1 egg white
1 teaspoon water
1 tablespoon sugar
1 (10-ounce) jar lemon curd (we tested with Dickinson's)
⅔ cup sour cream
¼ teaspoon ground ginger

¼ teaspoon almond extract
3 cups mixed berries (such as blueberries, blackberries, raspberries, or sliced strawberries)
¼ cup sliced almonds, toasted
2 tablespoons honey
Powdered sugar (optional)

Roll pastry into a 15- x 10-inch rectangle on a lightly floured surface. Place pastry on an ungreased baking sheet.

Cut a ½-inch-wide strip from each long side of pastry. Brush strips with water, and place moist side down on top of each long side of pastry rectangle, edges flush together. Repeat procedure on short sides of rectangle, trimming away excess pastry at corners. Prick pastry generously with a fork, excluding the border.

Combine egg white and 1 teaspoon water; brush border of pastry with egg mixture. Sprinkle sugar evenly over border. Bake at 375° for 20 minutes or until puffed and golden brown. Gently remove pastry from baking sheet, and cool completely on a wire rack.

Meanwhile, stir lemon curd in a medium bowl until smooth. Combine sour cream, ginger, and almond extract in a small bowl; fold into lemon curd. Cover and chill at least 4 hours.

To serve, transfer pastry shell to a serving platter. Spread filling over pastry. Top with berries and almonds; drizzle with honey. Sprinkle with powdered sugar, if desired. Yield: 8 servings.   Jan Hazel

Moon River Collection
The Landings Landlovers
Savannah, Georgia

Apple Dumplings

Buy a bag of small apples when preparing this fall treat so the apples will be relatively the same size. The red food coloring gives the apples a pretty pink hue but can be omitted, if you prefer.

1½ cups sugar
1½ cups water
¼ teaspoon ground cinnamon
¼ teaspoon ground nutmeg
8 drops red liquid food coloring (optional)
3 tablespoons butter or margarine
2 cups all-purpose flour
2 teaspoons baking powder
1 teaspoon salt

⅔ cup shortening
½ cup milk
6 small Granny Smith apples, peeled and cored
1½ teaspoons sugar
⅛ teaspoon ground cinnamon
⅛ teaspoon ground nutmeg
2 tablespoons butter or margarine
2 tablespoons sugar

Combine first 4 ingredients and, if desired, food coloring in a small saucepan. Bring to a boil; remove from heat, and add 3 tablespoons butter. Stir until butter melts; set syrup aside.

Combine flour, baking powder, and salt; cut in shortening with a pastry blender until crumbly. Add milk, stirring until dry ingredients are moistened. Roll into an 18- x 12-inch rectangle on a lightly floured work surface. Cut into 6 squares. Place an apple on each square. Sprinkle apples evenly with 1½ teaspoons sugar and ⅛ teaspoon each of cinnamon and nutmeg. Dot each apple with 1 teaspoon butter. Moisten edges of pastry with water. Bring corners to center, and pinch edges together. Place 1 inch apart in an ungreased 13- x 9-inch pan. Pour syrup over dumplings, and sprinkle with 2 tablespoons sugar. Bake at 375° for 40 minutes or until apples are tender. Yield: 6 servings.   Linda Burrichter

Christian Women's Fellowship
Oak Grove Christian Church
Shellsburg, Iowa

Rugalach

Traditional rugalach is usually made with a cream cheese dough, but our version contains sour cream. Use your favorite jam to create different flavors.

1 **cup butter or margarine, softened**
½ **cup sour cream**
2½ **cups all-purpose flour**
1 **cup sugar, divided**
1 **teaspoon ground cinnamon, divided**

½ **cup finely chopped pecans, divided**
¼ **cup raspberry jam, divided**

Beat butter and sour cream at medium speed with an electric mixer until creamy. Add flour, beating well.

Divide dough into 4 equal portions. Shape each portion into a flat round; wrap each round in wax paper. Cover and chill at least 2 hours.

Combine ¼ cup sugar and ¼ teaspoon cinnamon on work surface. Roll dough, 1 portion at a time, on cinnamon-sugar mixture into a 10-inch circle, turning dough once to incorporate cinnamon-sugar mixture on both sides. Sprinkle evenly with 2 tablespoons pecans, pressing lightly into dough. Cut dough into 12 wedges. Place ¼ teaspoon jam at wide end of each wedge. Roll up each wedge tightly, beginning at wide end, and seal points. Repeat procedure 3 times with remaining dough, cinnamon-sugar mixture, pecans, and jam. Place cookies, point side down, on ungreased baking sheets.

Bake at 375° for 16 to 18 minutes or until edges are lightly browned. Cool completely on wire racks. Yield: 4 dozen.   Marcia Halpern

Look What's Cooking . . .
Temple Sinai Sisterhood
Cranston, Rhode Island

Mini Cream Puffs

1 cup water
½ cup butter or margarine
1 cup all-purpose flour

4 large eggs
Vanilla Cream Pudding
Chocolate Icing

Combine water and butter in a medium saucepan; bring to a boil. Add flour, all at once, stirring vigorously over medium-high heat until mixture leaves sides of pan and forms a smooth ball. Remove pan from heat.

Add eggs, 1 at a time, beating thoroughly with a wooden spoon after each addition. Drop dough by tablespoonfuls onto ungreased baking sheets. Bake at 400° for 20 minutes or until puffed and golden. Cool away from drafts.

Cut off top of each cream puff; pull out and discard soft dough inside, if necessary, to form a small cavity. Fill bottom halves with about 1 tablespoon Vanilla Cream Pudding, and cover with top halves. Arrange cream puffs on a serving platter, and drizzle with Chocolate Icing. Serve immediately, or cover and chill. Yield: 3 dozen.

Vanilla Cream Pudding

⅓ cup sugar
2 tablespoons cornstarch
⅛ teaspoon salt
2 cups milk

2 egg yolks, lightly beaten
2 tablespoons butter or
  margarine
2 teaspoons vanilla extract

Combine first 3 ingredients in a medium saucepan; gradually stir in milk. Bring to a boil over medium heat, stirring constantly; boil, stirring constantly, 1 minute. Remove from heat.

Gradually stir about one-fourth of the hot mixture into yolks; add yolk mixture to remaining hot mixture, stirring constantly. Cook, stirring constantly, over medium heat 3 minutes.

Remove from heat; add butter and vanilla, stirring until butter melts. Cover with plastic wrap, and chill. Yield: 2¼ cups.

Chocolate Icing

1 (1-ounce) unsweetened
  chocolate square
1 teaspoon butter or
  margarine

1 cup sifted powdered sugar
2 tablespoons hot water

Melt chocolate and butter in a small saucepan over low heat, stirring often. Remove from heat, and whisk in powdered sugar and hot water until smooth. Yield: ½ cup.   Emily Powers

Fine Food from the Friends
Friends of the Superior Public Library, Inc.
Superior, Wisconsin

Apple-Pear Crisp

All this sweet and cinnamony fall dessert needs is a big scoop of vanilla ice cream to top it off.

⅓ cup sugar
2 tablespoons all-purpose flour
1 teaspoon ground cinnamon
4 Gala apples, peeled and sliced
4 Bosc pears, peeled and sliced

¾ cup uncooked quick-cooking oats
⅔ cup firmly packed light brown sugar
½ cup all-purpose flour
⅛ teaspoon salt
½ cup butter or margarine, cut into pieces

Combine first 3 ingredients in a large bowl. Add apple and pear slices, and toss until coated. Spoon fruit mixture into a greased 2-quart round baking dish; set aside.

Combine oats and next 3 ingredients; cut in butter with a pastry blender until crumbly. Sprinkle topping over fruit mixture. Bake at 375° for 50 minutes or until bubbly. Serve warm with vanilla ice cream, if desired. Yield: 6 to 8 servings.   Elizabeth Donnelly

Heaven's Bounty
Long Beach Catholic School Parents' Club
Long Beach, New York

Upside-Down Youngberry Cobbler

Youngberries are a type of blackberry with a dark red color and sweet, juice-packed flesh.

4 cups fresh youngberries or
　blackberries
1½ cups sugar, divided
1 teaspoon tapioca
¼ teaspoon lemon juice
¼ cup butter or margarine,
　softened

1 cup all-purpose flour
2 teaspoons baking powder
⅛ teaspoon salt
½ cup milk
Garnish: whipped cream

Combine berries, 1 cup sugar, tapioca, and lemon juice in a bowl; let stand 15 minutes.

Beat butter at medium speed with an electric mixer until creamy. Gradually add remaining ½ cup sugar, beating well. Combine flour, baking powder, and salt; gradually add to butter mixture alternately with milk, beginning and ending with flour mixture. Mix at low speed after each addition until blended.

Spoon batter into a greased 11- x 7-inch baking dish; spread evenly. Pour berry mixture over batter. Bake at 375° for 40 to 45 minutes or until golden. Garnish, if desired. Yield: 8 servings.　　Peggy Rowland

Future Generations
Robertson County Family and Community Education Clubs
County Extension Office
Springfield, Tennessee

Poultry

Buttermilk Picnic Chicken, page 244

Outdoor Roasted Chicken

1 (4-pound) whole chicken
2 tablespoons butter or margarine, softened
2 tablespoons Worcestershire sauce
3 garlic cloves, chopped
2 teaspoons Cajun seasoning
½ teaspoon salt
¼ teaspoon pepper
1 small onion, cut into wedges
1 small green bell pepper, cut into strips
1 celery rib, cut into 3-inch pieces
½ cup dry white wine
1 cup water

Remove giblets and neck from chicken; reserve for another use. Rinse chicken thoroughly under cold water, and pat dry with paper towels.

Rub butter on outside of chicken and inside cavity. Sprinkle Worcestershire sauce and next 4 ingredients evenly over outside and in cavity. Stuff cavity with onion, bell pepper, and celery. Tie ends of legs together with string, if necessary.

Fill an 8-inch pan with wine and water. Remove grill rack; place pan on left side of grill, and return rack.

Preheat gas grill to medium-high (350° to 400°), using both burners. After preheating, turn left burner off. Place chicken on rack over pan. Grill, covered with grill lid, 1½ to 2 hours or until a meat thermometer inserted in thigh registers 180°. Remove chicken from grill, and let stand 5 minutes before slicing. Yield: 4 servings.

Thyme to Entertain: Good Food and Southern Hospitality
The Charity League, Inc., of Paducah, Kentucky

Whole Roasted Chicken with Herbs and Wine

3 tablespoons olive oil,
  divided
1 small onion, chopped
1 carrot, chopped
1 celery rib, chopped
1 (6½-pound) whole chicken
6 garlic cloves, halved
6 fresh rosemary sprigs
1 teaspoon salt
1 teaspoon garlic powder

1 teaspoon paprika
½ teaspoon pepper
1½ cups dry red wine,
  divided
1 tablespoon butter or
  margarine, melted
1 tablespoon all-purpose flour
¼ teaspoon salt
¼ teaspoon pepper

Combine 2 tablespoons olive oil and next 3 ingredients; arrange in a shallow roasting pan.

Remove giblets and neck from chicken; reserve for another use. Rinse chicken thoroughly under cold water, and pat dry with paper towels. Place garlic and rosemary in cavity of chicken. Place chicken, breast side up, over vegetable mixture in pan. Rub chicken with remaining 1 tablespoon olive oil; sprinkle with 1 teaspoon salt and next 3 ingredients. Insert a meat thermometer into meaty portion of thigh, making sure it does not touch bone.

Bake, uncovered, at 400° for 1½ hours, basting once with pan drippings. Pour ¾ cup wine over chicken. Increase oven temperature to 425°, and bake 10 more minutes or until thermometer inserted in thigh registers 180°. Place chicken on a serving platter; cover and let stand 15 minutes before carving.

Meanwhile, pour pan drippings (about 1½ cups) into a medium saucepan. Stir in remaining ¾ cup wine, butter, flour, ¼ teaspoon each of salt and pepper into pan drippings; bring mixture to a boil over medium-high heat, stirring constantly. Cook 11 minutes or until thickened, stirring constantly. Serve sauce over chicken. Yield: 4 to 6 servings.

The Kosher Palette
Joseph Kushner Hebrew Academy
Livingston, New Jersey

Buttermilk Picnic Chicken

Buttermilk and seasonings give this oven "fried" chicken its savory goodness and delicious taste.

¾ cup buttermilk
2 teaspoons reduced-sodium chicken bouillon granules
1 teaspoon poultry seasoning
1 (3- to 4-pound) package chicken pieces (we tested with Pick-of-the-Chick)

1 cup all-purpose flour
1 tablespoon paprika
2 teaspoons seasoned salt
¼ teaspoon pepper
¼ cup butter or margarine, melted

Combine first 3 ingredients. Place chicken in a large heavy-duty zip-top plastic bag. Pour buttermilk mixture over chicken. Seal bag, and marinate in the refrigerator at least 8 hours, turning occasionally.

Combine flour and next 3 ingredients in a large heavy-duty zip-top plastic bag. Add chicken, a few pieces at a time, shaking bag to coat. Arrange chicken on a 15- x 10-inch jellyroll pan lined with aluminum foil. Drizzle chicken with melted butter. Bake at 350° for 1 hour or until golden. Yield: 6 to 8 servings.

Picnics, Potlucks & Prizewinners
Indiana 4-H Foundation, Inc.
Indianapolis, Indiana

Lemon Grilled Chicken

¾ cup butter or margarine
½ cup fresh lemon juice
⅓ cup water
2 garlic cloves, minced
2 tablespoons soy sauce
1 teaspoon Dijon mustard
1 teaspoon paprika

1 teaspoon honey
½ teaspoon salt
⅛ teaspoon ground red
  pepper
1 (3-pound) package chicken
  pieces (we tested with
  Pick-of-the-Chick)

Combine first 10 ingredients in a medium saucepan. Cook over medium heat, stirring constantly, until butter melts.

Coat food rack with cooking spray; place on grill over medium-high heat (350° to 400°). Place chicken on rack, and grill 30 minutes or until done, basting with marinade and turning occasionally. Yield: 6 to 8 servings.

Las Vegas: Glitter to Gourmet
The Junior League of Las Vegas, Nevada

Moroccan Chicken

This not-too-spicy, Middle Eastern-flavored dish calls for chicken thighs, which are moist and tender. Be sure to have plenty of mint and orange wedges for garnish.

2½ to 3 pounds skinned and
    boned chicken thighs
½ cup chopped onion
1 large garlic clove, chopped
1 tablespoon butter or
    margarine, melted
2 teaspoons grated orange
    rind
½ cup fresh orange juice

¼ teaspoon salt
¼ teaspoon ground
    cinnamon
⅛ teaspoon ground allspice
2 tablespoons honey
Couscous
Garnishes: orange wedges,
    fresh mint sprigs

Brown chicken, onion, and garlic in melted butter in a large skillet over medium-high heat until browned. Add orange rind, orange juice, and salt. Bring to a boil; cover, reduce heat, and simmer 5 minutes. Sprinkle chicken with cinnamon and allspice. Drizzle with honey. Cover and simmer 10 minutes or until chicken is done. Serve with Couscous. Garnish, if desired. Yield: 6 to 8 servings.

Couscous

2 cups water
2 tablespoons fresh lemon
    juice
1 tablespoon olive oil
½ teaspoon salt

⅛ teaspoon ground turmeric
1⅓ cups uncooked couscous
½ cup currants
½ cup chopped green onions

Bring first 5 ingredients to a boil in a medium saucepan. Stir in couscous and currants. Remove from heat, and cover. Let stand 5 minutes or until water is absorbed. Fluff with a fork, and stir in green onions. Yield: 5 cups.

Treasures of the Tropics
Hibiscus Children's Center
Jensen Beach, Florida

Chicken Avocado Melt

*Each tender chicken breast is baked with avocado slices and cheese,
and then topped with sour cream, green onions, and red bell pepper
for an eye-catching entrée and a taste sensation.*

4 (6-ounce) skinned and
  boned chicken breast halves
2 tablespoons cornstarch
1 teaspoon garlic salt
1 teaspoon ground cumin
1 large egg, lightly beaten
1 tablespoon water
⅔ cup yellow cornmeal
¼ cup vegetable oil

1 ripe avocado, sliced
1½ cups (6 ounces)
  shredded Monterey Jack
  cheese
½ cup sour cream
¼ cup chopped green onions
¼ cup chopped red bell
  pepper

Place chicken between 2 sheets of heavy-duty plastic wrap; flatten to
¼-inch thickness, using a meat mallet or rolling pin.

Combine cornstarch, garlic salt, and cumin in a large heavy-duty zip-
top plastic bag. Add chicken; seal and shake well to coat. Combine egg
and water in a small bowl; stir well with a wire whisk. Dip chicken in
egg mixture, and coat with cornmeal.

Cook chicken in hot oil in a large nonstick skillet over medium-high
heat 2 minutes on each side or until browned. Drain chicken on paper
towels.

Place chicken on a 15- x 10-inch jellyroll pan. Arrange avocado slices
evenly over chicken; sprinkle evenly with cheese.

Bake at 350° for 15 minutes or until chicken is done. Top evenly
with sour cream, green onions, and red bell pepper. Yield: 4 servings.

Made in the Shade
The Junior League of Greater Fort Lauderdale, Florida

Chicken with Goat Cheese

You can substitute porcini or portobello mushrooms in this recipe for the medley we used, depending on your tastes.

6 tablespoons butter or margarine, divided

4 skinned and boned chicken breast halves

6 ounces goat cheese, crumbled

1½ to 2 pounds sliced mushrooms (we tested with shiitake, cremini, and button mushrooms)

2 tablespoons all-purpose flour

2 cups beef broth

Melt 2 tablespoons butter in a large skillet over high heat; add chicken, and brown on both sides. Place chicken in a lightly greased 9-inch square baking dish. Sprinkle goat cheese over chicken.

Melt 2 tablespoons butter in skillet over medium-high heat. Sauté mushrooms until almost tender. Transfer to a bowl, and set aside.

Melt remaining 2 tablespoons butter in skillet over low heat; whisk in flour until smooth. Cook 1 minute, whisking constantly. Gradually whisk in broth; cook over medium heat 5 minutes, stirring constantly, until mixture is thickened and bubbly.

Stir mushrooms into sauce in skillet. Pour mushroom mixture over chicken and goat cheese. Cover and bake at 350° for 30 minutes or until chicken is done. Yield: 4 servings.   Mary Weiler

Share the Flavor: A Collection of Recipes from German Village
German Village Society
Columbus, Ohio

Poached Chicken with Black Beans and Salsa

1 cup chicken broth
6 skinned and boned chicken breast halves
¼ cup dry white wine
¼ teaspoon salt
¼ teaspoon black pepper

1 (15-ounce) can black beans, undrained
2 teaspoons balsamic vinegar
¼ teaspoon ground red pepper
Salsa

Bring broth to a boil in a large skillet; add chicken and next 3 ingredients. Return to a boil; cover, reduce heat, and simmer 15 minutes or until chicken is done. Set aside, and keep warm.

Process black beans, balsamic vinegar, and ground red pepper in a blender until smooth. Bring black bean mixture to a simmer in a saucepan over medium heat, stirring constantly. Cook until thoroughly heated. Serve over chicken; top with salsa. Yield: 6 servings.

Salsa

1 large tomato, chopped
1 serrano chile pepper, minced
1 small onion, minced

1 garlic clove, minced
½ cup chopped fresh cilantro
¼ teaspoon salt
¼ teaspoon pepper

Combine all ingredients in a bowl; stir well. Cover and chill 2 to 3 hours. Yield: 3 cups.

The Guild Collection: Recipes from Art Lovers
The Guild, The Museum of Fine Arts, Houston, Texas

Sautéed Chicken in Lemon Sauce

6 skinned and boned chicken
   breast halves
½ teaspoon salt, divided
¼ teaspoon pepper, divided
¼ cup butter or margarine
2 tablespoons dry vermouth
2 teaspoons grated lemon rind
2 tablespoons fresh lemon
   juice
¾ cup whipping cream
½ cup low-sodium chicken
   broth
½ cup freshly grated
   Parmesan cheese, divided
¼ cup chopped fresh parsley
Garnish: lemon wedges

Place chicken between 2 sheets of heavy-duty plastic wrap, and flatten to ½-inch thickness, using a meat mallet or rolling pin. Sprinkle with ¼ teaspoon salt and ⅛ teaspoon pepper.

Melt butter in a large skillet over medium-high heat. Add chicken; cook 3 to 5 minutes on each side or until golden. Remove chicken from skillet; set aside, and keep warm. Drain skillet.

Add vermouth, lemon rind, and lemon juice to skillet, and cook 1 minute, stirring to loosen particles from bottom of skillet. Stir in whipping cream and chicken broth. Bring to a boil; reduce heat, and simmer, uncovered, 5 to 6 minutes, stirring occasionally. Stir in ¼ cup Parmesan cheese, remaining ¼ teaspoon salt, and remaining ⅛ teaspoon pepper; simmer 1 minute, stirring constantly. Pour sauce over chicken; sprinkle with remaining ¼ cup Parmesan cheese and parsley. Garnish, if desired. Yield: 6 servings.   Patricia Gallucci

Dixon Fixins
Dixon Ambulatory Care Center
Westminster, Maryland

Greek Chicken Phyllo Pie

1 (3¾-pound) whole chicken
11 cups water
2 celery ribs, each cut into 4 pieces
1 large onion, chopped
2 bay leaves
2 teaspoons salt
¼ cup butter
⅓ cup all-purpose flour
3 large eggs, lightly beaten
¼ cup (1 ounce) freshly grated Romano cheese
¼ teaspoon pepper
⅛ teaspoon ground nutmeg
1 (16-ounce) package frozen phyllo pastry, thawed
1¼ cups butter, melted
Garnish: celery leaves

Combine first 6 ingredients in a large Dutch oven. Bring to a boil; cover, reduce heat, and simmer 30 minutes or until chicken is tender. Remove chicken; discard celery and bay leaves. Let chicken cool. Bone chicken, and coarsely chop meat. Set aside 3 cups broth; reserve remaining broth for another use.

Melt ¼ cup butter in a Dutch oven over medium heat. Whisk in flour until smooth. Cook 1 minute, whisking constantly. Gradually whisk in reserved 3 cups broth; cook over medium heat, whisking constantly, until slightly thickened. Gradually stir about one-fourth of hot mixture into eggs; add eggs to remaining hot mixture, stirring constantly. Stir in cheese, pepper, and nutmeg; cook over medium heat, stirring constantly, 3 minutes or until thickened. Set aside.

Place 1 sheet of phyllo in a buttered 13- x 9-inch pan, and brush lightly with melted butter. Layer 14 more sheets of phyllo over first sheet, lightly brushing each sheet with melted butter. Spread half of chicken mixture over phyllo.

Layer 12 more sheets of phyllo over chicken mixture, lightly brushing each sheet of phyllo with melted butter. Spread remaining chicken mixture over phyllo. Layer remaining phyllo over chicken mixture, lightly brushing each sheet with melted butter. Make ¼-inch-deep cuts in top of phyllo with a sharp knife to make 12 squares.

Bake, uncovered, at 375° for 1 hour or until golden. Let stand 10 minutes before serving. Cut into squares. Garnish, if desired. Yield: 12 servings.

Celebrating Heritage: Recipes and Reflections of Jean Richards Roddey
The Jean Richards Roddey Scholarship Committee
Seneca, South Carolina

Chicken Carbonara

Any type of pasta that lists cream and bacon as ingredients is bound to be good. Be sure to serve immediately or the creaminess will be lost.

8 ounces uncooked dried linguine
3 tablespoons vegetable oil
4 skinned and boned chicken breast halves, cut into ½-inch strips
1 large green bell pepper, cut into ½-inch strips
1 cup whipping cream
½ cup freshly grated Romano cheese
½ teaspoon dried thyme
½ teaspoon salt
½ teaspoon pepper
6 bacon slices, cooked and crumbled
2 tablespoons chopped fresh parsley

Cook linguine according to package directions; drain. Set aside, and keep warm.

Heat vegetable oil in a large skillet over medium-high heat. Add chicken, and sauté 3 to 4 minutes on each side or until done. Remove chicken; set aside, and keep warm.

Add bell pepper to skillet; cook 5 minutes or until tender, stirring occasionally. Add whipping cream, cheese, thyme, salt, pepper, and reserved chicken to skillet. Bring to a boil; reduce heat, and simmer, uncovered, 5 minutes or until slightly thickened. Stir in cooked pasta and bacon. Sprinkle with parsley. Serve immediately. Yield: 4 to 6 servings.

Debbi Baldini

Divine Offerings: Recipes and Hints for the Kitchen
St. Charles Presbyterian Women
St. Charles, Missouri

Chicken with Sun-Dried Tomatoes

You can use chicken tenders instead of chicken breasts in this dish richly flavored with dried tomatoes, white wine, and tarragon.

4 skinned and boned chicken breast halves, cut into strips
1½ tablespoons butter or margarine, melted
1 large shallot, minced
1 tablespoon Dijon mustard
1 cup heavy whipping cream

2 tablespoons dry white wine or vermouth
1½ tablespoons dried tarragon
1 (3-ounce) package dried tomatoes, chopped and hydrated

Sauté chicken strips in melted butter in a large skillet over medium-high heat 8 minutes or until lightly browned on both sides. Remove chicken from skillet, and set aside. Add shallot to skillet, and sauté 1 minute. Add mustard and remaining 4 ingredients to skillet. Cook over medium heat until sauce thickens slightly, stirring occasionally. Return chicken to skillet, and simmer until thoroughly heated. Serve with rice or pasta. Yield: 4 servings.

Faithfully Charleston
St. Michael's Episcopal Church
Charleston, South Carolina

Chicken Spaghetti

If you have some extra time on your hands, be sure to try this deliciously spicy cheese and chicken spaghetti. It makes enough for two dishes, perfect to keep one and give away the other to a friend.

12 skinned and boned chicken breast halves (about 4 pounds)
3 quarts water
1 teaspoon salt
16 ounces uncooked dried spaghetti
1 cup butter or margarine
2 (4.5-ounce) jars sliced mushrooms, undrained
1 medium onion, chopped
1 green bell pepper, chopped
4 celery ribs, chopped
2 garlic cloves, minced
1 cup all-purpose flour
1 cup half-and-half
2 (14-ounce) cans chicken broth
2 tablespoons chili powder
1 teaspoon salt
¼ teaspoon ground white pepper
¼ teaspoon ground red pepper
1 tablespoon Worcestershire sauce
3 cups (12 ounces) shredded Cheddar cheese

Place chicken, water, and 1 teaspoon salt in a Dutch oven. Bring to a boil; reduce heat, and simmer, uncovered, 30 minutes or until chicken is done. Remove chicken, reserving broth. Cut chicken into bite-size pieces. Bring broth to a boil. Cook spaghetti in broth according to package directions. Drain and set aside.

Melt butter in a large skillet. Add mushrooms, onion, bell pepper, celery, and garlic. Sauté 7 minutes or until vegetables are tender. Stir in flour. Gradually add half-and-half and canned broth. Cook over medium heat, stirring constantly, until sauce thickens. Stir in chili powder and next 4 ingredients.

Combine sauce, chicken, and spaghetti in a large bowl; mix well. Spoon mixture into a 15- x 10-inch baking dish or 2 (11- x 7-inch) baking dishes. Sprinkle with cheese. Bake at 350° for 30 minutes. Yield: 12 servings.

Secret Ingredients
The Junior League of Alexandria, Louisiana

Enstalada Depollo

This is the Mexican version of a chicken salad sandwich but on a tortilla instead of bread. You can make the mixture ahead and then assemble the sandwiches right before serving.

4 small skinned and boned chicken breast halves
1 (16-ounce) container sour cream
1 (4.5-ounce) can chopped green chiles
1 small onion, chopped
1 teaspoon garlic salt
⅛ teaspoon salt
⅛ teaspoon pepper

10 (8-inch) flour tortillas
1 (16-ounce) can refried beans
½ head iceberg lettuce, chopped (about 3 cups)
2 tomatoes, diced
1 (8-ounce) package shredded sharp Cheddar cheese
1 (4½-ounce) can chopped ripe olives

Cook chicken in water to cover in a large saucepan 15 minutes or until done. Cool chicken, and chop into bite-size pieces. Combine chicken, sour cream, and next 5 ingredients. Cover and chill until ready to assemble.

Warm tortillas according to package directions. Spread each tortilla with refried beans. Spread chicken mixture evenly over beans. Top each tortilla with lettuce, tomato, cheese, and olives. Roll up tortillas. Yield: 10 servings.

Patti Hambright

Sharing Our Best
Hackensack American Legion Auxiliary Unit 202
Hackensack, Minnesota

Tahitian Stir-Fry Chicken

You don't need a wok to assemble this pineapple-studded stir-fry, just a nonstick skillet and maybe some chopsticks for added flair.

1 (20-ounce) can pineapple chunks in syrup
1 cup uncooked basmati rice
⅓ cup low-sodium soy sauce
2 garlic cloves, minced
2 tablespoons cornstarch
2 tablespoons sugar
½ teaspoon black pepper
1 pound skinned and boned chicken breast halves, cut into 1-inch pieces

1½ cups sliced zucchini
2 red bell peppers, cut into ½-inch pieces
1 green bell pepper, cut into ½-inch pieces
1 small onion, sliced vertically

Drain pineapple, reserving syrup. Set pineapple chunks aside.

Cook rice according to package directions, using ⅓ cup pineapple syrup instead of ⅓ cup water; keep rice warm.

Stir together remaining ⅔ cup pineapple syrup, soy sauce, and next 4 ingredients in a small bowl. Set aside.

Coat chicken with cooking spray. Stir-fry chicken in a large nonstick skillet over medium-high heat 3 minutes or until browned. Add zucchini, bell peppers, and onion. Stir-fry 2 minutes or until vegetables are crisp-tender. Add soy sauce mixture to skillet, and stir-fry until sauce thickens. Stir in reserved pineapple chunks. Serve over rice. Yield: 6 servings.

Mary Cohn

Uncommonly Kosher
Yeshiva Parents of Hebrew Theological College
Skokie, Illinois

Penne with Chicken, Havarti, Artichokes, and Italian Tomatoes

1½ cups chopped onion
1 teaspoon minced garlic
6 tablespoons olive oil, divided
3 (28-ounce) cans whole tomatoes, drained
1 (14-ounce) can quartered artichoke hearts, drained
2 teaspoons dried basil
1½ teaspoons dried crushed red pepper
2 cups reduced-sodium chicken broth
½ teaspoon salt
¼ teaspoon black pepper
16 ounces uncooked dried penne pasta
2 cups chopped cooked chicken
2½ cups (10 ounces) shredded Havarti cheese
⅓ cup sliced kalamata olives
⅓ cup grated Parmesan cheese
½ cup finely chopped fresh basil

Sauté onion and garlic in 3 tablespoons hot oil in a large Dutch oven over medium-high heat 5 minutes or until tender. Add tomatoes, artichoke hearts, dried basil, and red pepper; bring to a boil, stirring to break up tomatoes. Add chicken broth, and return to a boil; reduce heat, and simmer, uncovered, 1 hour and 15 minutes or until sauce is thickened and reduced to 6 cups, stirring occasionally. Stir in salt and pepper.

Cook pasta according to package directions; drain.

Combine cooked pasta and remaining 3 tablespoons olive oil in a large bowl. Add tomato sauce, chicken, and Havarti cheese; stir well. Sprinkle with olives, Parmesan cheese, and chopped basil. Yield: 8 servings.

Creating a Stir
The Fayette County Medical Auxiliary
Lexington, Kentucky

Chicken Livers Stroganoff

1 onion, chopped
1 tablespoon vegetable oil
1 (8-ounce) package sliced
   fresh mushrooms
½ pound chicken livers
1 tablespoon all-purpose flour
6 tablespoons chicken broth
¼ cup dry white wine

2 tablespoons ketchup
¼ teaspoon salt
¼ teaspoon pepper
¼ teaspoon ground mace
½ cup sour cream
1 tablespoon chopped fresh
   dill

Sauté onion in hot oil in a large nonstick skillet over medium-high heat 5 minutes or until golden. Add mushrooms, and sauté 3 minutes. Add chicken livers; sauté 6 minutes.

Combine flour and next 6 ingredients, stirring until smooth. Stir flour mixture into liver mixture. Bring to a boil; cover, reduce heat, and simmer 10 minutes or until livers are done. Stir in sour cream and dill. Cook until thoroughly heated. Serve over brown rice, if desired. Yield: 2 servings.

Twice Treasured Recipes
The Bargain Box, Inc.
Hilton Head Island, South Carolina

Orange-Bourbon Turkey

8 oranges
1 (10- to 12-pound) turkey
1 cup water
½ cup bourbon
⅓ cup molasses
2 teaspoons salt
¼ cup bourbon

3 tablespoons all-purpose
flour
1 teaspoon salt
½ teaspoon pepper
Garnishes: orange slices, fresh
parsley sprigs

Cut oranges in half; squeeze juice from oranges (about 2 cups). Reserve rinds.

Remove giblets and neck from turkey, and rinse turkey with cold water; pat dry. Place turkey in a large shallow dish or roasting pan. Combine orange juice, water, ½ cup bourbon, and molasses; pour over turkey. Marinate in refrigerator 8 hours, turning occasionally. Drain body cavity well, reserving marinade.

Sprinkle 1 teaspoon salt over turkey. Sprinkle cavity with 1 teaspoon salt. Place reserved orange rinds in turkey cavity. Tie ends of legs together with string; tuck wing tips up and over back, and tuck under bird. Place turkey, breast side up, on a roasting rack coated with cooking spray.

Bake at 325° for 3 hours or until a meat thermometer inserted in thigh registers 180°. Cover turkey loosely with aluminum foil during the last 45 minutes of baking time, if necessary, to prevent over-browning. Let stand, loosely covered with foil, 10 minutes before carving. Discard orange rinds.

Place reserved marinade in a large saucepan; bring to a boil. Skim off foam. Reduce heat to medium; cook, stirring occasionally, 15 minutes or until liquid is reduced to 3½ cups. Whisk together ¼ cup bourbon and flour; gradually whisk into reserved marinade. Bring to a boil, and boil 1 minute, whisking constantly. Stir in 1 teaspoon salt and pepper.

Arrange turkey on a serving platter. Garnish, if desired. Yield: 15 servings.

Vintage Virginia: A History of Good Taste
The Virginia Dietetic Association
Centreville, Virginia

Golden Turkey Breast

1 (10-ounce) package frozen chopped spinach, thawed
1½ cups thinly sliced fresh shiitake mushrooms
½ cup finely chopped onion
2 tablespoons butter or margarine, melted
½ teaspoon salt
½ teaspoon sage
½ teaspoon dried marjoram
¼ teaspoon ground white pepper
1 cup dry white wine
1 (3-pound) boneless turkey breast half, skinned
¼ teaspoon salt
¼ teaspoon black pepper

Drain spinach in a wire-mesh strainer, using back of a spoon to squeeze out juice. Set spinach aside.

Sauté mushrooms and onion in melted butter in a large skillet 5 minutes. Stir in ½ teaspoon salt and next 3 ingredients. Stir in spinach and wine. Cook, stirring constantly, until wine evaporates. Remove from heat.

Butterfly turkey breast by making a lengthwise cut down center of 1 flat side, cutting to within ½ inch of other side. From bottom of cut, slice horizontally to ½ inch from left side; repeat procedure on right side. Open breast, and spoon ¾ cup spinach mixture lengthwise down center of breast. Tie breast securely with string at 1½-inch intervals. Combine ¼ teaspoon each of salt and black pepper; rub over turkey. Place on a lightly greased rack in a broiler pan. Bake, uncovered, at 325° for 1 hour and 5 minutes or until a meat thermometer inserted in center of breast registers 170°. Let stand 10 minutes before carving.

Heat remaining spinach mixture in skillet; place on a serving platter. Remove string from turkey, and cut into 1-inch-thick slices. Arrange slices over spinach mixture. Yield: 6 to 8 servings.

Café Weller . . . Tastes to Remember
Apple Corps of the Weller Health Education Center
Easton, Pennsylvania

Turkey Meat Loaf with Sun-Dried Tomatoes

Serve this moist and flavorful meat loaf with condiments such as chili sauce, cranberry sauce, or even salsa for variety. Any leftovers make a great sandwich.

1 pound ground turkey (dark and light meat)
12 dried tomatoes in oil, chopped (about ¼ cup)
1 large onion, chopped
1 large egg, lightly beaten
1 cup soft breadcrumbs (homemade) (we tested with Pepperidge Farm Hearty White Bread)

½ cup pine nuts, toasted
¼ cup milk
2 teaspoons chopped fresh rosemary
2 teaspoons chopped fresh oregano
1½ teaspoons salt
½ teaspoon pepper

Combine all ingredients in a large bowl; stir well. Place mixture in a 9- x 5-inch loafpan coated with cooking spray. Bake, uncovered, at 375° for 45 minutes or until a meat thermometer inserted in center registers 165°. Let stand 5 minutes before slicing. Serve with cranberry sauce, if desired. Yield: 4 to 6 servings.

Entirely Entertaining in the Bonnet House Style
Bonnet House Alliance
Ft. Lauderdale, Florida

Blackened Duck

12 ounces uncooked dried
angel hair pasta
2 (0.9-ounce) envelopes
béarnaise sauce mix (we
tested with McCormick)
12 skinned and boned duck
breast halves
⅓ cup butter or margarine,
melted

3 tablespoons Cajun
blackened seasoning
2 (14-ounce) cans quartered
artichoke hearts, drained
2 garlic cloves, chopped
1 (8-ounce) package sliced
fresh mushrooms
1 cup dry white wine

Cook pasta according to package directions; keep warm.

Prepare béarnaise sauce according to package directions; set aside, and keep warm.

Place a large cast-iron skillet over medium-high heat 10 minutes or until very hot. Brush duck with melted butter; sprinkle with seasoning. Place duck in hot skillet; cook 4 minutes on each side or until a meat thermometer registers 180°.

Combine artichoke hearts and remaining 3 ingredients in a large saucepan; cook over medium-high heat 4 minutes, stirring often.

Divide pasta among serving plates. Slice each duck breast into thin strips; arrange over pasta. Spoon artichoke mixture over duck; pour béarnaise sauce evenly over artichoke mixture. Yield: 6 servings.

Meet Me at the Garden Gate
The Junior League of Spartanburg, Inc.
Spartanburg, South Carolina

Salads

Fruit and Yogurt Layered Salad, page 264

Spiced Cranberry Ring

2 (3-ounce) packages
  raspberry-flavored gelatin
1½ cups boiling water
¼ teaspoon salt
¼ teaspoon ground
  cinnamon
Dash of ground cloves

1 (16-ounce) can whole-berry
  cranberry sauce
2 tablespoons grated orange
  rind
1 cup diced orange sections
1 cup chopped apple
½ cup chopped walnuts

Combine gelatin, boiling water, salt, cinnamon, and cloves in a large bowl; stir 2 minutes or until gelatin dissolves. Stir in cranberry sauce and orange rind. Chill 1½ hours or until consistency of unbeaten egg white.

Gently fold orange sections, apple, and walnuts into chilled gelatin mixture. Spoon mixture into a lightly greased 6-cup mold. Cover and chill at least 8 hours. Unmold onto a serving plate. Yield: 8 to 10 servings.

Maureen Jones

Sharing Recipes from Green Road Baptist Church
Green Road Baptist Church
Green Road, Kentucky

Fruit and Yogurt Layered Salad

Only the freshest fruit will do for this low-fat salad that looks best served in a trifle bowl so the layers are visible.

1 (8-ounce) container
  strawberry low-fat yogurt
¼ cup light cream cheese,
  softened
1 tablespoon sugar
2 teaspoons lemon juice
¼ teaspoon almond extract
1 (8-ounce) container frozen
  reduced-calorie whipped
  topping, thawed
2 cups diced red apple (we
  tested with Braeburn)

1 (15-ounce) can mandarin
  oranges, drained
3 ripe peaches, peeled and
  sliced
2 cups seedless green grapes
1 cup diced pear
2 cups sliced fresh strawberries
1 kiwifruit, peeled, halved,
  and sliced
3 whole fresh strawberries
1 cup fresh blueberries

Combine first 5 ingredients in a large bowl; beat at medium speed with an electric mixer until smooth. Add whipped topping; beat until thick and smooth.

Place apple in a 3-quart trifle bowl or deep glass bowl. Layer oranges, one-third of yogurt mixture, peaches, grapes, one-third of yogurt mixture, pear, sliced strawberries, and remaining yogurt mixture. Arrange kiwifruit around top edge of bowl. Cut 3 strawberries into fourths; arrange on top. Fill in remaining space with blueberries. Chill until ready to serve. Yield: about 12 servings.   Carol Fulton

Glen Haven Community Cookbook 1999
Glen Haven Area Volunteer Fire Department
Glen Haven, Colorado

Pear and Endive Salad

Belgian endive is a small cigar-shaped head of cream-colored, tightly packed, slightly bitter leaves. Here, it gets dressed up with toasted walnuts, ham, pears, and Gorgonzola cheese for an outstanding flavor combination.

2 **tablespoons Dijon mustard**
2 **tablespoons red wine vinegar**
¼ **cup vegetable oil**
⅛ **teaspoon salt**
⅛ **teaspoon pepper**
2 **Belgian endive, thinly sliced**
1 **(10-ounce) package fresh spinach, torn**

2 **pears, peeled, cored and cut into small pieces**
4 **ounces prosciutto or ham, cut into julienne strip**
½ **cup chopped walnuts, toasted**
2 **ounces Gorgonzola cheese, crumbled**

Whisk together first 5 ingredients in a small bowl; set aside.

Combine endive and remaining 5 ingredients in a salad bowl; toss well. Pour dressing over endive mixture, and toss gently. Serve immediately. Yield: 8 to 10 servings.

Cooking with Music: Celebrating the Tastes and Traditions of the Boston Symphony Orchestra
Boston Symphony Association of Volunteers
Boston, Massachusetts

Arugula Salad with Pears and Beets

The peppery taste of arugula is offset by the sweetness of pears and the tang of blue cheese in this refreshing twist on the basic dinner salad.

4 small beets
4½ tablespoons olive oil
3 tablespoons raspberry
   vinegar
¼ teaspoon salt
¼ teaspoon pepper

3 cups firmly packed arugula,
   trimmed
2 firm, ripe pears, sliced
½ cup crumbled blue cheese
¼ cup walnuts, chopped and
   toasted

Leave roots and 1 inch of stem on beets; discard greens. Scrub beets with a vegetable brush. Place in a 2-quart baking dish. Cover with water 1 inch above beets. Cover and bake at 400° for 40 minutes or until tender. Cool completely. Trim off roots and stems; peel off skins. Cut beets into wedges; set aside.

Whisk together olive oil, raspberry vinegar, salt, and pepper until smooth. Place arugula in a bowl, and drizzle with 2 tablespoons vinaigrette; toss to coat. Place arugula evenly on 4 salad plates.

Toss pear slices and beets with 2 tablespoons vinaigrette in a bowl; arrange over arugula. Sprinkle evenly with cheese and walnuts. Drizzle remaining vinaigrette over salads. Yield: 4 servings.

First Impressions: Dining with Distinction
The Junior League of Waterloo-Cedar Falls
Waterloo, Iowa

Spinach-Fruit Salad

If you aren't serving a large crowd, this recipe can easily be cut in half. If you use baby spinach, which is more tender and doesn't require removing the tough stems, prep time's a snap!

1 large cantaloupe
4 (7-ounce) packages baby spinach or 3 (10-ounce) packages spinach
1 cup thinly sliced red onion
1 cup seedless green grapes, halved
6 tablespoons sugar
3 tablespoons grated orange rind

2 tablespoons chopped red onion
¼ cup balsamic vinegar
¼ cup orange juice
¼ teaspoon pepper
½ cup vegetable oil
2 teaspoons poppy seeds

Cut cantaloupe into 1-inch pieces, and place in a large bowl. Add spinach, 1 cup onion, and grapes; cover and chill.

Process sugar and next 5 ingredients in a food processor until smooth. With processor running, gradually add oil through food chute; stir in poppy seeds. Cover and chill. Toss dressing with salad just before serving. Yield: 15 servings.

Diann Anderson

Cookin' with Pride
4th Infantry Division
Ft. Hood, Texas

Grilled Eggplant on Wilted Greens

Add even more grilled goodness to this salad by adding the red onion to the grill alongside the eggplant.

1 (1-pound) eggplant, peeled
1 tablespoon olive oil
½ teaspoon salt
½ teaspoon pepper
3 cups loosely packed
    gourmet mixed baby salad
    greens
1 small red onion, thinly
    sliced
1 teaspoon lemon juice
2 tablespoons extra-virgin
    olive oil
1 tablespoon reduced-sodium
    soy sauce
1 tablespoon seasoned rice
    vinegar

Cut eggplant crosswise into ½-inch-thick slices. Rub both sides of eggplant with 1 tablespoon olive oil; sprinkle with salt and pepper. Let stand 10 minutes. Coat food rack with cooking spray; place on grill over medium-high heat (350° to 400°). Place eggplant on rack, and grill 5 minutes on each side.

Place greens evenly on 6 salad plates. Top with eggplant and onion slices; drizzle with lemon juice.

Whisk together 2 tablespoons olive oil, soy sauce, and vinegar in a small bowl. Drizzle over salads; serve immediately. Yield: 6 servings.

Note: The younger the eggplant, the more tender the skin. If you buy a young eggplant, it's not necessary to peel the skin.

Sounds Delicious: The Flavor of Atlanta in Food & Music
Atlanta Symphony Orchestra
Atlanta, Georgia

Herb and Roasted Pepper Salad

Great over mixed greens or used as a condiment on sandwiches, this versatile mix abounds with textures and color, and can even be eaten alone.

2 large red bell peppers
2 large green bell peppers
2 large yellow bell peppers
1 (2¼-ounce) can sliced ripe olives
2 garlic cloves, minced
3 tablespoons olive oil
2 tablespoons balsamic vinegar
2 tablespoons sliced green onions

2 tablespoons capers
2 tablespoons chopped fresh basil
1 tablespoon chopped fresh oregano
¼ teaspoon pepper
¼ cup crumbled feta cheese
Lettuce leaves

Cut peppers in half lengthwise; discard seeds and membranes. Place peppers, skin side up, on a baking sheet; flatten with palm of hand. Broil peppers 3 inches from heat 20 minutes or until charred. Place peppers in a heavy-duty zip-top plastic bag; seal and let stand 15 minutes to loosen skins.

Peel peppers, and discard skins. Cut peppers into strips; place in a medium bowl or large heavy-duty zip-top plastic bag. Add olives and next 8 ingredients. Seal bag; marinate in refrigerator 8 hours. Add cheese, tossing gently. To serve, spoon pepper mixture onto lettuce leaves. Yield: 6 servings.   Dorothy Pero

Moon River Collection
The Landings Landlovers
Savannah, Georgia

Marinated Tomatoes, Cucumbers, and Feta Cheese

For authentic Italian flavor, use good quality olive oil and vinegar in this fresh vegetable salad.

½ cup olive oil
3 tablespoons red wine vinegar
3 to 4 fresh basil leaves, chopped
1 garlic clove, minced
1 teaspoon chopped fresh oregano
½ teaspoon salt
¼ teaspoon pepper
¼ teaspoon prepared mustard

4 tomatoes, sliced
1 red onion, sliced and separated into rings
1 cucumber, sliced
½ cup kalamata olives, pitted
½ cup crumbled feta cheese
2 tablespoons chopped fresh parsley

Combine first 8 ingredients in a jar; cover tightly, and shake vigorously. Alternate tomato, onion, and cucumber slices on a platter. Pour dressing over salad; top with olives. Cover and marinate in refrigerator 3 hours. Sprinkle with feta cheese and parsley just before serving. Yield: 6 to 8 servings.

Cooks of the Green Door
The League of Catholic Women
Minneapolis, Minnesota

Bacon Blue Salad

The leftover dressing is excellent on grilled or baked chicken.

½ cup freshly grated Parmesan cheese
6 tablespoons olive oil
6 tablespoons vegetable oil
¼ cup fresh lemon juice
3 garlic cloves, minced
1 teaspoon Worcestershire sauce

1 large head Romaine lettuce, torn (about 7 cups)
6 bacon slices, cooked and crumbled
1 (4-ounce) package crumbled blue cheese

Process first 6 ingredients in a blender or food processor until smooth.

Arrange lettuce in a large salad bowl; toss with desired amount of dressing. Cover and chill any remaining dressing for another use. Sprinkle salad with bacon and blue cheese. Serve immediately. Yield: 6 to 8 servings.

Thyme to Entertain: Good Food and Southern Hospitality
The Charity League, Inc., of Paducah, Kentucky

Crunchy Vegetable Salad

A picnic just wouldn't be complete without this veggie salad in a creamy sweet dressing. Be sure to serve it with a slotted spoon.

1 **small cauliflower, cut into florets**	⅓ **cup chopped celery**
1 **large bunch broccoli, cut into florets**	⅔ **cup mayonnaise**
	⅓ **cup vegetable oil**
2 **small zucchini**	⅓ **cup sugar**
3 **carrots, thinly sliced**	3 **tablespoons white vinegar**
1 **onion, finely chopped**	1 **teaspoon salt**
	Crumbled cooked bacon

Combine cauliflower and broccoli in a large bowl. Cut zucchini in half lengthwise, cut each half crosswise into thin slices. Add zucchini to broccoli mixture. Add carrot, onion, and celery; toss well.

Combine mayonnaise and next 4 ingredients in a small bowl. Add mayonnaise mixture to vegetables; toss well to coat. Cover and chill at least 8 hours.

Sprinkle with bacon just before serving. Serve with a slotted spoon. Yield: 10 to 12 servings.

The Bounty of Chester County: Heritage Edition
Chester County Agricultural Development Council
West Chester, Pennsylvania

Crunchy Gorgonzola Cheese Salad with Hazelnut Vinaigrette Dressing

If hazelnut oil isn't on your shelf, don't despair; substitute olive oil.

1 (10-ounce) package mixed salad greens
6 ounces Gorgonzola cheese, crumbled
2 cups pecan halves
2 tablespoons butter
1 tablespoon sugar
½ teaspoon salt
½ teaspoon pepper
¼ teaspoon ground red pepper

¼ cup orange juice
2 tablespoons red wine vinegar
2 teaspoons grated orange rind
2 teaspoons honey
1 teaspoon Dijon mustard
¼ cup hazelnut oil
¼ cup extra-virgin olive oil

Combine greens and cheese in a large bowl; set aside.

Combine pecans and next 5 ingredients; sauté in a large skillet 4 minutes or until toasted. Spread mixture evenly on a baking sheet or parchment paper; cool.

Whisk together orange juice and next 4 ingredients until blended. Gradually whisk in oils. Add pecans and desired amount of dressing to salad; toss well. Yield: 6 to 8 servings.   Lynette Earley

Our Daily Bread
First Presbyterian Church of Orlando—Weekday School
Orlando, Florida

"Hot" Spinach Salad with Goat Cheese

The warm mushroom mixture helps to melt the goat cheese so it's extra creamy with each bite.

1 (6-ounce) package sliced portobello mushrooms, cut in half
½ medium onion, thinly sliced
¼ cup olive oil
¾ cup pitted kalamata olives
6 cherry tomatoes, halved

¼ cup balsamic vinegar
1 (7-ounce) package baby spinach
¼ cup crumbled goat cheese
¼ teaspoon salt
⅛ teaspoon pepper

Sauté mushrooms and onion in hot oil over medium-high heat 3 minutes or until tender. Reduce heat to low; add olives, tomatoes, and vinegar; cook 10 minutes, stirring occasionally. Toss spinach with mushroom mixture in a large bowl.

Place salad on a serving platter; top with goat cheese, and sprinkle with salt and pepper. Serve immediately. Yield: 4 servings.

Faithfully Charleston
St. Michael's Episcopal Church
Charleston, South Carolina

Margarita Coleslaw

1 (10-ounce) can frozen margarita mix, thawed and undiluted
¼ cup white vinegar
¼ cup vegetable oil
2 tablespoons honey
1 teaspoon celery seeds

9 cups shredded green cabbage
3 cups shredded red cabbage
2 large Granny Smith apples, peeled and chopped
1 cup sweetened dried cranberries

Whisk together first 5 ingredients in a medium bowl. Cover and chill.

Combine green cabbage and remaining 3 ingredients. Add desired amount of dressing to coleslaw, and toss gently to coat. Serve immediately. Yield: 8 to 10 servings.

A Taste of Enchantment
The Junior League of Albuquerque, New Mexico

Blue Ridge Black Bean Salad

Need a good make-ahead dish for your next summer party? Then try this colorful salad dressed with a lime vinaigrette. It's perfect with grilled chicken or pork chops.

3 (15-ounce) cans black beans, rinsed and drained
2 (14.5-ounce) cans diced tomatoes, undrained
1 (11-ounce) can white shoepeg corn, drained
2 cups cooked brown rice

1 red bell pepper, chopped
1 green bell pepper, chopped
1 yellow bell pepper, chopped
1 small red onion, chopped
½ cup chopped fresh cilantro
Lime Vinaigrette

Combine first 9 ingredients in a large bowl; add Lime Vinaigrette, and toss gently. Cover salad, and chill at least 8 hours. Yield: 10 to 12 servings.

Lime Vinaigrette

2 tablespoons fresh lime juice
2 tablespoons balsamic vinegar
2 tablespoons olive oil
2 teaspoons ground cumin

¼ teaspoon dried crushed red pepper
⅛ teaspoon salt
⅛ teaspoon pepper

Whisk together all ingredients until smooth. Yield: about ⅓ cup.

Oh My Stars! Recipes That Shine
The Junior League of Roanoke Valley, Virginia

Black-Eyed Pea Salad

Serve this bacon- and pepper-studded salad on New Year's Day for good luck and great taste.

⅔ cup extra-virgin olive oil
⅓ cup white wine vinegar
1 garlic clove, crushed
½ teaspoon salt
½ teaspoon Dijon mustard
¼ teaspoon pepper
1 large tomato, seeded and chopped
1 green bell pepper, chopped
1 yellow bell pepper, chopped
6 fresh mushrooms, chopped
2 (16-ounce) cans black-eyed peas, rinsed and drained

1 (4-ounce) jar diced pimiento, drained
3 tablespoons chopped fresh cilantro
2 garlic cloves, minced
Lettuce leaves
Red cabbage leaves
2 tablespoons cooked and crumbled bacon
⅓ cup chopped green onions

Whisk together first 6 ingredients until blended; set aside.

Combine tomato, bell peppers, and mushrooms in a large bowl. Stir in peas, pimiento, cilantro, and garlic. Add vinaigrette, and toss gently to coat. Cover and chill at least 8 hours.

Line a serving platter with lettuce and cabbage leaves. Spoon salad onto leaves, using a slotted spoon. Sprinkle with bacon and green onions. Yield: 8 to 10 servings.

Art Fare: A Commemorative Celebration of Art & Food
The Toledo Museum of Art Aides
Toledo, Ohio

Mediterranean Couscous Salad

1 (14-ounce) can vegetable
  broth
1 cup uncooked couscous
1 (15-ounce) can chickpeas,
  drained
1 cup sliced green onions
½ cup dried cranberries,
  raisins, or chopped dried
  apricots
¼ cup chopped fresh parsley
1 tablespoon grated orange
  rind
¼ cup fresh orange juice
1 tablespoon vegetable oil
¼ cup crumbled feta cheese

Bring broth to a boil in a medium saucepan over medium-high heat. Stir in couscous, and remove from heat. Cover and let stand 5 minutes. Transfer couscous to a bowl, and fluff with a fork. Add chickpeas and next 3 ingredients; toss gently.

Whisk together orange rind, juice, and oil in a bowl. Add dressing to salad, and toss well. Sprinkle with feta cheese just before serving. Serve immediately. Yield: 4 servings.

Vintage Virginia: A History of Good Taste
The Virginia Dietetic Association
Centreville, Virginia

Marinated Antipasto Salad

The Italian flavors of antipasto are blended in a tasty salad that gets better the longer it marinates.

1 pound medium pasta shells,
  cooked, rinsed, and drained
12 ounces provolone cheese,
  diced
8 ounces hard salami, sliced
1 (6-ounce) can pitted ripe
  olives, drained and sliced
4 ounces sliced pepperoni
3 small tomatoes, cut into
  wedges
2 green bell peppers, cut into
  strips
2 celery ribs, sliced
¾ cup vegetable oil
½ cup red wine vinegar
3 tablespoons fresh oregano
  or 1 tablespoon dried
  oregano
1 tablespoon salt
1 teaspoon pepper

Combine first 8 ingredients in a large bowl.

Whisk together oil and remaining 4 ingredients in a small bowl. Pour over pasta mixture; toss to coat evenly. Cover and chill 8 to 10 hours, stirring occasionally. Yield: 12 to 15 servings.

Everything But the Entrée
The Junior League of Parkersburg, West Virginia

Italian Pasta Salad

Take advantage of summer's bounty of vegetables with this fresh pasta salad. Use different pasta shapes to shake up things a bit.

16 ounces uncooked dried rotini
4 garlic cloves, minced
1 (6-ounce) can chopped ripe olives
1 medium-size green bell pepper, chopped
1 medium tomato, chopped
1 small zucchini, chopped
2 cups broccoli florets
1½ cups finely chopped red onion
¾ cup freshly grated Parmesan cheese
1⅓ cups extra-virgin olive oil
⅔ cup red wine vinegar
2 teaspoons dry mustard
1½ teaspoons salt
½ teaspoon pepper

Cook pasta according to package directions; drain. Rinse with cold water, and drain again.

Combine pasta, garlic, and next 7 ingredients in a large bowl. Whisk together olive oil and remaining 4 ingredients in a small bowl until blended.

Pour 1½ cups dressing over pasta mixture; toss gently. Cover and chill at least 2 hours. Pour remaining dressing over pasta mixture before serving; toss gently. Yield: 12 servings.

America Celebrates Columbus
The Junior League of Columbus, Ohio

Greek Pasta Salad with Shrimp and Olives

For a perfect picnic, pack up this salad with some bread and wine.

12 ounces uncooked dried
    linguine
1 large tomato, chopped
1 large red bell pepper,
    seeded and chopped
4 green onions, chopped
3 large garlic cloves, chopped
4 ounces feta cheese, crumbled
½ cup chopped ripe olives

½ cup olive oil
¼ cup fresh lemon juice
2 tablespoons dry white wine
1 tablespoon dried thyme
¾ pound peeled, cooked
    shrimp
1 teaspoon salt
½ teaspoon pepper

Cook linguine according to package directions; drain. Rinse with cold water, and drain again.

Meanwhile, combine tomato and next 9 ingredients in a large bowl. Add linguine, shrimp, salt, and pepper. Toss gently. Yield: 5 servings.

Carolina Thyme
The Junior League of Durham and Orange Counties, Inc.
Durham, North Carolina

Asparagus Chicken Salad

Asparagus and bacon are surprise additions to this chunky chicken salad dressed with a mayonnaise and cottage cheese dressing. Serve on lettuce leaves for an elegant presentation.

¾ pound thin fresh
    asparagus
4 bacon slices
½ cup cottage cheese
½ cup mayonnaise
1 garlic clove, minced
2 teaspoons lemon juice

1 teaspoon salt
¼ teaspoon pepper
4 green onions, thinly sliced
¼ cup chopped fresh parsley
1 teaspoon chopped fresh dill
2 cups cubed cooked chicken
    breast

Snap off tough ends of asparagus; cut asparagus into ½-inch pieces. Arrange asparagus in a steamer basket over boiling water. Cover and steam 4 minutes or until crisp-tender. Plunge asparagus into ice water to stop the cooking process; drain and chill.

Cook bacon in a large skillet until crisp; remove bacon, and drain on paper towels. Crumble bacon, and set aside.

Whisk together cottage cheese and next 5 ingredients in a small bowl until smooth. Toss with asparagus, green onions, parsley, dill, and chicken. Cover and chill 2 hours. Toss crumbled bacon with salad just before serving. Yield: 6 servings.

A Taste Tour
Gingko Twig of Muhlenberg Hospital, Plainfield, New Jersey
Westfield, New Jersey

Chicken Salad Carlotta

Studded with four types of fruit, this chunky chicken salad gets an exotic flavor boost from mango chutney and curry. And it's lower in fat than traditional mayonnaise-based chicken salad.

4 skinned and boned chicken breast halves	2 tablespoons low-fat sour cream
1 cup chicken broth	2½ teaspoons curry powder
1 mango, peeled, seeded, and cut into ½-inch cubes	½ teaspoon salt
2 cups seedless green grapes	1 cup coarsely chopped fresh pineapple
½ cup golden raisins	1 cup mandarin oranges
¾ cup plain low-fat yogurt	1 cup chopped almonds
¼ cup minced fresh Italian parsley	Mixed salad greens
¼ cup mango chutney	1 cup flaked coconut

Place chicken in a 9-inch square pan, and cover with broth. Bake at 350° for 25 minutes or until chicken is done. Remove chicken, and cool; discard broth. Shred chicken into bite-size pieces, and place in a large bowl. Stir in mango, grapes, and raisins.

Combine yogurt and next 5 ingredients in a small bowl. Stir into chicken mixture. Cover and chill at least 3 hours. Stir in pineapple, oranges, and almonds just before serving. Serve on a bed of mixed salad greens, and sprinkle with coconut. Yield: 6 servings.

Twice Treasured Recipes
The Bargain Box, Inc.
Hilton Head Island, South Carolina

Linguine and Smoked Turkey Salad

For added convenience, look for cans of chopped baby corn in the Asian section of the grocery store, and use whatever pasta you have on hand.

16 ounces uncooked dried linguine

1 pound smoked turkey, diced (about 3 cups)

1 (10-ounce) package frozen sweet peas, thawed and drained

1 (14-ounce) can baby corn pieces, drained

1 red bell pepper, finely chopped

¼ cup vegetable oil

¼ cup soy sauce

⅓ cup sesame seeds

½ teaspoon salt

¼ teaspoon pepper

Cook linguine according to package directions; drain. Rinse with cold water, and drain again.

Combine linguine, turkey, and next 3 ingredients in a large bowl. Combine oil and remaining 4 ingredients in a small bowl. Pour over linguine mixture; toss well. Cover and chill until ready to serve. Yield: 8 to 10 servings. Linda Neiman

Uncommonly Kosher
Yeshiva Parents of Hebrew Theological College
Skokie, Illinois

Gorgonzola Salad Dressing

Reading this recipe, you might expect a creamy creation, but you'll discover a dressing with a vinaigrette consistency instead.

⅓ cup white vinegar
3 tablespoons mayonnaise
1 large garlic clove, pressed
1 teaspoon salt
½ teaspoon freshly ground
  pepper

½ teaspoon dry mustard
1 cup vegetable oil
3 ounces Gorgonzola or blue
  cheese

Whisk together first 6 ingredients in a small bowl. Slowly whisk in oil. Add cheese, breaking cheese apart while stirring. Stir well just before serving. Yield: 1½ cups.   Gerri Walker

V.C.O.S. Sharing Our Best
Volusia County Orchid Society, Inc.
DeLand, Florida

Minted Orange Salad Dressing

Yogurt and honey temper the tang of the orange and lemon juices in this dressing for fruit salad. And the mint adds a cool, refreshing zing.

3 tablespoons orange juice
2 tablespoons honey
1 tablespoon lemon juice

1 tablespoon minced fresh
  mint
1 cup plain yogurt

Whisk together first 4 ingredients in a bowl. Add yogurt; whisk until well blended. Cover and chill. Yield: 1½ cups.

A Taste of Enchantment
The Junior League of Albuquerque, New Mexico

Raspberry Vinaigrette

A handful of succulent raspberries and a splash of walnut oil are sweetened with a bit of honey and apple juice to create this fruity concoction.

½ cup fresh raspberries
1½ teaspoons walnut oil
¼ cup apple juice

2 tablespoons red wine vinegar
1 teaspoon honey

Mash raspberries in a medium bowl with a potato masher. Add oil and remaining ingredients; whisk until blended. Pour mixture through a wire-mesh strainer into a bowl, discarding seeds. Cover and chill. Yield: ⅔ cup.   Charlene Shumaker

The Western New York Federal Court Centennial Cookbook
U.S. District Court, Western District of New York
Buffalo, New York

Sherry Vinaigrette

Make sure to whisk this dressing right before serving because it tends to settle.

1 cup olive oil
½ cup balsamic vinegar
⅓ cup sugar
2 tablespoons dry sherry
1 garlic clove, minced

1 teaspoon freshly ground pepper
1 teaspoon dried Italian seasoning

Whisk together all ingredients in a small bowl. Yield: 1¾ cups.

Faithfully Charleston
St. Michael's Episcopal Church
Charleston, South Carolina

Sauces & Condiments

Scrumptious Sausage Spaghetti Sauce, page 285

Lemon Crema for Fruit (Krema Lemonion)

Served warm, this sauce is a lemony custard; when served cold, it resembles yogurt. Either way, it's perfect with sliced fruit.

¾ cup sugar
2 teaspoons cornstarch
1 cup evaporated milk
½ cup water

2 egg yolks, lightly beaten
1 teaspoon grated lemon rind
2 tablespoons fresh lemon juice

Combine sugar and cornstarch in a heavy medium-size saucepan. Gradually whisk in milk, water, and egg yolks with a wire whisk until blended; cook, whisking constantly, over medium-low heat 10 minutes. Bring to a boil; boil 7 minutes or until mixture thickens. Remove from heat, and cool slightly.

Stir in lemon rind and lemon juice. Serve sauce warm or chilled over fresh fruit. Yield: 1¾ cups.   Petroula Koukoumanos

Flavor It Greek! A Celebration of Food, Faith and Family
Philoptochos Society of Holy Trinity Greek Orthodox Church
Portland, Oregon

Mississippi Mud Sauce

¾ cup sugar
⅓ cup unsweetened cocoa
⅔ cup evaporated milk

¼ cup extracrunchy peanut butter

Stir together sugar and cocoa in a small saucepan; stir in evaporated milk. Bring to a boil over medium-high heat. Remove from heat, and stir in peanut butter. Serve warm over ice cream or pound cake. Yield: 1 cup.   JoAnn Hunter

Future Generations
Robertson County Family and Community Education Clubs
Springfield, Tennessee

Scrumptious Sausage Spaghetti Sauce

"Scrumptious" doesn't even begin to describe this delicious, versatile two-meat sauce with red wine and Italian seasonings. We found that it's even better the next day. Try it on pizza or in calzones, too.

8 ounces hot Italian sausage
8 ounces sweet Italian sausage
2 cups chopped onion
1½ cups diced celery
1 garlic clove, minced
2 (10¾-ounce) cans tomato
   puree
1 (14½-ounce) can Italian-style
   diced tomatoes, undrained
1 cup dry red wine
1 bay leaf

1 tablespoon chopped fresh
   parsley
1 tablespoon chopped fresh
   oregano
2 teaspoons salt
1 teaspoon sugar
¼ teaspoon ground cumin
¼ teaspoon ground red
   pepper
Hot cooked spaghetti

Remove and discard casings from sausage. Cook sausage in a Dutch oven over medium-high heat, stirring until it crumbles and is no longer pink. Remove sausage, reserving drippings in pan, and set sausage aside.

Add onion, celery, and garlic to drippings in pan; sauté 4 minutes or until tender, stirring occasionally.

Add sausage, tomato puree, and next 9 ingredients. Bring to a boil. Cover, reduce heat, and simmer 1 hour, stirring occasionally. Cool in pan 15 minutes. Pour sauce into a large bowl. Cover and chill 8 hours.

To serve, place spaghetti sauce in a large saucepan. Bring to a boil. Cover, reduce heat, and simmer 20 minutes or until thoroughly heated. Discard bay leaf. Serve over spaghetti. Yield: 6 cups.

Oh My Stars! Recipes That Shine
The Junior League of Roanoke Valley, Virginia

Lemon Cocktail Sauce

Not your traditional red cocktail sauce, this one zings with lemon juice and mustard.

6 tablespoons mayonnaise
2 tablespoons lemon juice
1 tablespoon prepared
  horseradish sauce

1 tablespoon minced onion
1 teaspoon prepared mustard

Combine all ingredients, stirring well. Cover and chill at least 30 minutes. Yield: ½ cup.

Note: This quick and simple sauce is great served with seafood and versatile enough to accompany asparagus, artichokes, or broccoli.

Twice Treasured Recipes
The Bargain Box, Inc.
Hilton Head Island, South Carolina

East Coast Tartar Sauce

If you're looking for a way to jazz up those weeknight fish sticks, this flavor-packed sauce will do the trick.

1 cup mayonnaise
2 tablespoons lemon juice
1 teaspoon Worcestershire
  sauce
Dash of hot sauce
¼ cup finely chopped dill
  pickle

¼ cup finely chopped fresh
  Italian parsley
2 tablespoons minced shallots
2 tablespoons capers
⅛ teaspoon salt
⅛ teaspoon pepper

Stir together first 4 ingredients in a medium bowl. Add dill pickle and remaining ingredients; stir gently. Cover and chill at least 1 hour. Yield: 1½ cups.

Sweet Pickin's
The Junior League of Fayetteville, North Carolina

Horseradish Sauce

No more tears! This is an easy sauce to whip together because it calls for prepared horseradish rather than tear-inducing grated fresh horseradish. It's great served with roast beef.

¼ cup prepared horseradish, drained
1 tablespoon white vinegar
¾ teaspoon salt

¼ teaspoon pepper
½ cup heavy whipping cream, whipped

Combine first 4 ingredients in a medium bowl. Gently fold in whipped cream. Yield: 1¼ cups. Rosemary Nebergall

Jubilee 2000 Recipe Collection
St. Alphonsus Liguori Parish—Hospitality Committee
Prospect Heights, Illinois

Lewis' Secret Sauce

We don't know who Lewis is, but we sure do love his sauce! Enjoy it as an accompaniment with cold shrimp, a topping on burgers, or as a dip for French fries and chicken fingers. Any way you eat it, it's delicious!

¼ cup dill pickle juice
¼ cup ketchup
¼ cup prepared mustard
2 tablespoons Ranch-style dressing

1 cup mayonnaise
⅛ teaspoon pepper

Pour pickle juice into a medium bowl. Whisk in ketchup and remaining ingredients until blended. Cover and chill. Yield: about 2 cups. Lewis Sloan, Jr.

Plate & Palette: A Collection of Fine Art and Food
Beaufort County Arts Council
Washington, North Carolina

Mike's Beer Batter

Since this batter is so thick, it's great for coating onion rings or other delicacies such as cheese or vegetables before frying.

2 large eggs	½ teaspoon salt
1 cup all-purpose baking mix	½ teaspoon dried thyme
½ cup beer	

Combine all ingredients in a bowl. Yield: 1 cup.   Kelli Dean

Cookin' with Pride
4th Infantry Division
Ft. Hood, Texas

Spicy Grilling Rub

A little goes a long way with this sweet and spicy rub; it's perfect on grilled shrimp and ribs, or even better, a fried turkey.

2 tablespoons light brown sugar	1½ teaspoons salt
2 tablespoons chili powder	1½ teaspoons ground white pepper
2 tablespoons ground black pepper	1½ teaspoons dried crushed red pepper
1 tablespoon paprika	1 teaspoon garlic powder

Combine all ingredients in a small bowl. Rub on chicken or pork before grilling. Yield: ⅔ cup.   Bill and Susan Fender

Note: Store in an airtight container in the refrigerator.

V.C.O.S. Sharing Our Best
Volusia County Orchid Society, Inc.
DeLand, Florida

Olive Salsa

Olives add a bit of saltiness to this twist on traditional salsa; serve with corn or tortilla chips for a fabulous appetizer.

1 (6-ounce) can ripe olives, chopped
¼ cup chopped green onions
¼ cup minced garlic
2 tomatoes, diced
2 (4.5-ounce) cans chopped green chiles, drained

¼ cup sweet onion, diced
¼ cup diced red bell pepper
¼ cup chopped fresh cilantro
1 tablespoon olive oil
2 teaspoons balsamic vinegar

Combine first 8 ingredients; stir in olive oil and vinegar. Cover and chill at least 6 hours. Serve at room temperature. Yield: 4½ cups.

Past and Present Meatless Treasures
Kaneohe Seventh-day Adventist Church
Kaneohe, Hawaii

Tomatillo Salsa

Serve this tart green salsa with chiles rellenos, egg dishes, fish, or chicken for a change from traditional red salsa.

8 fresh tomatillos, husks removed
2 jalapeño peppers, seeded and minced
3 tablespoons chopped fresh cilantro

2 tablespoons fresh lime juice
1 garlic clove, minced
½ teaspoon salt

Coarsely chop tomatillos. Combine tomatillos, jalapeño peppers, and remaining ingredients. Cover and chill at least 8 hours. Yield: 1½ cups.
Michael Anderson

Sharing Our Best
The Arrangement Hair Salon
Columbus, Ohio

Cranberry-Apricot Relish

The tangy flavor of cranberries and the sweetness of apricots provide the perfect balance of flavors in this relish that can be served with ham slices or over cream cheese for a delectable appetizer.

1 (12-ounce) package fresh
  cranberries (about 3 cups)
2 cups chopped dried apricots
1 cup golden raisins
1 cup sugar
1¾ cups water
½ teaspoon grated orange
  rind
¼ teaspoon ground ginger

Combine all ingredients in a 4-quart heavy saucepan. Bring to a boil. Cover, reduce heat, and simmer 20 minutes or until cranberries pop. Remove from heat; cool completely. Store in an airtight container in refrigerator up to 1 month. Yield: 3½ cups.   Lori Maldavir

Look What's Cooking . . .
Temple Sinai Sisterhood
Cranston, Rhode Island

Papaya-Tomato Relish

Add a little pizzazz to fish or grilled chicken with this colorful relish.

1 papaya, peeled, seeded, and
  diced
⅓ cup diced tomato
¼ cup chopped fresh parsley
¼ cup chopped fresh chives
¼ cup chopped sweet
  gherkins
¼ cup diced red bell pepper
3 tablespoons capers
¼ cup rice wine vinegar
1 garlic clove, minced
⅓ cup extra-virgin olive oil
¼ teaspoon salt
⅛ teaspoon pepper

Stir together first 7 ingredients in a medium bowl. Whisk together vinegar, garlic, and oil. Pour dressing over papaya mixture; sprinkle with salt and pepper. Toss gently. Yield: 2 cups.   Eileen Wall

On Course
Women Associates of the Buffalo Power Squadron
Lancaster, New York

Pine Nut Relish

This relish goes nicely with chicken or turkey. You also can serve it over cream cheese for a quick appetizer when guests drop in.

½ cup dried apricots, chopped

⅓ cup chopped onion

3 tablespoons dried tomatoes in oil, drained and chopped

2½ tablespoons honey

1 tablespoon peeled and minced fresh ginger

2 teaspoons chopped jalapeño pepper

⅔ cup seeded and chopped tomato

3 tablespoons pine nuts, toasted

1 tablespoon chopped fresh cilantro

¼ teaspoon salt

⅛ teaspoon pepper

Combine first 6 ingredients in a bowl. Cover and chill at least 8 hours.

Stir in tomato and remaining ingredients. Cover and chill. Serve at room temperature. Yield: 2 cups.

The Kosher Palette
Joseph Kushner Hebrew Academy
Livingston, New Jersey

Apple Chutney

2 Gala apples, chopped
½ cup chopped red bell
  pepper
½ cup apple cider vinegar
⅓ cup firmly packed light
  brown sugar
⅓ cup currants
¼ cup chopped green onions

1 tablespoon dried cranberries
1 teaspoon cumin seeds
¼ teaspoon dried crushed red
  pepper
¼ teaspoon ground allspice
¼ teaspoon ground cloves
¼ teaspoon black pepper

Combine all ingredients in a large saucepan. Bring to a boil; reduce heat, and simmer, uncovered, 23 minutes or until liquid is almost evaporated. Yield: 1½ cups.

Jamie Kornmeier

Cross Village: A Selection of Tastes, Art, and Memories
Cross Village Community Services
Cross Village, Michigan

Green Chile Chutney

Canned green chiles are usually a mild pepper but when combined with 3 types of fragrant, aromatic seeds and some spices, they give this chutney a little kick.

¼ cup olive oil
4 large onions, coarsely
  chopped (about 7 cups)
3 garlic cloves, minced
4 (4.5-ounce) cans chopped
  green chiles, undrained
1 tablespoon mustard seeds

1 tablespoon coriander seeds
1 tablespoon fennel seeds
1 teaspoon ground cumin
1 teaspoon ground cinnamon
1 cup white vinegar
1 cup sugar
1 tablespoon salt

Heat olive oil in a small Dutch oven over medium heat, and sauté onion and garlic 15 minutes or until soft. Increase heat to medium-high. Add green chiles and next 5 ingredients; cook 5 minutes, stirring often. Stir in vinegar, sugar, and salt. Bring to a boil; cook 15 minutes, stirring occasionally.

Pour into a sterilized container. Cool; store in refrigerator. Serve with roasted meats and poultry. Yield: 3¾ cups.

Seasons of Santa Fe
Kitchen Angels
Santa Fe, New Mexico

Three-Berry Spread

The nice part about this recipe is that you can use fresh or frozen berries, so you can make this spread all year around, for yourself and to give as gifts.

1¾ **cups fresh or frozen strawberries**
1¾ **cups fresh or frozen raspberries**
1½ **cups fresh or frozen blueberries**

1 **(1¾-ounce) package powdered pectin**
7 **cups sugar**

Crush berries in a large saucepan. Stir in pectin; bring to a boil over medium-high heat, stirring constantly. Stir in sugar; return to a boil. Boil 1 minute, stirring constantly. Remove from heat; skim off foam with a metal spoon.

Ladle hot mixture into hot jars, filling ½ inch from top. Remove air bubbles; wipe jar rims.

Cover jars at once with metal lids, and screw on bands. Process in boiling water bath 10 minutes. Yield: 7 half-pints.   Kamma Michaud

Recipes from the Heart of Maine
Friends of the Millinocket Memorial Library
Millinocket, Maine

Mango Marmalade

It's important to use ripe mangoes for the best flavor and color when making this supereasy marmalade. Use a vegetable peeler to quickly peel a mango.

4½ cups cubed mango (about 5 medium)

¼ cup finely chopped lemon rind (about 2 large lemons)

2 tablespoons fresh lemon juice

3 cups sugar

Cook mango in a 3-quart saucepan over medium-low heat 20 minutes, stirring often. (Watch closely to prevent sticking.)

Add lemon rind, lemon juice, and sugar to mango. Bring to a boil; cook, stirring constantly, 5 minutes. Pour into hot jars, filling to ½ inch from top; wipe jar rims. Cover at once with metal lids, and screw on bands. Cool; store in refrigerator. Yield: 9 (4-ounce) jars.

Ofukuro No Aji: Favorite Recipes from Mama's Kitchen
Hōkūlani Cultural Exchange Committee
(Hōkūlani Elementary School)
Honolulu, Hawaii

Soups & Stews

Turkey Chili, page 308

Chilled Creamy Peach Soup

This soup is wonderful served at the beginning of a meal or in a wine glass as a sipping dessert.

6 ripe peaches (about 2½ pounds), peeled and sliced
3 tablespoons lemon juice
½ cup sugar

1 teaspoon almond extract
2 cups half-and-half or whipping cream
½ cup sliced almonds, toasted

Process first 4 ingredients in a blender 2 minutes or until smooth. Add half-and-half; process on low until blended. Cover and chill until ready to serve. Ladle into serving bowls. Top with almonds just before serving. Yield: 5½ cups.

The Bounty of Chester County: Heritage Edition
Chester County Agricultural Development Council
West Chester, Pennsylvania

Cold and Creamy Cranberry Soup

Serve this refreshing pink soup as an appetizer or enjoy it as a dessert. Look for crème fraîche in the dairy aisle of larger supermarkets.

2 oranges
1 tablespoon butter
1¼ cups sugar
1 cup sherry
1 pound fresh or frozen cranberries (4 cups)
1 cup Riesling or other sweet white wine

1 (8-ounce) container sour cream
1 cup half-and-half
1 cup club soda
1 cup crème fraîche
16 pecan halves

Peel rind from oranges with a vegetable peeler. Cut rind into julienne strips. Juice oranges, and set aside.

Melt butter in a medium saucepan over medium heat. Add orange rind, and cook 2 minutes. Add sugar, sherry, and reserved orange juice. Bring to a boil; cook 2 minutes. Add cranberries; cover, reduce heat, and simmer 3 minutes. Let cool. Cover and chill 8 hours.

Process half each of chilled mixture and wine in a blender 1 minute. Add half each of sour cream and half-and-half; blend 1 minute. Pour pureed mixture through a wire-mesh strainer into a bowl. Discard rind and cranberry seeds. Repeat procedure with remaining half of ingredients.

Add club soda just before serving; stir well. Ladle soup into soup bowls. Top each serving with crème fraîche and pecan halves. Yield: 6 cups.   Rolf Gahlin

Cooks of the Green Door
The League of Catholic Women
Minneapolis, Minnesota

Green Velvet Soup

Leeks and asparagus provide the color, while potatoes contribute to the velvety smoothness of this richly textured soup that you can enjoy hot or cold.

1 **pound fresh asparagus**	½ **teaspoon salt**
2 **medium leeks, thinly sliced**	½ **teaspoon ground white**
¼ **cup butter or margarine**	**pepper**
3 **medium-size red potatoes,**	1 **cup whipping cream**
peeled and cubed	**Chopped fresh chives**
6 **cups chicken broth**	

Snap off tough ends of asparagus; cut asparagus into ½-inch pieces.

Sauté leeks in butter in a Dutch oven over medium-high heat 3 minutes. Add potato; sauté 3 minutes. Add asparagus, broth, salt, and pepper. Bring to a boil; reduce heat, and simmer, uncovered, 30 to 40 minutes or until vegetables are very tender.

Process mixture, in batches, in a food processor or blender until smooth, stopping to scrape down sides. Return to pan; stir in whipping cream. To serve, ladle soup into individual bowls. Sprinkle each serving with chopped chives. Yield: 10 cups.   Pam Campbell

Moon River Collection
The Landings Landlovers
Savannah, Georgia

Potato and Roquefort Swirl Soup

2 tablespoons butter or
  margarine
3 medium onions, thinly
  sliced
4 cups thinly sliced, peeled
  baking potato
½ cup thinly sliced leeks
3 cups chicken broth
1 cup chopped fresh
  watercress
¼ cup chopped fresh parsley
¼ cup chopped fresh dill
½ cup water
8 ounces Roquefort cheese,
  crumbled
1 cup heavy whipping cream
½ teaspoon salt
⅛ teaspoon ground white
  pepper

Melt butter in a large saucepan over medium heat; add onion, and sauté until tender. Add potato, leek, and chicken broth. Bring to a boil; cover, reduce heat, and simmer 15 minutes or until vegetables are tender. Process potato mixture in a blender until smooth, stopping to scrape down sides.

Combine 1 cup potato puree, watercress, parsley, dill, and water in a saucepan. Bring to a boil; cover, reduce heat, and simmer 15 minutes. Remove from heat; stir in cheese. Process cheese mixture in a blender until smooth, stopping to scrape down sides.

Add ¾ cup heavy whipping cream, salt, and pepper to remaining potato puree mixture; stir well. Add remaining ¼ cup heavy whipping cream to cheese mixture.

To serve, ladle soup into individual bowls. Add cheese mixture, and swirl with a knife. Serve warm, or cover and chill. Yield: 9½ cups.

Bravo! Recipes, Legends & Lore
University Musical Society
Ann Arbor, Michigan

Cream of Fennel Soup

If you like the flavor of licorice, you'll love it in this rich-tasting soup. If you've never given fennel a fair shake, this is a delicious way to try it.

3 pounds fennel (about
    5 medium bulbs)
¾ cup chopped onion
½ cup butter or margarine,
    melted
3 tablespoons dry vermouth
    (optional)
3 (14½-ounce) cans chicken
    broth

2½ cups milk
5 tablespoons butter or
    margarine
¼ cup all-purpose flour
1 cup heavy whipping cream
1 tablespoon lemon juice
½ teaspoon salt
½ teaspoon pepper

Rinse fennel thoroughly; reserve fronds for garnish. Trim stalks to within 1 inch of bulb; discard hard outside stalks. Quarter bulbs. Cook fennel and onion in melted butter in a large Dutch oven over medium-high heat 30 minutes or until tender, stirring often.

Add vermouth, if desired, and cook 1 minute. Add chicken broth and milk; simmer 30 minutes. Process fennel mixture, in batches, in a blender or food processor until pureed, stopping once to scrape down sides. Press mixture through a wire-mesh strainer, using back of a spoon; discard pulp. Return fennel mixture to Dutch oven; bring to a boil.

Melt 5 tablespoons butter in a small saucepan. Add flour, stirring until smooth; cook 1 minute, stirring constantly. Gradually stir flour mixture into fennel mixture; cook until thickened, stirring often. Add cream and remaining 3 ingredients; cook until thoroughly heated. Garnish with reserved fennel fronds, if desired. Yield: 7½ cups.

First Impressions: Dining with Distinction
The Junior League of Waterloo-Cedar Falls
Waterloo, Iowa

Beefy Barley Soup

2 pounds ground beef
2 (10¾-ounce) cans
   condensed beef broth,
   undiluted
1 (28-ounce) can diced
   tomatoes with basil, garlic,
   and oregano, undrained
4 carrots, sliced

4 celery ribs, sliced
1 large onion, chopped
1 cup water
⅔ cup uncooked barley
1 tablespoon dried parsley
   flakes
½ teaspoon salt
½ teaspoon pepper

Cook ground beef in a Dutch oven, stirring until it crumbles and is no longer pink; drain. Return meat to Dutch oven.

Add beef broth and remaining ingredients; bring to a boil. Cover, reduce heat, and simmer 1 hour, stirring occasionally. Yield: 12 cups.

It's a Snap!
The Haven of Grace
St. Louis, Missouri

Chicken Vegetable Soup

A homemade stock is the base for this vegetable-packed soup loaded with hearty ingredients such as parsnip, tomato, barley, and spinach.

14 cups water
3 pounds bone-in chicken
   breast halves, skinned
2 celery ribs, quartered
2 bay leaves
2 garlic cloves, halved
1 large onion, quartered
1 tablespoon black
   peppercorns
3 garlic cloves, minced
2 carrots, peeled and sliced
2 celery ribs, sliced
1 parsnip, sliced

1 small onion, chopped
1½ teaspoons chopped fresh
   thyme
1 tablespoon vegetable oil
½ cup uncooked barley
1 (28-ounce) can diced
   tomatoes with basil, garlic,
   and oregano, undrained
1 (6-ounce) package baby
   spinach
1½ teaspoons salt
¼ teaspoon pepper

Combine first 7 ingredients in a large Dutch oven. Bring to a boil; reduce heat, and simmer 1 hour. Remove chicken from Dutch oven with a slotted spoon; let chicken cool. Bone chicken, reserving bones, and coarsely chop meat. Set aside.

Add reserved bones to broth in Dutch oven. Bring to a boil; reduce heat, and simmer 1 hour. Pour broth through a wire-mesh strainer, discarding solids. Return broth to Dutch oven.

Sauté garlic and next 5 ingredients in oil in a large nonstick skillet over medium heat 1 minute. Add barley; cook 1 minute.

Add vegetable mixture, tomatoes, and reserved chicken to Dutch oven. Bring to a boil; cover, reduce heat, and simmer 1 hour. Stir in spinach, salt, and pepper; cook until spinach wilts. Yield: 17 cups.

To Your Health: Recipes for Healthy Living from Lahey Clinic
Lahey Clinic
Burlington, Massachusetts

Portuguese Kale Soup

This zesty soup needs only a dollop of sour cream to temper the kick from the chorizo sausage and spicy tomatoes.

½ **pound chorizo or smoked sausage, cut into ½-inch slices**
1 **large onion, coarsely chopped**
½ **pound new potatoes, diced**
2 **tablespoons olive oil**
1 **teaspoon ground cumin**
1 **teaspoon dried thyme**
1 **(14½-ounce) can diced tomatoes, undrained**

1 **(10-ounce) can diced tomatoes and green chiles, undrained**
1 **(15-ounce) can red kidney beans, undrained**
2 **cups chicken broth**
4 **cups coarsely chopped kale (about 1 bunch)**

Sauté sausage, onion, and potato in olive oil in a Dutch oven over medium-high heat until lightly browned. Add cumin and next 5 ingredients. Bring to a boil; reduce heat, and simmer, uncovered, 30 minutes. Add kale; cook 5 more minutes or until kale wilts. Yield: 8 cups.

The Guild Collection: Recipes from Art Lovers
The Guild, The Museum of Fine Arts, Houston, Texas

Sherried Oyster and Brie Soup

Brie adds body and introduces a depth of flavor to this rich and creamy soup.

1 cup cream sherry	2 tablespoons all-purpose flour
4 ounces Brie	3 cups beef broth
2 tablespoons butter or margarine	1 cup milk
1 pound fresh mushrooms, thinly sliced	1 cup heavy whipping cream
½ cup minced shallots	¼ teaspoon pepper
2 tablespoons fresh lemon juice	1 (16-ounce) container fresh Select oysters, drained
	Garnish: chopped fresh chives

Bring cream sherry to a boil over medium heat; reduce heat, and simmer 20 to 25 minutes or until reduced to ½ cup. Remove from heat, and set aside.

Remove and discard rind from Brie. Cube cheese, and set aside.

Melt butter in a Dutch oven over medium heat. Add mushrooms, shallots, and lemon juice; cook 4 to 5 minutes or until mushrooms are tender, stirring often. Sprinkle with flour; cook 1 minute, stirring constantly. Add sherry and broth. Bring to a boil; reduce heat, and simmer, uncovered, 20 minutes. Add Brie, stirring until cheese melts. Add milk, whipping cream, and pepper. Cook until thoroughly heated (do not boil). Reduce heat to low, and add oysters; cook 1 to 2 minutes or until edges of oysters begin to curl.

To serve, ladle into individual bowls. Serve immediately. Garnish, if desired. Yield: 7½ cups. Stan and Lelia Gentle

Look Who's Cooking in Louisville
Pitt Academy
Louisville, Kentucky

Lobster and Chive Bisque

This fancy bisque is studded with chunks of lobster, flavored with sherry, and thickened with cream for a luxurious taste and texture. Serve it with breadsticks and a simple green salad for a quick meal.

1 tablespoon minced onion
3 tablespoons butter or
　margarine
3 tablespoons all-purpose
　flour
3 cups milk
1 cup heavy whipping cream

½ cup dry sherry
1 teaspoon salt
⅛ teaspoon paprika
1 cup cooked lobster meat
　(about 1 pound)
2 tablespoons chopped fresh
　chives

Sauté onion in butter in a Dutch oven over medium heat 1 minute or until tender. Add flour, stirring until blended. Cook 1 minute, stirring constantly. Gradually add milk and next 4 ingredients. Bring just to a simmer; cook, uncovered, 15 to 18 minutes or until slightly thickened (do not boil). Stir in lobster meat and chives. Yield: 5 cups.

Secret Ingredients
The Junior League of Alexandria, Louisiana

Fish Chowder

Any type of white fish will do in this creamy down-home chowder.

4 cups water
3 medium potatoes, diced
1 cup sliced carrot
1 pound halibut or other white fish, cut into large chunks
1 medium onion, chopped
1 green bell pepper, chopped
1 cup chopped celery
2 tablespoons butter or margarine

2 tablespoons all-purpose flour
2 cups milk
1 (15.25-ounce) can whole kernel corn, undrained
1 teaspoon salt
1 cup half-and-half

Bring water to a boil in a Dutch oven; add potato, and cook 15 minutes. Add carrot and fish. Reduce heat, and simmer, uncovered, 10 minutes or until vegetables are tender.

Sauté onion, pepper, and celery in butter in a large skillet 8 minutes or until vegetables are soft. In a small bowl, whisk together flour and milk until blended; add flour mixture and corn to sautéed vegetables. Cook over medium-high heat until mixture begins to thicken, stirring often; add to potato and fish. Stir in salt and half-and-half; cook 3 minutes or until thoroughly heated. Yield: 14 cups.   Cindi Becker

Sharing Our Best
Hackensack American Legion Auxiliary Unit 202
Hackensack, Minnesota

Mexican Chicken-Corn Chowder

No one will leave the table hungry after a bowl of this cheesy chowder.

1½ pounds skinned and boned chicken breast halves, cut into bite-size pieces
½ cup chopped onion
1 garlic clove, minced
3 tablespoons butter or margarine
2 chicken bouillon cubes
1 cup hot water
½ teaspoon ground cumin
2 cups half-and-half
2 (14.75-ounce) cans cream-style corn
1 (4.5-ounce) can chopped green chiles
¼ teaspoon hot pepper sauce
2 cups (8 ounces) shredded Monterey Jack cheese

Sauté chicken, onion, and garlic in butter in a large Dutch oven 7 minutes or until chicken is lightly browned.

Dissolve bouillon cubes in hot water; add bouillon mixture and cumin to chicken mixture. Bring to a boil; cover, reduce heat, and simmer 3 minutes. Add half-and-half and remaining ingredients. Cook over low heat until thoroughly heated. Serve immediately. Yield: 10 cups.

Kaye Blodgett

Wildcat Valley: Recipes & Remembrances
Keats Lions Club
Manhattan, Kansas

Plum Spicy Beef Stew

We were extremely surprised by the depth of flavor that a can of plums added to this Asian-inspired stew. It's one of our favorite recipes in the book.

2 pounds beef stew meat, cut into 1-inch pieces
1 tablespoon vegetable oil
2 (15-ounce) cans purple plums in heavy syrup, undrained
⅔ cup soy sauce
¼ cup water
1 teaspoon ground ginger
¾ teaspoon salt
½ teaspoon ground cumin
3 large carrots, cut into thin strips
2 green onions, sliced
1 red bell pepper, cut into thin strips
1 (5-ounce) can sliced water chestnuts, drained
4 cups hot cooked rice

Brown beef in hot oil in a Dutch oven.

Drain plums, reserving syrup; discard pits. Process plums and syrup in a blender until smooth, stopping to scrape down sides. Add soy sauce and next 4 ingredients; process until smooth.

Add plum puree to Dutch oven. Bring to a boil; cover, reduce heat, and simmer 1 hour, stirring occasionally.

Add carrot, green onions, red pepper, and water chestnuts; cover and cook 45 minutes or until meat and vegetables are tender. Serve over rice. Yield: 8 cups (without the rice).   Susan Gloor

Of Books and Cooks
Woman's Book Club
Harrison, Arkansas

Trinidad Beef Stew

A twist on basic beef stew, this slightly sweet beef stew is flavored with molasses and ginger for an exotic flavor and loads of taste.

1 (3-pound) eye-of-round roast
3 tablespoons all-purpose
  flour
1 tablespoon vegetable oil
2 (14½-ounce) cans no-salt-
  added diced tomatoes
3 cups sliced onion
1¼ teaspoons pepper

1 teaspoon salt
2 cups water
⅓ cup white vinegar
3 tablespoons molasses
2½ cups thinly sliced carrot
½ cup raisins
½ teaspoon ground ginger

Dredge beef in flour. Brown beef on all sides in hot oil in a Dutch oven over medium-high heat. Stir in tomatoes and next 6 ingredients. Bring to a boil; cover, reduce heat, and simmer 1 hour and 15 minutes or until beef is tender, stirring occasionally. Stir in carrot, raisins, and ginger. Simmer 30 more minutes or until carrot is tender, stirring occasionally.

Remove beef to a platter, and shred, using 2 forks. Return beef to Dutch oven, and stir gently. Cook just until thoroughly heated, stirring often. Yield: 9 cups.

To Your Health: Recipes for Healthy Living from Lahey Clinic
Lahey Clinic
Burlington, Massachusetts

Turkey Chili

Where's the beef? It's not in this chili! Ground turkey and turkey sausage give this chili its meaty flavor. We promise you'll never miss the beef.

1 onion, chopped
1 green bell pepper, chopped
1 pound ground turkey
1 pound ground turkey
  sausage
1 teaspoon vegetable oil
1 (16-ounce) can chili beans
2 cups tomato sauce

2 cups tomato juice
1 garlic clove, minced
1 (1.75-ounce) envelope chili
  seasoning mix
1 (10-ounce) can diced
  tomatoes and green chiles
1 teaspoon sugar

Cook first 4 ingredients in hot oil in a Dutch oven over medium heat, stirring until meat crumbles and is no longer pink; drain. Add chili beans and remaining ingredients to Dutch oven; bring to a boil. Reduce heat, and simmer, uncovered, 30 minutes, stirring constantly. Yield: 8 cups.   Judy Manka

The Gala of Good Taste: 10th Anniversary Commemorative Cookbook
Mental Health Association in Reno County
Hutchinson, Kansas

Vegetables

Parmesan Potato Sticks, page 316

Elegant Broccoli and Walnuts

These simple ingredients turn plain broccoli into a showy side dish.

2 **pounds fresh broccoli**	1 **cup chopped walnuts**
1 **pound bacon**	¾ **cup sliced green onions**

Remove leaves from broccoli; cut off tough ends of stalks, and discard. Cut off broccoli florets. Place florets in a steamer basket over boiling water; cover and steam 6 minutes or until crisp-tender. Set aside, and keep warm.

Cook bacon in a skillet until crisp; remove bacon, and drain on paper towels, reserving 1 tablespoon drippings in skillet. Crumble bacon, and set aside. Cook walnuts in reserved drippings, stirring constantly, over medium heat 3 minutes. Add green onions, and cook 1 minute or until soft.

Transfer warm broccoli to a serving platter; spoon walnut mixture over broccoli. Sprinkle with bacon, and serve immediately. Yield: 6 to 8 servings.

Creating a Stir
The Lexington Medical Society Auxiliary
Lexington, Kentucky

Caper-Lemon Brussels Sprouts

Think you're not a fan of Brussels sprouts? One taste of these browned beauties sprinkled with Parmesan cheese and you'll be hooked.

1½ **pounds fresh Brussels sprouts**	1½ **tablespoons fresh lemon juice**
3 **tablespoons olive oil**	¼ **cup freshly grated Parmesan cheese**
2 **tablespoons drained capers, rinsed**	

Wash Brussels sprouts; remove discolored leaves. Cut off stem ends; cut sprouts in half lengthwise. Arrange sprouts in a steamer basket over boiling water. Cover and steam 7 to 8 minutes or until crisp-tender. Remove from heat.

Sauté sprouts in hot olive oil in a large skillet over medium-high heat 3 to 4 minutes or until lightly browned. Stir in capers and lemon juice; shake pan to coat. Transfer sprouts to a serving dish; sprinkle with Parmesan cheese. Yield: 4 servings.

California Fresh Harvest: A Seasonal Journey through Northern California
The Junior League of Oakland-East Bay
Lafayette, California

Danish Red Cabbage

The deep red color and not-too-sweet flavor make this a colorful side dish when paired with pork or turkey. It's even better when prepared the day before and then served so the flavors have a chance to develop.

¼ cup butter or margarine
3 pounds red cabbage, coarsely
 shredded (about 2 heads)
½ cup water

¼ cup cider vinegar
2 tablespoons currant jelly
1 tablespoon sugar
1 teaspoon salt

Melt butter in a Dutch oven over medium-high heat. Add cabbage, tossing to coat. Stir in water and vinegar. Cover and cook over medium heat 10 minutes or until tender, stirring occasionally.

Combine jelly, sugar, and salt in a small bowl; stir well. Add jelly mixture to cabbage. Cover and cook 5 more minutes. Yield: 7 servings.

Twice Treasured Recipes
The Bargain Box, Inc.
Hilton Head Island, South Carolina

Fried Carrot Balls

Entice your children to eat their vegetables with these carrot balls that resemble hush puppies in appearance.

1 (1-pound) package carrots
2 cups water
2 tablespoons butter or margarine
2 tablespoons all-purpose flour
⅔ cup milk
½ teaspoon salt
¼ teaspoon pepper
2 tablespoons chopped fresh parsley

1 tablespoon minced onion
1 tablespoon sugar
1 cup all-purpose flour
2 large eggs, lightly beaten
3 tablespoons whipping cream
2 cups fine, dry breadcrumbs (store-bought)
Vegetable oil

Finely chop carrots. Place in a large saucepan, and add water. Bring to a boil; cover, reduce heat, and simmer 13 minutes or until tender. Drain well.

Melt butter in a heavy saucepan over low heat; whisk in 2 tablespoons flour until smooth. Cook, whisking constantly, 1 minute. Gradually whisk in milk; cook, whisking constantly, over medium heat until mixture is thickened and bubbly. Stir in salt and pepper. Add carrot, parsley, onion, and sugar. Shape mixture into 1½-inch balls. Dredge carrot balls in 1 cup flour. Combine eggs and whipping cream. Dip balls in egg mixture, and coat with breadcrumbs.

Pour oil to a depth of 2 inches into a large heavy skillet. Fry carrot balls in hot oil over high heat until lightly browned. Drain on paper towels. Yield: 1 dozen.

Mattie Carroll

A Dab of This and a Dab of That
Bethlehem Baptist Church Senior Missionary
Ninety Six, South Carolina

Elegant Eggplant

Ever eaten eggplant? This creamy casserole is a delicious way to introduce your family to it. Choose eggplant with firm, smooth, glossy skin and a bright green stem.

1 large eggplant, peeled and chopped (about 6 cups)	2 cups soft breadcrumbs (homemade)
¼ cup water	2 tablespoons butter or margarine, melted
½ teaspoon dried marjoram	1 large tomato, peeled and chopped
¼ teaspoon salt	
⅓ cup chopped fresh parsley	½ cup half-and-half
¼ cup chopped onion	¼ cup freshly grated Parmesan cheese
2 tablespoons butter or margarine	

Combine eggplant, water, marjoram, and salt in a medium saucepan; bring to a boil over medium-high heat. Cover, reduce heat, and simmer 8 to 10 minutes or until tender; drain. Stir in parsley; set aside.

Sauté onion in 2 tablespoons butter in a small skillet until tender. Add onion to eggplant mixture.

Combine breadcrumbs and 2 tablespoons melted butter in a small bowl. Layer half of eggplant mixture, half of tomato, and 1 cup breadcrumb mixture in a lightly greased 8-inch square baking dish. Repeat layers, ending with breadcrumb mixture. Pour half-and-half over layers, and sprinkle with Parmesan cheese. Bake, uncovered, at 375° for 40 minutes. Yield: 6 servings.

First Impressions: Dining with Distinction
The Junior League of Waterloo-Cedar Falls
Waterloo, Iowa

Caramelized Onion Pudding

Onions never tasted as good as they do in this sinfully rich, creamy pudding.

¼ cup butter
3 cups sliced onion (about
  2 small onions)
3 large eggs
2 cups heavy whipping cream
2 tablespoons all-purpose
  flour

2 tablespoons sugar
1 teaspoon salt
1 teaspoon baking powder
1 (4-ounce) package crumbled
  goat cheese

Melt butter in a large nonstick skillet over medium heat. Add onion; sauté 28 minutes or until onion is browned. Remove from heat, and set aside.

Beat eggs and next 5 ingredients with an electric mixer until smooth. Stir in goat cheese and onion. Pour onion mixture into a greased 11- x 7-inch baking dish.

Bake, uncovered, at 350° for 35 minutes or until golden. Yield: 6 servings. Kathy Cary

Splendor in the Bluegrass
The Junior League of Louisville, Kentucky

Elvira's Fried Black-Eyed Pea Patties

Serve these right out of the skillet with some homemade chowchow.

1 (15-ounce) can black-eyed
  peas, drained
1½ cups chopped onion
⅓ cup self-rising flour
1 large egg, lightly beaten

¼ teaspoon seasoned
  pepper
⅛ teaspoon salt
½ cup vegetable oil, divided

Mash peas in a medium bowl. Add onion and next 4 ingredients; stir well.

Pour ¼ cup oil into a large heavy skillet. Place over medium-high heat until hot. Drop half of pea mixture by heaping tablespoonfuls into hot oil, shaping into patties. Fry 2 to 3 minutes on each side or until golden. Drain on paper towels. Repeat procedure with remaining ¼ cup oil and pea mixture. Yield: 1 dozen.

From Black Tie to Blackeyed Peas: Savannah's Savory Secrets
St. Joseph's Foundation of Savannah, Inc.
Savannah, Georgia

Sautéed Peas with Walnuts

Honey lends a touch of sweetness and walnuts add a bit of crunch to these dressed-up peas.

1 tablespoon unsalted butter	2 drops of hot sauce
1 large shallot, minced	½ teaspoon salt
¼ cup chicken broth	¼ teaspoon pepper
2 teaspoons honey	½ cup chopped toasted
1 (10-ounce) package frozen	walnuts
petite sweet green peas,	
thawed	

Melt butter in a large skillet over medium-low heat. Add shallot; cook 3 minutes, stirring occasionally. Add chicken broth, honey, and peas. Cook over medium-high heat 3 minutes or until peas are tender and liquid evaporates. Stir in hot sauce, salt, and pepper. Remove from heat, and stir in walnuts. Serve immediately. Yield: 3 to 4 servings.

America Celebrates Columbus
The Junior League of Columbus, Ohio

Red Potatoes with Artichokes and Feta Cheese

Roasting the potatoes and artichokes for 55 minutes makes them tender and gives the flavors a chance to meld.

2 pounds small red potatoes, unpeeled and quartered
2 (14-ounce) cans artichoke hearts, drained and halved
2 garlic cloves, minced
2 tablespoons chopped fresh thyme

1 tablespoon olive oil
½ teaspoon salt
½ teaspoon pepper
1 (4-ounce) package crumbled feta cheese

Combine first 7 ingredients in a large bowl or large heavy-duty, zip-top plastic bag. Stir mixture in bowl, or seal bag, and shake well to coat. Arrange potato mixture in a well-greased 13- x 9-inch baking dish. Bake, uncovered, at 425° for 55 minutes or until potato is tender, stirring occasionally. Add cheese; toss gently. Yield: 8 servings.

Settings on the Dock of the Bay
ASSISTANCE LEAGUE® of the Bay Area
Houston, Texas

Parmesan Potato Sticks

Homemade fries are crisper and better tasting than the frozen variety. These are coated in cheese and spices, then baked to a golden brown.

6 small baking potatoes (about 3 pounds)
3 to 4 cups cold water
1 teaspoon salt

¾ cup butter or margarine, melted
Parmesan Coating

Scrub potatoes. Cut lengthwise into ½-inch slices; turn and stack potato slices, cut sides down. Cut lengthwise into ½-inch sticks. Place potato sticks in a large bowl. Combine cold water and salt; pour over potatoes to cover. Let stand 5 minutes. Drain well; spread on paper towels to absorb water. Pat dry with paper towels.

Dip potato sticks in melted butter; roll in Parmesan Coating. Place in a single layer on ungreased baking sheets (do not let potato sticks touch). Bake at 400° for 30 minutes; turn potatoes, and bake 10 more minutes or until golden. Yield: 4 to 6 servings.

Parmesan Coating

1 **cup fine, dry breadcrumbs (store-bought)**	1 **teaspoon dried parsley flakes**
1 **cup grated Parmesan cheese**	½ **teaspoon paprika**
1 **teaspoon salt**	¼ **teaspoon garlic powder**
	¼ **teaspoon pepper**

Combine all ingredients in a bowl. Yield: 2¼ cups.

Specialties of the Haus
TCM International, Inc.
Indianapolis, Indiana

Spinach Soufflé

This dish boasts three types of cheeses and is so rich and cheesy that it doesn't rise like a regular soufflé.

1 **(10-ounce) package frozen chopped spinach, thawed and drained**	¼ **teaspoon pepper**
3 **large eggs, lightly beaten**	1 **(16-ounce) container small-curd cottage cheese**
¼ **cup all-purpose flour**	4 **ounces sharp Cheddar cheese, cubed**
¼ **cup butter or margarine, melted**	4 **ounces American cheese, cubed**
½ **teaspoon salt**	

Combine first 6 ingredients in a bowl; fold in cheeses. Pour into a lightly greased 1½-quart baking dish. Bake at 350° for 50 to 55 minutes or until set. Yield: 6 servings.   Dorothy Brinker

Menus & Memories
University of Oklahoma Women's Association
Norman, Oklahoma

Glorified Stuffed Tomatoes

3 large ripe tomatoes
1 teaspoon Creole seasoning
1 (10-ounce) package frozen
   chopped spinach, thawed
1 (3-ounce) package cream
   cheese, softened
1 cup grated Parmesan cheese
1 tablespoon butter, softened
1 tablespoon chopped fresh
   oregano

2 tablespoons sour cream
1 (4-ounce) jar marinated
   artichoke hearts, drained
   and chopped
6 green onions, chopped
½ cup Italian-seasoned
   breadcrumbs (store-bought)
2 tablespoons butter, melted

Cut each tomato in half crosswise; carefully scoop out pulp. Reserve pulp from 2 tomatoes. Invert tomato shells onto paper towels to drain. Sprinkle inside of tomatoes with Creole seasoning.

Drain spinach well, pressing between paper towels.

Combine cream cheese and next 4 ingredients, stirring until smooth. Add reserved tomato pulp, spinach, artichokes, and green onions. Spoon ½ cup spinach mixture into each tomato shell. Place in an ungreased 13- x 9-inch baking dish.

Combine breadcrumbs and melted butter. Sprinkle 1 tablespoon breadcrumb mixture over each stuffed tomato. Bake at 350° for 35 minutes or until topping is golden brown. Yield: 6 servings.

Thyme to Entertain: Good Food and Southern Hospitality
The Charity League, Inc., of Paducah, Kentucky

Turnip Casserole

Don't limit your vegetable choices to just a few. Add a little adventure to meal time, and try this turnip surprise.

1 pound medium turnips, peeled and cut into ½-inch cubes (3 cups)

2 medium onions, coarsely chopped (about 2⅓ cups)

¼ cup sugar

½ teaspoon salt

⅛ teaspoon ground white pepper

⅛ teaspoon ground red pepper

⅔ cups soft breadcrumbs (homemade)

½ teaspoon paprika

1 tablespoon butter or margarine, melted

3 tablespoons all-purpose flour

1 cup milk

1 tablespoon butter or margarine

2 cups (8 ounces) shredded American cheese

Cook turnip and onion in boiling salted water to cover 10 minutes or just until tender. Drain; return vegetables to pan. Stir in sugar, salt and peppers. Set aside, and keep warm.

Combine breadcrumbs and paprika; add 1 tablespoon melted butter. Toss well, and set aside.

Place flour in a medium saucepan. Gradually add milk, stirring until smooth. Add 1 tablespoon butter. Place pan over medium heat; cook, stirring constantly, until thickened. Gradually add cheese. Stir until cheese melts. Stir cheese sauce into turnip mixture; pour into a greased 11- x 7-inch baking dish. Sprinkle with breadcrumb mixture. Bake, uncovered, at 400° for 20 minutes or until bubbly. Yield: 6 servings.   Lillian Burris

Recipes & Remembrances
Parkview Nursing and Rehabilitation Center
Wilmington, Delaware

Acknowledgments

Each of the community cookbooks listed is represented by recipes appearing in *America's Best Recipes*. The copyright is held by the sponsoring organization whose mailing address is included.

202's Totally Tempting Treasures, American Legion Auxiliary Green-Pierce Unit 202, 1101 E. Scott St., Wichita Falls, TX 76301

Always in Season, Junior League of Salt Lake City, Inc., 526 E. 300 S, Salt Lake City, UT 84102

America Celebrates Columbus, The Junior League of Columbus, Inc., 583 Franklin Ave., Columbus, OH 43215-4715

An Acquired Taste, Winchester Thurston School, 555 Morewood Ave., Pittsburgh, PA 15213

Art Fare: A Commemorative Celebration of Art & Food, Toledo Museum of Art Aides, P.O. Box 1013, Toledo, OH 43697

At Your Service: Southern Recipes, Places and Traditions, Junior League of Gwinnett and North Fulton Counties, Inc., 6700 Sugarloaf Pkwy., Ste. 500, Duluth, GA 30097

Austin Entertains, Junior League of Austin, 5416 Parkcrest Dr., Ste. 100, Austin, TX 78731

Beyond Cotton Country, Junior League of Morgan County, 109 2nd Ave. NE, Decatur, AL 35601

Bless This Food: A Collection of Prayers & Recipes, Steel Lake Presbyterian Church—Women's Ministries, 1829 S. 308th St., Federal Way, WA 98003

The Bounty of Chester County: Heritage Edition, Chester County Agricultural Development Council/Government Services Center, Ste. 270, 601 Westtown Rd., West Chester, PA 19380-0990

Bravo! Recipes, Legends & Lore, University Musical Society, 881 N. University Ave., Ann Arbor, MI 48109-1011

Bread from the Brook, The Church at Brook Hills, 3145 Brook Highland Pkwy., Birmingham, AL 35242

Breakfast in Cairo, Dinner in Rome, International School of Minnesota Foundation, 6385 Beach Rd., Eden Prairie, MN 55344

Business is Cookin' with FBLA, Lakeview Future Business Leaders of America, 3744 83rd St., Columbus, NE 68601

Café Weller . . . Tastes to Remember, Apple Corps of the Weller Health Education Center, 325 Northhampton St., Easton, PA 18042

California Fresh Harvest: A Seasonal Journey through Northern California, Junior League of Oakland-East Bay, Inc., 3732 Mt. Diablo Blvd., Ste. 365, Lafayette, CA 94549

Carolina Thyme, Junior League of Durham and Orange Counties, Inc., 900 S. Duke St., Durham, NC 27707

Celebrating Heritage: Recipes and Reflections of Jean Richards Roddey, The Jean Richards Roddey Scholarship Committee, P.O. Box 2023, Seneca, SC 29679

Chautauqua Celebrations, Wythe Arts Council, Ltd., P.O. Box 911, Wytheville, VA 24382

Christian Women's Fellowship, Oak Grove Christian Church, 6101 32nd Ave., Shellsburg, IA 52332

Cooking for Good, West End Charities, 211 N. Record St. S-109, Dallas, TX 75202

Cooking Seasoned with Love, Upsala Community Presbyterian Church, 101 Upsala Rd., Sanford, FL 32771

Cooking Up Memories, St. Paul's Episcopal Church, 305 W. Seventh St., Chattanooga, TN 37402

Cooking with Care, HospiceCare of the Piedmont, Inc., 408 W. Alexander Ave., Greenwood, SC 29646

Cooking with Class, Forest Hills Elementary School PTO, 1133 Andrews Rd., Lake Oswego, OR 97034

Cooking with Class, Timber Lake Booster Club, P.O. Box 62, Timber Lake, SD 57656

Cooking with Friends, Brunswick Community Hospital, 1 Medical Center Dr., Supply, NC 28462

Cooking with Music: Celebrating the Tastes and Traditions of the Boston Symphony Orchestra, Boston Symphony Association of Volunteers, Symphony Hall, 301 Massachusetts Ave., Boston, MA 02115

Cooking with the Original Search Engine, Fort Worth Public Library All Staff Association, 1300 NE 35th St., Fort Worth, TX 76106-4552

Cookin' with Friends, National Presbyterian School Class of 2000, 4121 Nebraska Ave. NW, Washington, DC 20016

Cookin' with Pride, 4th Infantry Division, Ironhorse Gift Shop, P.O. Box 5009, Ft. Hood, TX 76544

Cooks of the Green Door, The League of Catholic Women, 207 S. 9th St., Minneapolis, MN 55402

Creating a Stir, The Lexington Medical Society Auxiliary, 2628 Wilhite Dr., Ste. 201, Lexington, KY 40503-3304

Cross Village: A Selection of Tastes, Art, and Memories, Cross Village Community Services, P.O. Box 104, Cross Village, MI 49723

A Dab of This and a Dab of That, Bethlehem Baptist Church Senior Missionary, 303 E. Main St., Ninety Six, SC 29666

De Nuestra Mesa: Our Food, Wine, and Tradition, New Hope Charities, Inc., 626 N. Dixie Hwy., West Palm Beach, FL 33401

The Dining Car, Service League of Denison, 418 W. Main, Denison, TX 75020

Divine Offerings: Recipes and Hints for the Kitchen, St. Charles Presbyterian Women, 131 Gamble St., St. Charles, MO 63301

Dixon Fixins, Dixon Ambulatory Care Center, 291 Stoner Ave., Westminster, MD 21157

Down Home Dining in Mississippi, Mississippi Homemaker Volunteers, Inc., 715 Markette St., Water Valley, MS 38965

Embden Centennial Cookbook, St. John Lutheran Church, 14721 40th St. SE, Wheatland, ND 58079

Entertaining Thoughts . . ., Junior League of the Lehigh Valley, Inc., 2200 Avenue A, Ste. 101, Bethlehem, PA 18017

Entirely Entertaining in the Bonnet House Style, Bonnet House Alliance, 900 N. Birch Rd., Ft. Lauderdale, FL 33346

Everything But the Entrée, Junior League of Parkersburg, Inc., 1301 Murdoch Ave., Parkersburg, WV 26101

Faithfully Charleston, St. Michael's Episcopal Church, 14 St. Michael's Alley, Charleston, SC 29401

Feeding the Flock, St. Philips Episcopal Church, 3860 SE California, Topeka, KS 66609

Fine Food from the Friends, Friends of the Superior Public Library, Inc., 1530 Tower Ave., Superior, WI 54880

First Impressions: Dining with Distinction, Junior League of Waterloo-Cedar Falls, Inc., 847 W. 4th St., Waterloo, IA 50702

Flavor It Greek! A Celebration of Food, Faith and Family, Philoptochos Society of Holy Trinity Greek Orthodox Church, 3131 NE Glisan St., Portland, OR 97232

Flavors of the Gardens, Callaway Gardens, P.O. Box 2000, Pine Mountain, GA 31822-2000

Flavors of the Tenderloin, Sidewalk Clean-Up, Recycling & Urban Beautification (SCRUB), 1278 44th Ave., San Francisco, CA 94122

Forget Me Not: Recipes and Stories to Remember, Hospice and Palliative Care of Greensboro, 2500 Summit Ave., Greensboro, NC 27405

From Black Tie to Blackeyed Peas: Savannah's Savory Secrets, St. Joseph's Foundation of Savannah, Inc., 11705 Mercy Blvd., Savannah, GA 31419

Future Generations, Robertson County Family and Community Education Clubs, County Extension Office, 514 Hill St., Springfield, TN 37172

The Gala of Good Taste: 10th Anniversary Commemorative Cookbook, Mental Health Association in Reno County, P.O. Box 2021, Hutchinson, KS 67504-2021

Gifts from Our Heart, Mercy Special Learning Center, 830 S. Woodward St., Allentown, PA 18103-3440

Glen Haven Community Cookbook 1999, Glen Haven Area Volunteer Fire Department, P.O. Box 88, Glen Haven, CO 80532

Good Food, Served Right, Traditional Arts in Upstate New York, 2 W. Main St., Canton, NY 13617

The Guild Collection: Recipes from Art Lovers, The Guild, Museum of Fine Arts, 1001 Bissonnet, Houston, TX 77005

The Heart of Pittsburgh, Sacred Heart Elementary School PTG, 325 Emerson St., Pittsburgh, PA 15206

Heaven's Bounty, Long Beach Catholic School Parents' Club, Long Beach Catholic School, 735 W. Broadway, Long Beach, NY 11561

Homemade with Love, Swanton-Missisquoi Valley Lions Club, P.O. Box 376, Highgate Center, VT 05459

It's About Time: Recipes, Reflections, Realities, National Association Teachers of Family and Consumer Sciences, 2604 Kiwanis Dr., Bowling Green, KY 42104-4229

It's a Snap!, The Haven of Grace, 1133 Benton St., St. Louis, MO 63106

Jubilee 2000 Recipe Collection, St. Alphonsus Liguori Parish—Hospitality Committee, 411 N. Wheeling Rd., Prospect Heights, IL 60070

Key Ingredients, Le Bonheur Club, Inc., 1047 Cresthaven Rd., Memphis, TN 38119

The Kosher Palette, Joseph Kushner Hebrew Academy, 110 S. Orange Ave., Livingston, NJ 07039

Lake Waccamaw United Methodist Church Cookbook, Lake Waccamaw United Methodist Church, 506 Lake Shore Dr., Lake Waccamaw, NC 28450

Las Vegas: Glitter to Gourmet, Junior League of Las Vegas, 6126 W. Charleston Blvd., Las Vegas, NV 89146

Lighthouse Secrets: A Collection of Recipes from the Nation's Oldest City, Junior Service League of St. Augustine, Inc., P.O. Box 244, St. Augustine, FL 32080

A Little DAPS of This . . . A Little DAPS of That, Dallas Area Parkinsonism Society (DAPS), 3003 LBJ Freeway, Ste. 125E, Dallas, TX 75234-7755

Look What's Cooking . . ., Temple Sinai Sisterhood, 30 Hagen Ave., Cranston, RI 02920

Look Who Came to Dinner, Junior Auxiliary of Amory, Inc., 1603 Woodview Cir., Amory, MS 38821

Look Who's Cooking in Louisville, Pitt Academy, 4605 Poplar Level Rd., Louisville, KY 40213

Made in the Shade, Junior League of Greater Fort Lauderdale, 704 SE 1st St., Fort Lauderdale, FL 33301

McInnis Bobcat Favorites, McInnis Elementary PTA, 5175 N. U.S. Hwy. 17, DeLeon Springs, FL 32130

Mealtime and Memories, Stumptown Mennonite Church Women, 2813 Stumptown Rd., Bird-in-Hand, PA 17505

Meet Me at the Garden Gate, Junior League of Spartanburg, Inc., 615 E. Main St., Spartanburg, SC 29302

Meet Us in the Kitchen, Junior League of St. Louis, 10435 Clayton Rd., St. Louis, MO 63131

Menus & Memories, The University of Oklahoma Women's Association, 100 Timberdell Rd., OU Foundation, Norman, OK 73072

Molto Bene, Salvatore Mancini Lodge #2440, 66 Hunter Run, North Providence, RI 02904

Moon River Collection, The Landings Landlovers, 50 Shellwind Dr., Savannah, GA 31411

More Enchanted Eating from the West Shore, Friends of the Symphony, P.O. Box 1603, Muskegon, MI 49443

Of Books and Cooks, Woman's Book Club, 202 Magnolia, Harrison, AR 72601

Ofukuro No Aji: Favorite Recipes from Mama's Kitchen, Hōkūlani Cultural Exchange Committee (Hōkūlani Elementary School), 2940 Kamakini St., Honolulu, HI 96816

Oh My Stars! Recipes That Shine, Junior League of Roanoke Valley, Inc., 541 Luck Ave., Ste. 317, Roanoke, VA 24016

On Course, Women Associates of the Buffalo Power Squadron, P.O. Box 45, Lancaster, NY 14086-0045

Our Daily Bread, First Presbyterian Church of Orlando—Weekday School, 106 E. Church St., Orlando, FL 32801

Panthers' Pantry, Children's Educational Foundation, 16436 Paula Rd., Madera, CA 93638

Past and Present Meatless Treasures, Kaneohe Seventh-day Adventist Church, 45-566 Mahinui Rd., Kaneohe, HI 96744

Picnics, Potlucks & Prizewinners, Indiana 4-H Foundation, Inc., 225 S. East St., Ste. 760, Indianapolis, IN 46202

Plate & Palette: A Collection of Fine Art and Food, Beaufort County Arts Council, 108 Gladden St., P.O. Box 634, Washington, NC 27889

Ragin Cajun Cookbook, Beacon Club of University of Louisiana at Lafayette, P.O. Box 44010, Lafayette, LA 70504-4010

Recipes & Remembrances, Parkview Nursing and Rehabilitation Center, 2801 W. 6th St., Wilmington, DE 19805

Recipes from the Heart, Littleton Regional Hospital Helping Hands, 600 St. Johnsbury Rd., Littleton, NH 03561

Recipes from the Heart of Maine, Friends of the Millinocket Memorial Library, 5 Maine Ave., Millinocket, ME 04462

Ropin' the Flavors of Texas, Junior League of Victoria, Inc., 202 N. Main St., Victoria, TX 77901

Savoring the Seasons: Riverside, The Craven Regional Medical Center Foundation, P.O. Box 1576, New Bern, NC 28563

Savor the Flavor: Delightfully Vegetarian, Portland Adventist Community Services, 11020 NE Halsey St., Portland, OR 97220

Savor the Moment, Junior League of Boca Raton, Inc., 1181 S. Rogers Cir., Ste. 2A, Boca Raton, FL 33487

Seasons of Santa Fe, Kitchen Angels, 1222 Siler Rd., Santa Fe, NM 87507

Secret Ingredients, Junior League of Alexandria, Inc., 1082 Alexandria Mall, 3437 Masonic Dr., Alexandria, LA 71301

Settings on the Dock of the Bay, ASSISTANCE LEAGUE® of the Bay Area, P.O. Box 590153, Houston, TX 77259-0153

Share the Flavor: A Collection of Recipes from German Village, German Village Society, 588 S. 3rd St., Columbus, OH 43215

Sharing Our Best, The Arrangement Hair Salon, 2982 E. Broad St., Columbus, OH 43209

Sharing Our Best, Bull Run Parent Teacher Club, 41515 SE Thomas Rd., Sandy, OR 97055

Sharing Our Best, Hackensack American Legion Auxiliary Unit 202, 202 1st St., P.O. Box 414, Hackensack, MN 56452

Sharing Recipes from Green Road Baptist Church, Green Road Baptist Church, HC 83 Box 210, Green Road, KY 40946

Sounds Delicious: The Flavor of Atlanta in Food & Music, Atlanta Symphony Orchestra, 1293 Peachtree St., Ste. 300, Atlanta, GA 30309-3552

Southern Elegance: A Second Course, Junior League of Gaston County, Inc., 2950 S. Union Rd., Ste. A, Gastonia, NC 28054

Specialties of the Haus, TCM International, Inc., 6337 Hollister Dr., Indianapolis, IN 46224

Splendor in the Bluegrass, Junior League of Louisville, Inc., 501 S. Second St., Louisville, KY 40202

St. Andrew's Cooks Again, Presbyterian Women of St. Andrew, 1350 N. 23rd St., Beaumont, TX 77706

Start Your Ovens: Cooking the Way It Ought'a Be, Junior League of Bristol, TN/VA, 519 State St., Bristol, VA 24201

A Sunsational Encore, Junior League of Greater Orlando, 125 N. Lucerne Cir. E, Orlando, FL 32801

Sweet Pickin's, Junior League of Fayetteville, Inc., 2605 Fort Bragg Rd., Fayetteville, NC 28303

Tapestry: A Weaving of Food, Culture and Tradition, Junior Welfare League of Rock Hill, 958 W. Main St., Rock Hill, SC 29730

A Taste of Enchantment, Junior League of Albuquerque, 5301 Central Ave. NE, Ste. 1100, Albuquerque, NM 87108

A Taste Tour, Gingko Twig of Muhlenberg Hospital, Plainfield, New Jersey, 809 Village Green, Westfield, NJ 07090

Thyme to Entertain: Good Food and Southern Hospitality, The Charity League, Inc., 1921 Broadway, Paducah, KY 42001

A Thyme to Remember, Dallas County Medical Society Alliance, 5500 Swiss Ave., Dallas, TX 75214

To Your Health: Recipes for Healthy Living from Lahey Clinic, Lahey Clinic, 41 Mall Rd., Burlington, MA 01805

Treasures of the Tropics, Hibiscus Children's Center, 2400 NE Dixie Hwy., Jensen Beach, FL 34957

Tucson Treasures: Recipes & Reflections, Tucson Medical Center Auxiliary, 5301 E. Grant Rd., Tucson, AZ 85712

Twice Treasured Recipes, The Bargain Box, Inc., 546 William Hilton Pkwy., Hilton Head Island, SC 29928

Uncommonly Kosher, Yeshiva Parents of Hebrew Theological College, 7135 N. Carpenter Rd., Skokie, IL 60077

V.C.O.S. Sharing Our Best, Volusia County Orchid Society, Inc., P.O. Box 4282, DeLand, FL 32723-4282

Vintage Virginia: A History of Good Taste, The Virginia Dietetic Association, P.O. Box 439, Centreville, VA 20122

Walking with Christ, First Baptist Church, c/o Shirley W. Brinkley, 342 Pineview Dr., Mount Airy, NC 27030

The Western New York Federal Court Centennial Cookbook, U.S. District Court, Western District of New York, 68 Court St., Room 304, Buffalo, NY 14202

What Can I Bring?, Junior League of Northern Virginia, Inc., 7921 Jones Branch Dr., Ste. 320, McLean, VA 22102

Wildcat Valley: Recipes & Remembrances, Keats Lions Club, 4970 Anderson Ave., Manhattan, KS 66503

Yuletide on Hilton Head: A Heritage of Island Flavors, United Way of Beaufort County, P.O. Box 22961, Hilton Head Island, SC 29925

Index

Your Community Cookbook Could Win an Award

Each fall on Avery Island, Louisiana, the McIlhenny Company sponsors the Tabasco® Community Cookbook Awards competition for service organizations nationwide. All community cookbooks published within the last two years are eligible for this annual event that celebrates the history and preservation of local culinary traditions.

The editors of *America's Best Recipes* congratulate the winners of the 13th Annual Tabasco® Community Cookbook Awards and are proud to feature many of their recipes in this volume. The McIlhenny Company awarded prize money to the winning entries of the 2002 competition. The first place winner received $2,500, followed by $1000 for second place, and $750 for third. Each regional winner was awarded $500. Proceeds from the sales of each cookbook support the programs and purpose of each sponsoring organization.

The 2002 Tabasco® Community Cookbook Awards Winners:

- **First Place Winner:** *Kona on My Plate,* Kona Outdoor Circle, Kailua-Kona, HI
- **Second Place Winner:** *Tastes of Jewish Tradition,* Harry & Rose Samson Jewish Community Center of Milwaukee, WI
- **Third Place Winner:** *Colorado Colore: A Palate of Tastes,* The Junior League of Denver, CO
- **New England:** *Woods Hole Cooks Something Up,* Woods Hole Historical Museum, Woods Hole, MA
- **Mid-Atlantic:** *Sensational Shellfish: The Best of North Fork,* Friends of SPAT, Southold, NY
- **South:** *First Come, First Served . . . in Savannah,* St. Andrews School Parent Teacher Organization, Savannah, GA
- **Midwest:** *Celebrating 300 Years of Detroit Cooking: 1701 to 2001,* Detroit Historical Society Guild, Eastpointe, MI
- **Southwest:** *Austin Entertains,* The Junior League of Austin, TX
- **West:** *Secrets of Salsa,* The Mexican Women of Anderson Valley, Boonville, CA
- **Special Merit:** *Preserving the Past,* Sherman Garden Club, Sherman, CT
- **Walter S. McIlhenny Hall of Fame 2002:** *Three Rivers Cookbook III,* Child Health Association of Sewickley, PA
- **Walter S. McIlhenny Hall of Fame 2002:** *Simply Classic,* The Junior League of Seattle, WA

For information on the Tabasco® Community Cookbook Awards or for an awards entry form, send a self-addressed stamped #10 (legal size) envelope to

Tabasco Community Cookbook Awards
% Hunter Public Relations
41 Madison Ave.
New York, NY 10010-2202

For a free booklet about producing a community cookbook, send a self-addressed stamped #10 (legal size) envelope to

Compiling Culinary History
% Hunter Public Relations
41 Madison Ave.
New York, NY 10010-2202